Alternate Translation

of the

NEW TESTAMENT

(Selected Scriptures)

For My Parents
Louis and Evelyn Goldstein
My daughter, Maria
My granddaughters, Sarina & Juliette

DEDICATION

FOR: The Lord Jesus, the One who fully equipped me . . . .

TO: his Body . . . .

    Come, my beloved, let us go forth into the field; let us lodge in the villages.

    The mandrakes give a smell, and at our gates are all manner of pleasant fruits, new and old, which I have laid up for thee, O my beloved.

    Let us get up early to the vineyards; let us see if the vine flourish, whether the tender grape appear, and the pomegranates bud forth: there will I give thee my loves. (Song Of Solomon 7:11-13).

    Many waters cannot quench love, neither can the floods drown it: ***IF A MAN WOULD GIVE ALL THE SUBSTANCE OF HIS HOUSE FOR LOVE, THE WOMAN WOULD BE PRONOUNCED GUILTY FOR THE PURPOSE OF PERFECTING HER*** (Song Of Solomon 8:7).

Copyright © 2014 by Living Epistles Ministries
All rights reserved under International Copyright Law.
Published @ Long Island, NY December 2025

ISBN: 13: 978-0692309735
ISBN: 10: 069230973X

Alternate Translation of The New Testament
Sheila R. Vitale

No part of this book may be reproduced, in any form, without written permission from the publisher

Requests for permission to reproduce selections from this book should be mailed to:

Living Epistles Ministries
Sheila R. Vitale
P O Box 562
Port Jefferson Station, NY 11776-0562 USA
(631) 331-1493

TABLE OF AUTHORITIES

1. **Brown Driver & Briggs' Hebrew Lexicon**, Woodside Bible Fellowship, Ontario, Canada, Licensed From The Institute for Creation Research.

2. **Englishman's Greek-Hebrew Concordance**.

3. **Gesenius' Hebrew and Chaldee Lexicon to the Old Testament** Scriptures, Baker Book House, Grand Rapids, Michigan.

4. **The Interlinear Bible** (Jay P. Green, Sr.), Hendrickson Publisher's, Peabody, Massachusetts 01961-3473.

5. **The Interlinear Bible (transliterated)**, Biblesoft and International Bible Translators, Inc.

6. **Nave's Topical Bible**.

7. **Nelson's Bible Dictionary**, Thomas Nelson, Inc., Publishers, Nashville, Tennessee.

8. **Strong's Exhaustive Concordance** (James Strong) Thomas Nelson, Inc., Publishers, Nashville, Tennessee.

9. **Strong's Hebrew And Chaldee Dictionary** (James Strong), Thomas Nelson, Inc., Publishers, Nashville, Tennessee.

10. **Strong's Greek Dictionary** (James Strong), Thomas Nelson, Inc., Publishers, Nashville, Tennessee.

11. **The New Thayer's Greek-English Lexicon Of The New Testament**, Hendrickson Publisher's, Peabody, Massachusetts 01961-3473.

12. **Unger's Bible Dictionary** (Merrill F. Unger), The Moody Bible Institute of Chicago, Chicago, Illinois 60610.

13. **1979 Authorized Version** (AV), The On-Line Bible

14. **Stephanus Greek Text**, The On-Line Bible

15. **Green's Literal Translation**, The On-Line Bible

Numbers In Brackets [###] Indicate The Message # in Which Alternate Translation Was Researched And Worked Up. [Version Date: 08/05/2024]

Living Epistles Ministries

Sheila R. Vitale
Pastor, Teacher, Founder
PO Box 562
Port Jefferson Station, NY 11776 USA

Alternate Translation®
of the
NEW TESTAMENT©

**Selected Scriptures
Translated, Edited and compiled by
Sheila R. Vitale**

**Alternate Translation®
of the
NEW TESTAMENT©**

THE ALTERNATE TRANSLATION BIBLE

1. Is An Esoteric Interpretation of the Scripture.

2. Is Not Intended To Replace Traditional Translations.

For More information, See,
Facts About The Alternate Translation Bible
At the end of this Volume

Living Epistles Ministries
Sheila R. Vitale
Pastor, Teacher & Founder

Ministry Staff
Anthony Milton, Teacher (South Carolina)
Brooke Paige, Teacher (New York)
Dele Adegbite, Teacher (London-Nigeria)
Margaret Mobolaji-Lawal, Leader (Lagos, Nigeria)
Sandra Aldrich (MN) (July 7, 1975 – April 18, 2021)

Administrative Staff
Susan Panebianco, Office Manager

Editorial Staff
Rose Herczeg, Editor

Technical Staff
Lape Mobolaji-Lawal, Database Administrator

Ministry Illustrators
Cecilia H. Bryant (Oct. 18, 1921 – Oct. 23, 2013)
Fidelis Onwubueke

Music Staff
Don Gervais, Singer, Lyricist and Guitarist
(June 30, 1956 – October 21, 2024)
June Eble, Singer, Lyricist and Clarinetist
(July 20, 1931 – Jan. 24, 2024)
Rita L. Rora, Singer, Lyricist and Guitarist

Table of Contents

PREFACE I
- WHY ANOTHER TRANSLATION? I
- MULTIPLE VERSIONS III
- PREPARING TO TRANSLATE IV
- ALTERNATE TRANSLATIONS ARE PROGRESSIVE V
- THE WORD OF GOD IS ALIVE V

MATTHEW 1
- CHAPTER 1 1
- CHAPTER 3 2
- CHAPTER 4 2
- CHAPTER 5 6
- CHAPTER 6 7
- CHAPTER 7 8
- CHAPTER 8 9
- CHAPTER 10 13
- CHAPTER 11 15
- CHAPTER 12 16
- CHAPTER 13 20
- CHAPTER 14 22
- CHAPTER 16 26
- CHAPTER 17 27
- CHAPTER 19 28
- CHAPTER 20 29
- CHAPTER 21 30
- CHAPTER 22 38
- CHAPTER 23 39
- CHAPTER 24 40
- CHAPTER 25 47
- CHAPTER 26 50
- CHAPTER 27 57

MARK 61
- CHAPTER 1 61
- CHAPTER 2 61
- CHAPTER 3 63
- CHAPTER 4 65
- CHAPTER 5 66
- CHAPTER 6 71
- CHAPTER 9 72
- CHAPTER 10 74

- Chapter 12 77
- Chapter 13 77
- Chapter 14 79
- Chapter 15 80

LUKE 81

- Chapter 1 81
- Chapter 2 83
- Chapter 4 89
- Chapter 6 90
- Chapter 7 90
- Chapter 8 92
- Chapter 11 92
- Chapter 10 93
- Chapter 11 94
- Chapter 12 94
- Chapter 13 103
- Chapter 16 104
- Chapter 17 107
- Chapter 20 111
- Chapter 22 111
- Chapter 23 112

JOHN 113

- Chapter 1 113
- Chapter 2 116
- Chapter 3 118
- Chapter 4 120
- Chapter 5 127
- Chapter 6 128
- Chapter 7 133
- Chapter 10 134
- Chapter 12 134
- Chapter 13 135
- Chapter 14 136
- Chapter 18 137
- Chapter 19 137
- Chapter 21 138

ACTS 145

- Chapter 1 145
- Chapter 3 145
- Chapter 4 146
- Chapter 5 147
- Chapter 7 149
- Chapter 8 150
- Chapter 9 151

CHAPTER 13	151
CHAPTER 17	152
CHAPTER 26	152
CHAPTER 28	153

ROMANS 155

CHAPTER 1	155
CHAPTER 2	160
CHAPTER 3	165
CHAPTER 5	171
CHAPTER 6	174
CHAPTER 7	175
CHAPTER 8	175
CHAPTER 9	180
CHAPTER 10	181
CHAPTER 11	185
CHAPTER 12	196
CHAPTER 13	197
CHAPTER 14	199

1ST CORINTHIANS 201

CHAPTER 1	201
CHAPTER 3	201
CHAPTER 4	202
CHAPTER 5	202
CHAPTER 7	203
CHAPTER 8	204
CHAPTER 10	207
CHAPTER 11	208
CHAPTER 13	218
CHAPTER 15	220
CHAPTER 16	226

2ND CORINTHIANS 227

CHAPTER 3	227
CHAPTER 4	229
CHAPTER 5	229
CHAPTER 7	232
CHAPTER 8	233
CHAPTER 12	234
CHAPTER 13	234

GALATIANS 237

CHAPTER 2	237
CHAPTER 3	239
CHAPTER 4	239
CHAPTER 5	240

CHAPTER 6 241
EPHESIANS **243**
    CHAPTER 1 243
    CHAPTER 2 247
    CHAPTER 3 250
    CHAPTER 4 254
    CHAPTER 5 259
    CHAPTER 6 263

PHILIPPIANS **271**
    CHAPTER 1 271
    CHAPTER 2 271
    CHAPTER 3 272

COLOSSIANS **277**
    CHAPTER 1 277
    CHAPTER 2 283
    CHAPTER 3 289
    CHAPTER 4 295

1ST THESSALONIANS **297**
    CHAPTER 1 297
    CHAPTER 4 297
    CHAPTER 5 298

2ND THESSALONIANS **301**
    CHAPTER 1 301
    CHAPTER 2 305
    CHAPTER 3 309

1ST TIMOTHY **313**
    CHAPTER 2 313
    CHAPTER 3 314
    CHAPTER 4 314
    CHAPTER 5 315

TITUS **317**
    CHAPTER 2 317
    CHAPTER 3 317

HEBREWS **319**
    CHAPTER 1 319
    CHAPTER 2 323
    CHAPTER 3 328
    CHAPTER 5 328
    CHAPTER 6 329

CHAPTER 8 330
CHAPTER 9 331
CHAPTER 10 333
CHAPTER 11 335
CHAPTER 12 336
CHAPTER 13 337

JAMES **339**

CHAPTER 1 339
CHAPTER 4 340
CHAPTER 5 341

1ST PETER **343**

CHAPTER 1 343
CHAPTER 2 347
CHAPTER 3 347
CHAPTER 4 349

2ND PETER **351**

CHAPTER 1 351
CHAPTER 2 351
CHAPTER 3 353

1ST JOHN **357**

CHAPTER 2 357
CHAPTER 5 359

JUDE **367**

CHAPTER 1 367

END NOTE **373**

APPENDICES **377**

MATTHEW 379
MARK 386
LUKE 390
JOHN 403
ACTS 413
ROMANS 414
1 CORINTHIANS 415
2 CORINTHIANS 416
1 TIMOTHY 418
1 JOHN 419

FACTS ABOUT THE ALTERNATE TRANSLATION BIBLE **423**

A BRIEF HISTORY OF THE ALTERNATE TRANSLATION BIBLE 423
WHAT IS THE ALTERNATE TRANSLATION BIBLE? 424

QUESTIONS & ANSWERS 426
ABOUT THE AUTHOR **431**

The Alternate Translation Bible© (ATB)

The Old Testament

Alternate Translation of the Old Testament©
Alternate Translation, Exodus, Chapter 32
   (Crime of the Calf)©
Alternate Translation, Daniel, Chapter 8©
Alternate Translation, Daniel, Chapter 11©

The New Testament

Alternate Translation of the New Testament©
Alternate Translation, 2 Thessalonians, Chapter 2
   (Sophia)©
Alternate Translation, 1st John, Chapter 5©
Alternate Translation, The Book of Colossians
   (To The Church At Colosse) ©
Alternate Translation, The Book of Corinthians, Chapter 11
   (Corinthian Confusion) ©
Alternate Translation, The Book of Jude
   (The Common Salvation)©
Alternate Translation of The Book of the Revelation of
   Jesus Christ to St. John©
Traducción Alternada del Libro de Revelación de Jesucristo©

THE ALTERNATE TRANSLATION BIBLE

1. Is An Esoteric Understanding Of The Scripture.
2. Is Not Intended To Replace Traditional Translations.

For More information, See,
Facts About The Alternate Translation Bible
At the end of this Volume

PREFACE

Why Another Translation?

The King James Translators were not spiritual men. They were scholars who, themselves, perceived the Deity of the Scripture as an unforgiving, punishing God. But there is another Message, a spiritual understanding of the Scripture called *the Doctrine of Christ*, which reveals a loving God, whose sole intention towards mankind is to deliver us from destruction and death.

There are many definitions for each word in the English dictionary and many translations for each Hebrew and Greek word in the original text of the Scripture.

The King James Translators dealt with the problem of one Hebrew source word appearing several times in a single Chapter, by using a different English word each time that the Hebrew word appears. The English word choices of the translator, then, are directly related to: 1) his knowledge of the Word of God, 2) the degree to which he is influenced by the Spirit of Revelation and 3) the accepted understanding of the Word of God at the time.

The Spirit of Revelation influences the translator to choose legitimate *Alternate Translations* from the Hebrew and Greek lexicons listed in the front of the *Alternate Translation Bible*, to express the spiritual intent of the Scripture. The Alternate English Translations for some of the Hebrew and Greek words in the Scripture are just as legitimate as the choices made by the King James Translators, but they render a radically different and much more positive Translation than the Authorized Version.

Alternate Translation Of The New Testament/ Preface

Multiple English translations for the same Hebrew or Greek word in the King James text are perfectly legitimate examples of Translator's License, and simply prove our point: *The King James Translators, themselves, used multiple definitions of the same Hebrew and Greek Word.*

The *Alternate Translation Bible* is a Spiritual Translation of the Scripture that is as legitimate to the Spiritual Mind as the King James translation is to the Carnal Mind. The *Alternate Translation Bi*ble sounds radically different from the King James and other translations, because it must be Spiritually Discerned (1 Cor. 2:14).

A knowledge of the True Intent of the author of the Scripture and a desire to understand the message that he intended to convey, should be the top priority for all genuine seekers of *Truth*.

God is the Living Word that feeds Mankind through imperfect vessels. Beware of idolatry for the King James, or any other Translation, because *all translations* are the work of imperfect mortal men. Seek God and He will direct your paths (Pro. 3:6).

May the Spirit of Truth expose all of our wrong thinking, and may the Truth intended by the author of the Word cleave to our heart and mind, because the Spirit of Truth awakens our potential for Eternal Life (1 Cor 15:4).

Romans 8:1-14

1. THERE IS THEREFORE NOW NO CONDEMNATION TO THEM WHICH ARE IN CHRIST JESUS, WHO WALK NOT AFTER THE FLESH, BUT AFTER THE SPIRIT.

2. FOR THE LAW OF THE SPIRIT OF LIFE IN CHRIST JESUS HATH MADE ME FREE FROM THE LAW OF SIN AND DEATH.

3. FOR WHAT THE LAW COULD NOT DO, IN THAT IT WAS WEAK THROUGH THE FLESH, GOD SENDING HIS OWN SON IN THE LIKENESS OF SINFUL FLESH, AND FOR SIN, CONDEMNED SIN IN THE FLESH:

Alternate Translation Of The New Testament/ Preface

4. THAT THE RIGHTEOUSNESS OF THE LAW MIGHT BE FULFILLED IN US, WHO WALK NOT AFTER THE FLESH, BUT AFTER THE SPIRIT.

5. FOR THEY THAT ARE AFTER THE FLESH DO MIND THE THINGS OF THE FLESH; BUT THEY THAT ARE AFTER THE SPIRIT THE THINGS OF THE SPIRIT.

6. FOR TO BE CARNALLY MINDED IS DEATH; BUT TO BE SPIRITUALLY MINDED IS LIFE AND PEACE.

7. BECAUSE THE CARNAL MIND IS ENMITY AGAINST GOD: FOR IT IS NOT SUBJECT TO THE LAW OF GOD, NEITHER INDEED CAN BE.

8. SO THEN THEY THAT ARE IN THE FLESH CANNOT PLEASE GOD.

9. BUT YE ARE NOT IN THE FLESH, BUT IN THE SPIRIT, IF SO BE THAT THE SPIRIT OF GOD DWELL IN YOU. NOW IF ANY MAN HAVE NOT THE SPIRIT OF CHRIST, HE IS NONE OF HIS.

10. AND IF CHRIST BE IN YOU, THE BODY IS DEAD BECAUSE OF SIN; BUT THE SPIRIT IS LIFE BECAUSE OF RIGHTEOUSNESS.

11. BUT IF THE SPIRIT OF HIM THAT RAISED UP JESUS FROM THE DEAD DWELL IN YOU, HE THAT RAISED UP CHRIST FROM THE DEAD SHALL ALSO QUICKEN YOUR MORTAL BODIES BY HIS SPIRIT THAT DWELLETH IN YOU.

12. THEREFORE, BRETHREN, WE ARE DEBTORS, NOT TO THE FLESH, TO LIVE AFTER THE FLESH.

13. FOR IF YE LIVE AFTER THE FLESH, YE SHALL DIE: BUT IF YE THROUGH THE SPIRIT DO MORTIFY THE DEEDS OF THE BODY, YE SHALL LIVE.

Multiple Versions

There are many instances of multiple versions of a Scripture verse, or a series of verses. The translator has included this redundancy so that the reader can experience the progression of her understanding of the Scripture over the years. The number within the brackets that precedes each translation is the number of the Message that produced the translation. The names of the Messages are listed in the *LEM Media Catalogue*, which can be viewed on the *LEM Website*:

http://www.lemdatabase.org/lem/CatalogueFiles/LEM-MediaCatalogue.pdf

Alternate Translation Of The New Testament/ Preface

Some numbers within brackets have a "C" after them, which indicates that the translation is the product of a *Christ-Centered Kabbalah* Message. The names of *CCK* Messages are listed in the *CCK Media Catalogue*, which can be viewed on the *CCK Website*:

http://www.lemdatabase.org/lem/CatalogueFiles/CCK-MediaCatalogue.pdf

Also, if there are any illustrations associated with the work-up(s) of the translation(s), links to those illustrations have been inserted next to the *linked Message Names* on the *LEM or the CCK Website*. (See, *Alternate Translations Are Progressive*.)

http://livingepistles.org/#parentVerticalTab1

http://christ-centeredkabbalah.org/#tl3

In addition, fully-annotated versions of *Alternate Translations* (references and bookmarks) are included wherever an *Alternate Translation* has been made into a book. The name of the book is noted between the brackets, instead of the Message Number, wherever the translation has been made into a book.

Preparing To Translate

Three Hebrew-English dictionaries, three Interlinear Texts, and multiple Bible Dictionaries (see, Table of Authorities at the beginning of this book) are used to search out the meaning of each Hebrew and Greek word of the *Alternate Translation Bible*. English dictionaries, encyclopedias and search engines are also employed to acquire as much information as possible about obviously, and not so obviously related topics, revealed through the *Alternate Translations*. Each word and verse is seriously prayed over to discover God's spiritual message behind the written words.

References and footnotes are attached to some translations. Others have only references, and many are not annotated. Footnotes for new translations have not been included since 2016, but references are always included if the *Alternate Translation* is annotated. Some fully annotated *Alternate Translations* (footnotes and references) have been made into books. Transcripts of other *Alternate Translations* which are fully annotated are available for sale from the publisher.

The research material for each *Alternate Translation* is faithfully preserved in the Archival Notes for the Living Epistles Ministries or Christ-Centered Kabbalah Message where it was rendered.

It is not unusual for the verse structure of the *Alternate Translations* to be rearranged so that they can be read as one continuous message. Accordingly, some paragraph numbers are out of order (*3* before *2*, for example) and some paragraphs are divided into *a* and *b* and interspersed (*2a, 3a, 2b, 3b*, for example).

Alternate Translations Are Progressive

Alternate Translations are rendered for each verse in its entirety. After that, all of the translated verses are read together as one whole revelation to confirm their synchronicity, reveal additional, deep nuances of the whole revelation, and to expose any inconsistencies or errors.

Alternate Translations are progressive in that the *Alternate Translation* for each verse is affected by the *Alternate Translations* for previous and subsequent verses. A newly translated verse, for example, will be influenced by previous *Alternate Translations*, and sometimes the *Alternate Translation* for the new verse causes changes in previously translated verses.

The Word of God Is Alive

The *Alternate Translation* of one whole chapter of Scripture is a living organism that evolves and grows in scope. The Spirit of Revelation refines the *Alternate Translations* as the translator reads and re-reads them. Eventually, all of the thoughts, understanding and influences of the Carnal Mind are removed, and the optimal understanding for that particular time is reached.

Written words are vessels that clothe the spiritual word, just like the body is a vessel that carries the soul in this world. It might even be said that the spiritual understanding of a written word is the soul of that written word.

Unveiling the spiritual meaning of a word shatters its hard exterior, so that the spiritual contents flow out and blend with the spiritual contents of the other vessels. Then, *The Spirit of Revelation* takes hold of the Word of God in this *liquid form,* goes beyond the letter of the Word, and reveals the esoteric message of the Word of God for a particular people, at an appointed time.

Sheila R. Vitale

Alternate Translation

of the

NEW TESTAMENT
(Selected Scriptures)

Alternate Translation of The New Testament/ Matthew

THE GOSPEL OF MATTHEW

Chapter 1

[591]
1.18   Now, these are the circumstances surrounding Jesus' birth: When Mary, [Jesus'] mother, was betrothed to Joseph, the Holy Spirit possessed her womb before they came together, and

1.19a   Joseph, who was a justified [spiritual] male, was disposed to dismiss [Mary's account of her experience with Gabriel], rather than expose her to public ridicule, or flattery, and

1.20a   Behold, an angel of the Lord shined into [Joseph's] dream [state, or trance, as he meditated], saying, **Joseph, son of David**, do not be afraid to learn from, [or believe] Mary, your wife,

1.19b   [But, rather], be encouraged by these things, [that she says],

1.20b   Because the Holy Spirit has regenerated^{R-1} [Righteous Adam], within her, and

$^{R-1}$ Matt 19:28

1.21   She shall produce a son from [your physical] seed [who] shall deliver his people from their sins, and you shall call him by the name of **JESUS**.

1.22   Now, all this happened to bring to pass what the Lord spoke by the prophet [Isaiah], saying,

1

1.23 Behold, a virtuous [R-1] woman[R-2] shall be with child[R-3] and shall produce a son,[R-4] and they shall call his name **Emmanuel**, which is translated, ***God in the midst of us***,[R-5] [and]

[R-1] Rev 14:4
[R-2] Rev 12:1-2
[R-3] Rev 12:5
[R-4] Matt 1:21, 25
[R-5] Jn 7:38

1.24 Joseph, now being fully awakened from the powerlessness of [spiritual] death, did what the angel of the Lord [told him to do, he believed Mary], his wife, and learned from [her about the son that they were to bring into the world],

1.25 But [Joseph] did not comprehend [the exalted] place from which [Jesus, Mary's] firstborn son, was called into existence, until the end of [her pregnancy, when] she called him by the name, JESUS.

Chapter 3

[15.1]
3.16-17 And when Jesus was baptized, righteousness and equality with God sprang up out of His spiritual substance. And, lo, the eyesight of His spiritual mind was restored to Him, and He perceived the Spirit of God rooting in Him, taking up residence in Him, and appearing in Him, and a voice from heaven saying, lo, this is my Son, the Beloved, the reconciled One, in whom I have found payment of the debt.

Chapter 4

[219.3]
4.01 Then, the Spirit [of Elijah][R-1] led Jesus[R-2] into the place between the eyebrows,[R-3] [where] Righteous [Adam, Jesus'

Alternate Translation of The New Testament/ Matthew

other] side, which is beyond Satan's influence [is located, to equip Jesus] for the spiritual battle [that] disciplines the Devil, [the personality that is in agreement with their carnal mind],

R-1 Matt 17:12
R-2 Rom. 8:11
R-3 Ex 13:16

4.02   [Now, Jesus] was fasting from the thoughts of [Satan, the enforcer of the Sowing & Reaping Judgment,[1] who is also the unconscious part of the carnal mind], and from the lusts[R] of [the carnal mind, the mortal] dimension on the right side of the heart center [within himself, but] afterward [Jesus] began to pine away[R] [because his carnal mind was still active],

R 2 Pet 1:4

4.03   And Satan, the enforcer of the Sowing & Reaping Judgment, [and] the unconscious part of [Jesus'] carnal mind, approached Jesus aggressively, saying, if you really are the Son of God, command [Abel], the spiritual genetic material[2] [of God within you], to be gathered together with [the Spirit of Elijah within you], and [let them] rise [into the place between the eyebrows of the righteous side of mankind within you, where they become spiritual] bread,[3]

4.04   And [Jesus] answered [Satan, the unconscious part of the carnal mind that he received from Mary], saying, preaching

---

[1] *SATAN, THE ENFORCER OF THE SOWING & REAPING JUDGMENT,* **IS A TRANSLATION OF** *STRONG'S* **#3985, TRANSLATED** *TEMPTED* **IN MATT. 4:1, AND** *TEMPTER* **IN MATT. 4:3.** (Read entire footnote in Appendices)

[2] ***Spiritual genetic material*** is an interpretation of the English word ***stone***, which can signify the pit of a fruit, which contains the entire genetic blueprint of the whole tree. (Read entire footnote in Appendices)

[3] ***Spiritual bread*** signifies a man who is so possessed by the Word of God, that his wisdom, teaching and counsel ***feeds*** Christ in other men. (Read entire footnote in Appendices)

3

Alternate Translation of The New Testament/ Matthew

doctrine to the mind [of God]⁴ forms the unmarried Christ Jesus,⁵ but [Righteous Adam] the whole Word of God,⁶ draws down [Elohim's] life force from above, [and]

    4.05   Then [the Spirit of Elijah] established an intimate [spiritual] connection with [Abel, the good side of Cain and Abel, the dual, mortal foundation⁷ that Jesus received from Mary],

    And [Righteous Adam], the head of [Abel, within the man, Jesus], his temple,⁸ stood up in [the left side of [Jesus'] heart, the entranceway to the Holy City,ᴿ because the Devil, [the personality that agrees with the carnal mind, had arisen within Jesus, and]

                                          ᴿ Rev 21:2

---

⁴   **The whole Mind of God** is Righteous Adam above married to Righteous Adam below. In the New Testament. The Lord Jesus Christ is Righteous Adam above, and Christ Jesus is Righteous Adam below.

⁵   **Righteous Adam** is called **Christ Jesus** when he is regenerated in a man by Jesus' Holy Spirit. **Abel** is the descendant of Righteous Adam, who went to sleep after the Woman committed adultery with the Snake (Gen 2:21). (Read entire footnote in Appendices)

⁶   The **whole Word of God** includes the knowledge (1) that Satan is the unconscious part of the carnal mind that all mortal men are born with, (2) that Christ must be formed in the individual, (3) that the Holy Spirit is not Christ, and (4) that the Mind of Christ must overthrow the carnal mind, (Read entire footnote in Appendices)

⁷   Cain and Abel, the mortal foundation of fallen mankind, form the individual personality (soul).

⁸   The physical body is the temple of the Holy Spirit (1 Cor 6:19), and the Body of Christ, which is the Mind of Christ, is the temple of God (Elohim). (Read entire footnote in Appendices)

Alternate Translation of The New Testament/ Matthew

4.06 Then [the Devil][9] said, if I am really Elohim's Son,[10] [I should be able] to throw [Abel, the part of me that is] underneath [Cain, up to the place that he fell down from,[11] because] it is written concerning [Righteous Adam], the Angel [of the Lord],

Indeed, [Jehovah] has given [Abel, my] left hand[12] [of judgment to be the authority over Cain, my] personality, to ascend upwards [to Elohim], so that [Satan, the unconscious part of] the carnal mind, can never surge against [Righteous Adam], the Son of God, [again].[13]

---

[9] **The Devil** is the personality that agrees with the carnal mind.

The use of the word **Devil** suggests that, for the moment, Jesus had fallen under the influence of his carnal mind.

[10] Jesus of Nazareth was still a mortal man when Satan, the unconscious part of the carnal mind that Jesus inherited from Mary, tested him. Jesus became **The Christ** after he brought that carnal mind into submission to the regenerated Adam (see, **Note #4**) within himself (Rom 1:4), and Righteous Adam was rejoined to Jehovah above though the mediatorship of the Spirit of Elijah (Matt 11:14). (Read entire footnote in Appendices)

[11] The carnal mind that Jesus inherited from Mary told Jesus that he had the power to reconnect his earthen self to the God world above by means of an earthly power. (Read entire footnote in Appendices)

[12] The right hand of Righteous Adam gives spiritual gifts to the personality (mortal soul), and his left hand ministers corrective judgment to the carnal mind (Sowing & Reaping Judgment) and to the young God Mind (White Throne Judgment).

[13] Christ was killed by the Serpent, the progenitor of the carnal mind, in the previous age (Rom 5:8-9[AT]). (Read entire footnote in Appendices)

Alternate Translation of The New Testament/ Matthew

4.07   And [Righteous Adam within] Jesus said to *Satan's nature [that Jesus' inherited from Mary], it is wrong to use the written, [letter*[R-1] *of] the Word of God to test [Christ, who is your] lord,*[R-2]

[R-1] 2 Cor 3:6
[R-2] Ps 110:1

4.08   But the Devil [approached Jesus] intimately, again, [this time] from the very high [spiritual] mountain [of the place between the eyebrows], and [showed Jesus how] he ruled over all the kingdoms of the world [who agreed with] his opinion,

4.09   *[And the Devil said to Jesus], I will give [you the power that you need] to complete [Cain and Abel, your mortal foundation],*[14] *if you will bring these [disciples of yours] down [from the high place that the Spirit of Elijah raised them up to, and convince them] to worship*[15] *me,*

4.10   And Jesus said to Satan, get behind [Righteous Adam within me], because it is written, *you shall worship the Lord, your God, and him only shall you serve,*

4.11   And then the Devil departed from Jesus, and angels came, and could be seen ministering to him.

Chapter 5

[Message # Unknown]

5.26   Believe me when I tell you that you will not escape from [Satan and Leviathan], your carnal mind, until you deliver

---

[14]   Satan ascended to that high place in verse 8 to demonstrate to Jesus that he could provide the power from above to below, that is needed to reconnect mankind to the God world.

[15]   **Submission** is the true expression of worship.

[fallen Adam], the beast, that is your other self, over [to the White Throne Judgment].

Chapter 6

[Message # Unknown]
    6.09a   Therefore, this is how you should pray to our Father in Heaven,

    6.10a   May the Kingdom [of God], your heaven[ly mind], appear in us, and generate the motives of

    6.09b   Your holy nature

    6.10b   Within our earthen [personalities],

    6.13b   Because we acknowledge that the Kingdom [of God] is the miracle-working power of this [New] Age,

    6.11   And that we need the [spiritual] bread[R-1] that you give us for this [New] Day,[R-2]

    [R-1] Jn 6:51
    [R-2] Mk 14:25 (AT)

    6.12   To [help us] to forgive those who have sinned against us, so that you can forgive our moral [weaknesses, which appear]

    6.13   When we experience Satan's evil [thoughts] driving us from within.

[1246.8.C]
    6.23   If all [three parts of the earthen] soul [which is a part of] the body, are separated from [Christ, the spiritual intellectual soul that is a part of] the body, is full of dark [thoughts], so, if the [en]light[ened part of] the soul, [is not relaying the enlightened thoughts of Christ to the emotional heart part of the soul], the

dark [images in the emotional heart part of] that soul are very great.

Chapter 7

[42.15]
    7.13   Enter into [the power of spiritual manhood] through [Righteous Adam's spiritual] dimension, because [the astral plane, Leviathan's] visible, but spiritually flat, dimension, leads to moral and spiritual ruin.

    [Many are experiencing the thoughts of Satan, the unconscious part of the carnal mind], which is in the Serpent's image,[R] but [Satan's thoughts] lead to moral and spiritual ruin, so make sure that you enter in[to spiritual manhood] through [the thoughts of] Righteous Adam, the [one] who requires you to confess your sins, repent and experience the birth pangs associated with spiritual purification, before he gives you spiritual power].

                                           [R] Matt 10:22 (AT)
                                              Matt 12:26 (AT)

    7.14   [You need the spiritual strength of Righteous Adam, the doorway to] true spiritual life, [because he is the only one strong enough to pressure Satan and Leviathan, your carnal mind, into the correct moral relationship with himself, but the lifestyle that leads to such a moral relationship] is afflictive and emotionally painful, [so only those who have cast[R] down Satan, the weight of their sin nature], are able to perceive it [and conform to it].

                                                         [R] Rom 13:12

Alternate Translation of The New Testament/ Matthew

Chapter 8

[Message # Unknown]

8.11   I am telling you that many shall come from the eternal realm, and from the inhabited world, and shall join Abraham, Isaac and Jacob in the kingdom of heaven,

8.12   But the children of *the outer kingdom* shall be cast into the darkness where [Satan, the Serpent's] tooth, chews them up, [and Leviathan consumes them, despite] their loud cries [for Jesus to help them].

8.18   Now, when Jesus perceived that there was an intense spiritual[16] [atmosphere] surrounding him, He called out [to his disciples] to pierce into the unconscious [part of their carnal mind],

8.19   And a certain scribe agreed, saying, Master, I will follow you wherever you go,

8.20   And Jesus said to [the scribe, Cain], the [spiritual] jackal[17] [who is the conscious part of the carnal mind, which is

---

[16]   The Greek word translated **multitudes, Strong's #3793,** is derived from **Strong's #2192,** which can be translated, **hum,** and the Aramaic word used for **multitudes** in the **Greek New Testament, Strong's #1995,** can be translated, **emotion of mind (Gesenius).**

Both **hum** (vibration), and **emotion of mind,** suggest spiritual activity.

[17]   The Greek work translated **fox, Strong's #258,** appears in the New Testament four times, and means **a fox,** or a **cunning person.**

Footnote Continued

the black] hole[R-1] [that Adam fell into, feeds off of the energy of Abel], the bird of the [spiritual] atmosphere, [Adam's dead descendant who] he has [possessed since Adam died, but [Jesus], the [regenerated][R-2] Son of Adam,[18] Abel's][19] head has [the authority] to lie [with him in the same place that Satan[20] lies with hum];

[R-1] Lk 2:8 (AT)
[R-2] Matt 19:28

8.21   Then another of [Jesus'] disciples said to him, Lord, let me go into the unconscious [part of the carnal mind of] the first Adam, the Christ [of the previous age, who died for our sins and] was buried, [and raise Abel from the dead],[R]

[R] 1 Cor 15:3

8.22   And Jesus said to him, you must die [to your carnal nature before you can raise] the dead [Christ who died for our sins and] was buried [under these animal bodies], so follow me,

---

On the other hand, **Gesenius** says that the Hebrew word translated **fox, Strong's #7776,** is derived from the root, **sheol**, which means the **pit** or **underground hole** (where the animal dwells), and that **jackal** is more likely the word intended in this context, because jackals devour dead bodies.

[18]   **Strong's #444**, translated, **man**, means, **man-faced creature**, which suggests the regenerated Adam, the complete man. **Strong's 435**, also translated **man**, is the Greek word that means **male person**.

[19]   The regenerated Adam within Jesus had spiritual sexual intercourse with the dead Abel, Adam's root system, within the disciples, and Abel rose from the dead within the disciples, with a new name, Christ (1 Cor 15:3). (Read entire footnote in Appendices)

[20]   Satan has spiritual sexual intercourse with Cain, the Serpent's root system within mortal man, and the carnal mind is formed in that place, i.e., in that man.

Alternate Translation of The New Testament/ Matthew

[1165.1.C (574.2.C)]

    8.23   And he entered into the spiritual dimension of the Ark, and his disciples followed him into the spiritual dimension [of the Ark, and they were in] the spiritual dimension [of the ark together],

    8.24   And a great storm arose in the unconscious part of the carnal mind, and waves [of the energy of the disciples'] mortal foundation covered the Ark, [the spiritual dimension of God within the disciples], insomuch so that [Abel within the disciples] went to sleep,

    8.25   And [the disciples] approached [Adam], the spiritual dimension [of God within Jesus, to ask him] to awaken [Abel within them], saying, Lord, [if you do not] save [Abel within us], we will be destroyed,[21]

    8.26   And [Adam spoke through Jesus and] said to [the sons of] Elohim in the spiritual dimension [of God], you are afraid because [Abraham's seed, the source of] your faith, is immature;[R] Then [Adam] arose [within Jesus] and rebuked [Satan], the spirit [that enforces Jehovah's righteous Sowing & Reaping Judgment] from the unconscious part of the carnal mind,[22] and great tranquility began to issue forth [from within the disciples],

[R] Matt 14:31(ATB)

    8.27   And the [spiritually] mature men were amazed [to hear that their faith was immature]; Indeed, [when they heard it] they said, "What kind of character does this man have, that even [Satan], the spirit [that enforces Jehovah's righteous Sowing & Reaping Judgment] from the unconscious part of the carnal mind, obeys him?

---

    [21]   Their resurrected spiritual life would be destroyed.

    [22]   The storm was Satan's legal response to the disciple's fear.

Alternate Translation of The New Testament/ Matthew

8.28   And [Adam] entered into the spiritual dimension [of God within Jesus], and [from there] pierced through [to the Mind of God within Jesus] into the carnal mind of [the disciples and] encountered [Satan and Leviathan], the two demonized [principalities] that issued forth from [the adultery of the woman who] was tricked [by the fallen angel, who] destroyed [Adam's] spiritual dimension [in order to acquire the bodies of humanity] which became their graves,[R] and Satan and Leviathan] were so exceedingly fierce that no mortal man who follows the lifestyle of this world [could restrain them],

[R] Ez 31:15

8.29   But when they beheld [Adam], they shrieked [in terror][R] saying, "What do you want with us? Has the son of God come to the same place [where we contended] with the Adam who came] before him, to torture *us* this time?"

[R] Matt 14:30, 26 (ATB)

8.30   And while the group [of disciples who were spiritual] male hogs were feeding on the spiritual doctrine of the Orchard in the unconscious part of God's mind, which is] a good distance away from their carnal mind, [Adam, who had entered their carnal mind through their soul tie with Jesus', was encountering Satan and Leviathan, the principalities of the demonized hybrid mind within the disciples],

8.31   And the demons [generated by Satan and Leviathan, the hybrid mind that issued from the adulteress woman who transgressed the Law within the disciples], implored Jesus in the unconscious part of the carnal mind, saying, "If you cast us out [how will that] group of male hogs [ever] repent?"

8.32   And [Adam] said, "Go out from the unconscious part of the carnal mind [of the disciples and reveal yourselves to them]," and they came out [from where they were hiding] and went into [the conscious mind of] the group of male hogs [who were feeding on spiritual doctrine in the Orchard, the Garden of God], and [the disciples who were] male hogs, saw [in the spiritual understanding of the Word, that they were the woman that was tricked into committing adultery with a fallen angel and

Alternate Translation of The New Testament/ Matthew

gave birth to Leviathan, the hybrid offspring that destroyed Adam's spiritual world and possessed his material bodies], and the whole group of souls [who were in] the high spiritual place where their sins were covered by Adam, the tabernacle that God dwelt in, assaulted [the demonic thoughts of Satan, the other principality that issued from the adulteress woman and a fallen angel, and] they plunged down from [the mind of the disciples which was in the Garden of God, and were dissolved in Satan's] sea, and died.

8.33   And the disciples that were grazing [in the Garden of God] that shunned [the thoughts of Satan], went into the spiritual city [of Jerusalem], and spoke publicly about everything that happened,

8.34   And there it was! All [the inhabitants of spiritual Jerusalem] came out [of the city] to meet Adam, the spiritual dimension [of God within the disciples], and when they saw him they implored [him] to change places with [Satan and Leviathan within] the borders [of their bodies also].

Chapter 10

[798.1.C]
10.14   And whosoever shall not accept you, or [not] pay attention to your words, violently shake their carnal mind [that clings to] the dust, [until Abel] withdraws [from Cain],

[798.3.C]
10.22   And [the carnal mind of] mortal man, which is in the Serpent's image,[R-1] shall hate you, because [you are living out of the mind of] Christ Jesus; but be content, because the [personality that is married to] the mortal mind that is overthrown,[R-2] is the [personality that] is saved.

[R-1] Matt 7:13 (AT)
12:26 (AT)
[R-2] Ez.1:28 (AT)

Alternate Translation of The New Testament/ Matthew

10.23   When one [person, who is an Israelite] city [for spiritual life], persecutes you, shun them, [and go on to the next person]; I am telling you the truth, you shall not have executed your duty to [all] Israelites [who are] cities [for spiritual life], until each individual shall have become the son of man.

10.27   What I relate [to you] from within the darkness [of the carnal mind], you expound in the light [of Kabbalah]; and what you hear with the ear [of the Spirit], you preach from above the highest place [that the carnal mind can rise to];

10.28   Do not teach [only] about [the Son of God], who has the authority to kill the body, but saves [the personality, the nefesh grade of] soul, but also recognize [the Spirit of his Mother], the fire that destroys the body and the [nefesh grade of] soul, [but saves the spirit].

10.29   By no means [is it possible] that one of the two small birds, [the cherubim who are] one 10th [of Majesty (Malchut) of the God World of Emanation, who] is sold to the ground, should fall without the father being concerned for them

10.30   Indeed, He is very concerned [about] you [because] you are the many hairs of his head, [which must] all be accounted for

10.31   Therefore, [you who are] the many [hairs of the head of Ancient Adam] should not be afraid, [because] the cherubim will carry you through,

10.32   [Wherefore], Whosoever of the whole [first Adam] agrees to be a part of me, [the one who stands] in front of the regenerated female Adam, also agrees that the ego, or personality, of himself is a part of [Elijah, the one who stands] in front of [Ancient Adam], my father which is in heaven, and

10.33   Indeed, whosoever of the whole [first Adam] denies [that they are a part of] me [who stands in] front of the

Alternate Translation of The New Testament/ Matthew

regenerated female Adam, also denies that the ego, or personality of himself [stands] in front of my father which is in heaven.

10.34   Do not think that I am come to bring peace on the earth: I come not to bring peace, but [I come with] a [circumcising] sword,

10.35   To bring division, the fallen female Adam against [Leviathan], his father, and the daughter [who married the serpent], against [Satan], her mother, and [the female cherub], the bride, from [Satan], her mother-in-law.

10.38   Whoever I take to myself to deliver [from the problems that they cried out to me about], and does not follow me, will be weighed in the balances.

Chapter 11

[978.3.C]
11.07   Elohim went out [of the God world into Israel] to visit the spiritual plant [that Jehovah planted, because] they were a dry [and thirsty land] wavering [between two opinions];

11.08   Indeed, [when] Elohim went out [from the God world into Israel], he perceived [that] the houses clothing [the primordial] kings were effeminate, and that Adam was also clothed in effeminate personalities.

11.09   Yes, Elohim went out [of the God World, into Israel so that the people would have the opportunity] to recognize a [true] prophet; But I say to you, [they saw] much more than a prophet.

[Message # Unknown]
11.17   You wail and mourn [because the prophets] have pierced and wounded you, but you do not repent,

Alternate Translation of The New Testament/ Matthew

11.16 It is as if you were children under the age of 12 [who continue] to sit in a public place [thinking that their] mother is calling to someone else, [but the truth is that] . . .

[994.1C]
11.19 The Son of man came in communion with the Father, and you say, look at that man, he hangs out with tax collectors and sinners, and is greedy for spiritual power; But the wisdom [that that man speaks] justifies [his behavior, because it indicates that his motives are of God].

Chapter 12

[513.4]
12.01 [Righteous Adam], the other dimension [which is] the [spiritual] cornfield within Jesus, the Sabbath Day, crossed over [into the conscious part of Jesus' mind], because [Jesus'] disciples were hungry [for spiritual food], and [Christ within the disciples] had begun to draw upon [Righteous Adam], the edible [spiritual] corn [within Jesus], and to consume him,

12.02 But when the Pharisees saw [Jesus'] disciples [learning the Doctrine of Christ, the Pharisees] said to [Jesus], are you aware that what you are doing is lawful only on the [spiritual] Sabbath day?

12.03 And [Righteous Adam within Jesus] said to [the Pharisees], have you not read what [Righteous Adam] did when [Abel/Christ] in the midst of David was hungry [for spiritual food]?

12.04 [Righteous Adam], Elohim's household [within David], exposed the Leviathan, [David's] sin nature, [because] it is unlawful for [Leviathan] to consume [Righteous Adam, the heavenly bread, which is] only [for Christ, Elohim's] priest, until [Righteous Adam] marries Christ within them],

12.05   Or have you not read in the law how [Righteous Adam], the collective mind [which is] the priest of [the personalities who are] the Sabbath Day, penetrates into the [personality that is becoming] the Sabbath [Day], and makes him sinless?

12.06   So, I am telling you that the collective mind [of Righteous Adam Christ Jesus] is greater than [Satan and Leviathan, the carnal mind that is joined] to the same personality,

12.07   And [that you would not have] condemned [Jesus and accused of him of] sin, if you understood that Leviathan must be sacrificed [before] the mercy [of Righteous Adam can be expressed through you,

12.08   Because [when Christ], the Son of Righteous Adam, controls [Leviathan within a personality, that personality] becomes the Sabbath Day.[23]

[218.2]
12.25   Now, Jesus was aware of what [the Pharisees] were thinking, [so Jesus] said to them, the personality that fails to subject her emotions and passions by uniting them with the [Christ] mind, [which is her renewed] conscience, is stripped of spiritual power, and dies,

12.26   So, how shall the Kingdom of God appear in you Pharisees, when [Satan and Leviathan], your [carnal] mind, which is in the image of the Serpent,[R] drives me away [and] separates you from Righteous Adam, your [true] head,

[R] Matt 7:13 (AT)
Matt 10:22 (AT)

---

[23]   According to the Jewish Sages, Ze'ir Anpin and Nukva, two of the personifications of the nature of God, join periodically in a spiritual marital union called the **Sabbath Day**, which union results in the birth of new souls engraved with the nature of God, and the outpouring of great blessings.

Alternate Translation of The New Testament/ Matthew

12.27a   And, furthermore, rather than thinking that I am casting out demons by Baal-ze-bub to justify your denial that I am the Christ, try the spirit on your own sons [of Israel],

12.28a   [But before you try the spirit on them] understand that the man who the Spirit of God is appearing in,[R]

[R] 1 Jn 4:3

12.29a   Enters into [the personality that is] Leviathan's wife,[24] [R] and seizes [Abel, who is] bound [underneath Cain within that personality], and separates [Abel from Cain],

[R] Is 40:1-2 (AT)

12.27b   [But, the man] who casts out demons [by Satan, the spirit of the carnal mind, is overcome by the demons within himself],[R]

[R] Acts 19:13-17

12.29b   And at the time that [these contrasting deliverance ministries] appear, [the Serpent's] household will be destroyed.[R]

[R] Jn 8:44

12.28b   Now, [according to this test], if I cast out demons by the Spirit of God, then [you must acknowledge that] the Kingdom of God is come unto you [through me, Jesus],

12.30   But, the personalities who oppose me are so completely penetrated by [Leviathan, the subconscious part of] the carnal mind, that [Satan has stolen] their opportunity to choose to be reconciled to me.

12.31   Therefore, every hurtful word arising out of Cain, the foundation of] mortal man's sin nature, shall be forgiven,[R-1] but Satan, that blaspheming spirit[R-2] [which is the unconscious

---

[24]   Leviathan, the Devil and Satan, are present-day expressions of the Ancient Serpent who appeared in the Garden. They are all spiritual females (Rev 20:2). (Read entire footnote in Appendices)

Alternate Translation of The New Testament/ Matthew

part of mortal man's carnal mind, the one] who [generates the thoughts of mortal man], shall not be forgiven.**R-3**

R-1 Lk 23:34
R-2 Matt 4:1 (AT)
R-3 Rev 20:10

12.32   Therefore, [the personality] that takes authority over [Abel],**R-1** the Son of Adam, shall be forgiven by [Righteous Adam],**R-2** but Leviathan, [Satan's] mouthpiece,**R-3** shall not be forgiven in this age, or in the age to come,

R-1 Jn 8:28
R-2 Matt 9:6
R-3 Rev 13:15

12.33   So, since our attitudes and behavior reveal whether we are the offspring of [Righteous Adam], or [the offspring of] the Serpent, if you are truly the offspring of [Righteous Adam],**R** the Tree of Life, let Elohim's good nature be seen in your attitudes and in your behavior; but if the Tree of the Knowledge of Good and Evil, which is the Serpent's evil nature, appears in your attitudes and behavior, [then] you must be the offspring of [Satan and Leviathan],

R Zech 11:12 (AT)

12.34   [But all] you offspring of the Serpent! How can hurtful men like you speak good things, when the true motives and attitudes of your heart naturally overflow into your mouth [to expose you]?

12.35   A man with a good nature expresses helpful and healing attitudes [through] his emotions; but a man with an evil nature expresses hurtful and destructive attitudes [through] his emotions.

12.36   So, I say unto you, in the day that the Sons of God judge [Satan and Leviathan], your carnal mind, the truth shall be revealed concerning every dead doctrine [that] you preach by [Leviathan, the subconscious part of the carnal mind of] mortal man,

Alternate Translation of The New Testament/   Matthew

12.37   Because in the Day of Judgment, the *truly* justified ones shall speak miracle-working Words, but the condemned ones shall be powerless,

12.39   And the generation [that] commits adultery [with Satan and Leviathan, their carnal mind, while] they seek for [Adam's righteous] mark, or nature, shall be [engraved with] the Serpent's mark, or nature, [if Righteous Adam], the [mind with the] mark, or nature that Jonas the prophet had, [does not regenerate in them].

[840.8.C]
12.43   When the morally impure spirit goes out of [the completed, fallen] Adam, he is sent where there is no moisture to blend the earth into the clay that he needs to incarnate a material body, so that he can rest from the labor that keeps him from dissolving, but does not find [the moisture of Jehovah's breath in the other dimensions that are reflected as outer space]

12.44   Then he says, I will return to my house from where I issued forth, and when he arrived, he found that [the woman] was swept clean and reset in the right moral order, and that she was on vacation (empty).

12.45   . . . and they enter in and dwell there permanently, and the last [fallen] Adam shall be worse than the first [fallen] Adam, and this is how it shall be for that wicked generation

Chapter 13

[818.11.C]
4 and 19   When a teacher sows [the Message of the Kingdom of God] in the hearts [of the students who] are following the lifestyle of this world, those] seeds extend [only as far as the conscious part of the carnal mind of those personalities, so when] some do not understand [the message of the Kingdom of God, Satan], that wicked bird [of the other

Alternate Translation of The New Testament/ Matthew

side], comes and forcibly seizes the Word [of the Kingdom] that was sown [in their heart], and consumes it; [But] some [of the personalities] who are treading the path of this [present] life understand [the message of the Kingdom of God, even though] the seeds extend[ed only into the conscious part of the carnal mind],

5 and 20 [Because, when those] same seeds [which were consumed by the wicked bird in some of the personalities] fell on the earth[en personalities who] understood the Word [of God concerning the Kingdom, those seeds pierced] straight through [the conscious part of the mind of those] earth[en personalities, and] extended [all the way to the soul that Jehovah gave to Abraham], the Rock [that accompanied the Hebrew children when they left Egypt, and throughout their journey, which Rock is] the root [of the Tree of Life within those personalities], and they received the joy [of the Holy Spirit, even though those seeds] did not germinate immediately where [those personalities] did not have very much knowledge of esoteric doctrine,

6 and 21 But, [the joy of the Holy Spirit] exists [only] temporarily, because when [the Rock], the Sun [of Righteousness in the teacher who sowed the seed], arises to drive [Satan, the evil bird in the unconscious part of the mind] under [the authority of] the Word [of God within the teacher, those personalities] are offended, and stumble [over the Rock that they cannot perceive within the teacher], and when [the Spirit of] Truth [within the teacher exposes the sins of those personalities], they persecute [him, and, then, the Rock within the teacher, rains down] fiery judgment [upon those personalities, and the soul tie between the teacher and the personalities] withers, [and the earthen personalities of the personalities, can no longer **suck the oil and the water from the spiritual Rock** within the teacher who sowed the seed within them, and]

7 and 22 Also, some of the seeds [that] fell on the carnal mind [of the personalities] who heard the Word [about the Kingdom of God that] extended [as far as the Rock within

them], did spring up, [but] were, nevertheless, strangled [by Satan and Cain], the sharp pointed stones [of their carnal mind, which had already pierced through their earthen personalities and [married them to Leviathan, their other side, even the one who] distracted them with the cares of this age and the delusion of wealth, [so] they did not bear the fruit of [the Rock within the teacher],

8 and 23 But the seed of the Rock [that accompanied the Hebrew children when they left Egypt], that fell down upon the good ground [of the personalities who pursued the spiritual life of Jehovah], that extended into some of [the personalities whose lifestyle] was virtuous, heard the Word [about the Kingdom of God], and understood it, and conceived, and brought forth fruit [in three degrees]:

An **hundred**fold, [which is] Understanding,

Sixtyfold, [which is], indeed, [the Spirit of] Truth, and

Thirtyfold, [which is] the Rock of the other [world, the seed that imposes the DNA of the higher world upon the lower world]

Chapter 14

[1165.1.C (674.5.C)]

14.14   And [Jesus] went forth and saw a large throng [of people], and was moved by his compassion for them, to relieve them of their diseases,

14.15   And when the ability to heal departed from [Jesus'] disciples, they came [to him] saying,

"The spirit [of healing] has dried up. The time for [ministry] must be over, [so let us] disburse the crowd that they may go to the village and buy kosher food for themselves,"

Alternate Translation of The New Testament/ Matthew

14.16a   But Jesus said,

"The Spirit has not departed [yet because]

14.18   "[Adam] told [me] he is willing to bring the Spirit [of Truth to the people that are] here, [so]

14.16b   "Feed them," and

14.17   They said,

"We can minister the letter but not the Spirit of the Word, [because] the people [that are] here only have the second [grade] of soul," [25]

14.20a   [So, Adam entered into the mind of the disciples through their soul tie with Jesus and] filled [them] up [with the authority to] complete [the people of the crowd, to give them a spiritual intellectual soul, so that] all of them could eat [the spiritual understanding of the Word [of God], and

14.19   [Adam, who was within the disciples through their soul tie with Jesus], commanded the resurrected Abel [within the disciples] to seize [Abel within the people of] the crowd [that the disciples] ministered the letter of the Word to, [so that Abel] could recover [his spiritual sight] and marry [Cain within the people;

And Abel stood up in the people who] submitted [to Adam, and Adam] circumcised[R] [Cain, the personality of the carnal mind], away from [Satan, and] the disciples gave [the spiritual understanding of] the letter of the Word to the crowd, and the personalities of the crowd that submitted to Adam] ate the spiritual understanding of the Word, and

[R] Col 2:11

---

[25] The first grade of soul is the personality, and the second grade of soul is the human spirit. The third grade of soul, the spiritual intellectual soul, is needed to understand spiritual doctrine.

Alternate Translation of The New Testament/ Matthew

14.20b [Adam] forgave the sins [of the people who consumed^R the Spirit of the Word, which is his flesh], and

^R Jn 6:53

14.21 The women, as well as the mortal males [that submitted to Adam], ate the spiritual wisdom about the [holy] child^R that [the disciples] ministered [to the crowd], and

^R Acts 4:27
Rev 12:5

14.22 Immediately [after that, Jesus] impressed upon the disciples [how important it was that] they enter into the ark, [their] other, [spiritual mind], and go forward [with the development [of their] spiritual side, [and then] he dismissed the crowd, and

14.23 After [Jesus] dismissed the crowd, he went into a high place in the Spirit; And prayed that God should permit the disciples to descend into the depth of Adam's spiritual authority, because] the night was approaching^R [when he would be taken from the earth and, at the present time], he was the only one who could descend into [the depth of Adam's spiritual authority to resurrect Abel and circumcise Cain away from Satan];

^R Jn 9:4

14.24 Now the Ark, [the other, spiritual mind of God], was a great [distance away from] the community of Israel, [26] [where] the bodies [of the people who were under the Law] were [experiencing] the pain of resisting [the thoughts of Cain, the personality of the carnal mind, who] was already opposing [their efforts to keep the Law] by impregnating the unconscious part of the mind with unstable [thoughts]; and

14.25 In the early hours of the morning, [when Adam] was walking around in the spiritual dimension [of Jesus' mind, which is directly below] the unconscious part of the carnal mind, and

---

[26] The correct translation of the Greek word is "stadium," which we have interpreted to mean "the community of Israel."

Alternate Translation of The New Testament/ Matthew

14..26 [Satan, the personality of] the unconscious part of the carnal mind, saw [Adam] walking around in the spiritual dimension of [Jesus'] mind, she became agitated and shrieked [in terror],[R] and the disciples [heard it, and] were afraid, saying,

"It is a ghost,"

[R] Vs 30
Matt 8:29 (ATB)

14.27 But Jessus spoke, instantly, [from] the spiritual dimension of [the unconscious] mind, saying,

"Be strong and courageous, and do not be afraid,[R] [because it is Satan, the personality of the unconscious mind, that became agitated and shrieked when she saw that] I [was walking around in the spiritual dimension of Jesus' mind]," and

[R] Deut 31:6

14.28 Peter responded from the ark, [his other, spiritual mind], and said,

"Lord, if [it was] you [who just spoke to me], allow me to enter into [the spiritual dimension of] mind, where [I do not have the authority] to go," and

14.29 [Jesus] said "come," and Peter descended out of the ark, [his other, spiritual mind], and walked into the spiritual dimension [that] Jesus went into,

14.30 But when [Peter] saw the power of the Spirit [of Judgment that rules in the spiritual dimension of Righteous Adam's mind] he became alarmed, and [Abel within Peter] began to plunge down [into the unconscious part of the carnal mind, and Cain, who is attached to Abel], shrieked [in terror [R] when she saw Satan, the enforcer of the Sowing & Reaping Judgment], and [Peter] said, "Lord save me," and

[R] Vs 26
Matt 8: 29 (ATB)

14.31 Immediately, Jesus extended [his] mind [towards Peter, and Adam] seized [Abel while he was still in] the spiritual dimension of [Jesus' mind, and Jesus] said to [Adam] in the spiritual dimension of [the unconscious] mind, "Why did [Abel within Peter] waver?" [And Adam said," Because Peter's] faith is [still] very small; [27] [R] and

[R] 8:26 (ATB)

14.32   When they came from the spiritual dimension of [the unconscious] mind into the ark, [the other, spiritual mind of God], the Spirit [of Adam's Righteous Judgment that blows in the spiritual dimension of the unconscious], rested.

Chapter 16

[447]
16.18   And I am also letting you know, Peter, that [Christ in] you is the little rock, but [that the Shekinah above is] the [big] rock who restores the [higher spirituality], where my people are gathered together with [the glorified Jesus Christ, the one who prevents] Satan, the door to the underworld, from catching them [and bringing them back under her control], and

16.19   I will give you [Christ], the vital, crucial element [that enables you] to possess the Kingdom of Heaven, [which is] the visible, spiritual world, and [to overcome Cain], your earth[en foundation], the chain [that] binds you to [Satan and the Devil, your carnal mind];

Indeed, [the Shekinah] in your earth[en personality] shall be loosed from [Satan, who speaks from the spiritual place that belongs to Christ Jesus, the Kingdom of] Heaven;[R]

[R] 2 Thes 2:4

16.20   Then [Jesus] identified Satan, [the unconscious part of the carnal mind within] his disciples, [and drove her down

---

[27] "Faith" before Jesus' resurrection is "Abraham's seed"; After the resurrection, it is called, "Christ." Abraham's seed which was to be strengthened through Jesus' resurrection, was still very immature.

Alternate Translation of The New Testament/ Matthew

under his authority, so that his disciples] could recognize that he was the Christ, and

16.21 From that time, Jesus began to reveal to his disciples that he would go to Jerusalem and suffer many things [at the hands of] the elders, and the chief priests and scribes, and be killed, and rise again, [and ascend out of this world], which is the Ancient Serpent's dimension, and

16.22 Then [Satan, the unconscious part of] Peter['s mortal mind], took authority over [Peter] and taught him, saying, "[God is] merciful, [He would not let] Satan do this to the Lord,"

16.23 But, then, Peter's [personality] turned into Righteous Adam, his other self, [who is Jesus'] relative, [and] said to Satan, "Go down under [my authority], because [you agree with the thoughts of Satan and Leviathan, the unconscious and subconscious parts of the carnal mind of] mortal man."

Chapter 17

[1203.1]
17.24 [But it] came to Peter in the unconscious part of the mind, [that the only begotten Son], the young lion [that was standing up] in the unconscious part of the mind, would forgive the sins [of the people that] approached [Jesus], and [Peter] said,

"Master, are you not [going] to satisfy the debt these people owe to the Egyptian god, *Suchos*, and make them your own?"

17.25 And [the only begotten Son] said, "Yes."

And, when they came into the house, Jesus anticipated [Peter's question about his death and resurrection in] the unconscious part of the mind, and said,

Alternate Translation of The New Testament/ Matthew

"What do you think, Simon? Who do the kings of the earth take the last bit of money from [to pay their] taxes, their own children, or strangers?"

17.26 [And Peter] said, "Of strangers."

And Jesus said to [Peter]

"Then, without doubt, the children [of God] are not slaves, but are free [from indebtedness to other gods] in the unconscious part of the mind;

17.27 "Nevertheless, in order to [ensure that the children] do not stumble in [the darkness of] the unconscious part of the mind, go and cast a hook into the abyss, and take away [the sins of] the first fish that ascends [through understanding] into the unconscious part of the mind, and opens [its] mouth [to speak about what it learned, and], then, takes [what it has received] and gives it to me and you in the unconscious part of the mind [so that we might] find salvation [also]."

Chapter 19

[OLM 07 12 00]

19.28 And Jesus said to them, I assure you [that] it is true that the Son of [Righteous] Adam shall be regenerated within you who follow my path, and [that the Son of Righteous Adam] shall marry you, and [the Son of Righteous Adam] shall marry the glorified [Jesus Christ], the [only] Potentate,[R] who resides permanently above the heart, [and above Satan and Leviathan], the powers of [the underworld].

[R] 1 Tim 6:15

Alternate Translation of The New Testament/ Matthew

Chapter 20

[524.2]
20.20   Then, the mother of the children [who] God [gave as a] gift [to humanity], desiring [to marry Abel] in the midst of her sons, approached [Satan and] worshiped [Satan],

20.21   And [Satan] said [to Leviathan in the mother], what do you want? [And Leviathan within the mother] said [to Satan], grant me permission to marry [Abel], my second son [within the disciples, who is] united with [Jesus], the beginning [of Jehovah's] blessing [to humanity], because [Cain within the disciples is already] united with [me, Leviathan], the beginning of Satan's kingdom [of darkness],

20.22   But Jesus responded to [the children who are Jehovah's gift to humanity, not their mother], saying, I know what Leviathan [within] you desires, [but] can you drink [from Elijah], the [glorified] vessel that I am permitted to draw energy from? [And Jesus' disciples] said [to Jesus], we can deal [with the stress associated with infolding the glorified Elijah's energy],

20.23   And [Jesus] said to [his disciples], indeed, my father, [the glorified Elijah], will prepare [Leviathan], my [opponent], to deliver up Cain, the beginning of the Kingdom of Darkness [within the disciples], to [Righteous Adam], the[ir] other [mind, and Righteous Adam] shall marry [Christ], the beginning of [Jehovah's] blessings [to mankind within you], and you will drink from [the Spirit of the glorified Elijah], the cup, [that I drink from, and Righteous Adam shall drive Cain, the fiery serpent within you, down] under [Abel],

20.24   And when [Jesus' disciples who were under] the law heard [that they would have to face Satan and Leviathan, their sin nature, and overcome them, Cain within the disciples]

Alternate Translation of The New Testament/   Matthew

was moved with indignation against [Abel, their] second [born] brother [within Jesus],

20.25   But Jesus called [forth the Christ nature in the disciples by] saying, *you know that [Satan], the Prince [of this world], dominates the gentiles, and [that Leviathan] wields a powerful authority over them,*

20.26   But it shall not be so for you. Indeed, it shall come to pass [that the glorified Elijah, the right hand of] the great [God, Jehovah], shall appear in whoever amongst you prefers [Righteous Adam over Leviathan, and the glorified Elijah will strengthen you] to attend to [Satan and Leviathan],

20.27   And [the glorified Elijah] will be the chief of whosoever amongst you prefers [Righteous Adam over Leviathan], and you, [the personality], will be [the glorified Elijah's] servant,

20.28   [And] Satan will appear to teach [you], just like [she appeared to Jesus], the Son of [Ancient] Adam, but [Jesus] delivered up [Leviathan], his [flesh] life, to redeem the many [Abels trapped within mortal humanity, and the glorified Elijah strengthened Jesus] to attend to [Satan and Leviathan],

20.29   And the spiritual [man, Elijah, the right hand of] the great [God, Jehovah], accompanied [Jesus and the disciples as] they departed from [spiritual] Jericho.

Chapter 21

[1206.6.C]

Jesus Approaches Jerusalem

21.01a   And as they approached Jerusalem, the City [where souls* dwell with Jehovah in] Peace, they came to Bethpage, [a village of] immature personalities [who] were not yet dwelling

Alternate Translation of The New Testament/ Matthew

peacefully [with Jehovah in the Sphere of Wisdom], the high place where [spiritual] olive [trees [R-1] grow], and

* "Souls" are also called "personalities."

[R-1] Rom 11:17
Vs 8 & 18

One Personality Saved

21.02   [The only begotten Son of the Father[R] in] the unconscious part of the mind [of Jesus of Nazareth] said,

[R-1] 2 Jn 3

"Go into the Village [which] is [just] ahead of [you], and immediately you will find an animal personality [that Jehovah loves], bound to [the lusts of her] animal body in the unconscious part of the mind; Release her and bring [her] to me,

21.03   "And if any one says anything to you [about what you are doing], you shall say,

"The Lord, [the only begotten Son of the Father] in the unconscious part of the mind [of Jesus of Nazareth], demands that [this personality] be set apart [from the animal nature of her body in] the unconscious pat of the mind, immediately," and, [then], bring her to me;

21.01b   And Jesus* sent [the] two [new] [R-1] disciples [into the Village of Bethpage],

* The Name, "Jesus" includes the only begotten Son of the Father (2Jn 3) in the unconscious part of the mind of Jesus of Nazareth.

[R-1] Matt 20:30-34

Announce The Fulfillment of Prophecy

21.04   And all this happened so that [what] the prophet [Zechariah] spoke should come to pass when he said,

Alternate Translation of The New Testament/ Matthew

21.05 "Tell the daughter of the Sphere of Wisdom: [R-1]

"[Christ], your king, the less than one-year old son [of the Son of the Sphere of Wisdom, who came riding in] a male donkey, is coming to marry you, a young male donkey [that he is bringing] under [his] yoke, [R-2]

"Look [for him always and everywhere, so that you are sure to recognize him when he appears]!"[R-3]

[R-1] Vs 19
[R-2] Matt 11:29
[R-3] Zech 9:9

21.06 And [the two new] disciples went and did what Jesus arranged for them to do,

21.07 And brought [Jehovah's beloved animal personality that was bound to the lusts of an animal body in the unconscious part of the mind] to [Jesus, and the only begotten Son of the Father within Jesus of Nazareth] married [her in] the unconscious part of the mind, and put [the nature of the Son of the Father] on top of [the animal nature] in the unconscious part of the mind, [and that personality became] the outer clothing [of the only begotten Son of the Father],

One Convert Becomes A Crowd

Immature Personalities

21.08 And [the only begotten Son of the Father within Jesus of Nazareth] spread himself[R-1] [from that personality into] a very large crowd of [repentant personalities of the Village of Bethpage, who were] leading [a spiritually immature] lifestyle,[R-2]

[and they became] the outer clothing [of the only begotten Son of the Father], and

Students of The Higher Wisdom

The others, [who] were students of the [spiritual olive] trees ^{R-3} [that were dwelling peacefully with Jehovah in the Sphere of Wisdom], beat their breasts^{R-4} in repentance to prepare [themselves for the spiritually ascended] lifestyle ^{R-5} [of the only begotten Son of the Father],

^{R-1} Gen 2:7
Jn 20:22
^{R-2} Jn 14:6
^{R-3} Vs 1 & 18
^{R-4} Lk 23:48
^{R-5} 1 Pet 1:16

The Crowd Announces Jesus

21.09   And the crowd [of personalities] that was [standing] in front of [the only begotten Son of the Father] in the unconscious part of the mind, [who were now] following [a lifestyle of repentance and submission to the Father] in the unconscious part of the mind, cried out [as their personalities entered into Jerusalem, the City of Souls that dwell in Peace with Jehovah], saying,

"Salvation is here, the Supreme God is here to save us [through] the Son of David [who comes to bless us in the Name of Jehovah], the Lord,"

An Emotional Reaction to The Spirit

21.10   And when [the only begotten Son of the Father, who is] in the unconscious part of the mind of [Jesus of Nazareth] came into Jerusalem, all [the personalities of spiritual Jerusalem], the city [of personalities that were dwelling peacefully with Jehovah in the Sphere of Wisdom], became agitated and disturbed in their mind, saying,

Alternate Translation of The New Testament/   Matthew

"Who is this?"

21.11   And the crowd [of repentant, spiritually immature personalities and students of the priests and scholars] said,

"This is the prophet Jesus of Nazareth of Galilee,"

The Existing Authority Is Overthrown

21.12   And Jesus went into the temple, and [the only begotten Son of the Father within Jesus of Nazareth, the seat of Jesus' authority to teach the Law], overthrew the seats [of the authority of the chief priests and] the scholars, the teachers of the Law, who were selling ^{R-1} the Holy Spirit for money, and cast everyone out of the temple that was buying [the Holy Spirit],

^{R-1} Rev 18:11-13
^{R-2} Rev 18:13

21.13   And [the only begotten Son of the Father who was] in the unconscious part of the mind of [Jesus of Nazareth], said to [the chief priests and the scholars],

"It is written,

" 'My house shall be called a house of prayer,' ^R

^{R-1} Is 56:7

"But you have made it [into] a cave of spiritual thieves,"

The Weak & Infirm Healed

21.14   And [the personalities of Jerusalem who] were physically blind, ignorant, stupid or slow to understand, and [the personalities of Jerusalem who] were physically crippled or fallen in the unconscious part of the mind, came to the temple, and [the only begotten Son of the Father] in the unconscious part of the mind [of Jesus of Nazareth], healed them, ^R

^R Is 35:5-6

Alternate Translation of The New Testament/ Matthew

The Existing Authority Complains

21.15   And when the chief priests and the scholars saw the miracles that [Jesus] did, and [heard] the students [of the priests and scholars] crying out in the temple, saying,

"Salvation is here, [the Supreme God is here to save us through] the Son of David [who comes to bless us in the Name of the Jehovah],"

They resented it, ^R

^R Matt 27:18, Mk 15:10

Priests and Scholars Rebuked

21.16   And said [to Jesus] out of their spiritual mind,

"Do you hear what these [students of the priests and scholars] are saying?"

And Jesus said, out of [the only begotten Son of the Father, his] spiritual mind,

"Yes.

"Have you never read concerning [this matter that]

" 'The complete story [of the salvation of Israel] shall come out of the mouth of [spiritual] infants [who] suck [this wisdom out of Jehovah, the Rock of their Salvation]?' " ^R

^R Deut 32:13

21.17   And [Jesus] left them, and went out of the City [of Jerusalem, where souls dwell peacefully with Jehovah] in the unconscious part of the mind, and went into Bethany, [where many of the personalities were depressed because they believed the thoughts of] the carnal mind, and he stayed in the field with the sheep ᴿ [that were] there;

ᴿ Gen 2:21 (ATB)
Jn 10:7

Jesus Hungers for Spiritual Fellowship

21.18   Now, [as the only begotten Son of the Father], the Morning [Star^{R-1} in the unconscious part of the mind of Jesus of Nazareth, returned to Jerusalem], he was hungering ᴿ⁻² [to taste the fruit of the spiritual olive trees that were dwelling peaceably with Jehovah in the Sphere of Wisdom], ᴿ⁻³

ᴿ⁻¹ Rev 2:28
ᴿ⁻² Matt 5:6
Jn 6:35
ᴿ⁻³ Vs 1 & 8

No Fruit in Jerusalem

21.19   But when he came [to Jerusalem, the spiritual city of personalities that were dwelling peaceably with Jehovah in the Sphere of Wisdom, in] the unconscious part of the mind, he perceived only a shoot [of a spiritual olive tree]; There was no fruit [in Jerusalem, even though the personalities that were dwelling there were] united [with daughter of the Sphere of Wisdom] ᴿ in the unconscious part of the mind, [and the only begotten Son of the Father] in the unconscious part of the mind of Jesus [of Nazareth], said

ᴿ Zech 9:9
Vs 5

Another Age

"[Let] the present [age] shrivel up [in the personalities that are dwelling peaceably in the Sphere of Wisdom] in the unconscious part of the mind, and let [the next] age be born in [them] without any further delay,"

21.20   And when the disciples understood [that Jesus had commanded the present age within the personalities that were dwelling peaceably in the Sphere of Wisdom to come to an end], they were astonished, saying,

"How soon [shall the present age within the personalities in] Israel [that are dwelling peaceably in the Sphere of Wisdom] wither away?"

21.21   And Jesus answered, saying in the unconscious part of the mind,

A New Covenant

"I am telling you the truth, if you have an intimate relationship with God and do not doubt [that the next age will be born in the personalities in] Israel [that are dwelling peaceably in the Sphere of Wisdom], not only shall [it be] done, but, if you say to [Death], [R-1] the insurmountable [consequence for sin under the Levitical Law], [R-2]

" 'This [personality] is forgiven, [R-3] let it be cast into the sea[R-4] [of undifferentiated potential, to be reformed[R-5] by the only begotten Son of the Father],'

"It shall be done [also],

[R-1] 1 Cor 15:55
[R-2] Deut 28
[R-3] Zech 3:4
[R-4] Mic 2:19
[R-5] Jer 18:4

The Great Commission

21.22   "And [when] you are intimate with God, you shall ask for all these things that [I just told you about], believing [that] they are possible, and you shall take [away the sins of the personalities in] Israel [that are dwelling peaceably in the Sphere of Wisdom]."

Alternate Translation of The New Testament/ Matthew

Chapter 22

[455.2]

22.15   Then the Pharisees went forth to figure out how they could confuse the Living Word in the unconscious part of [Jesus' mind],

22.16   And [the Pharisees] sent their disciples amongst the Herodians [to mock Jesus] saying, "Master, we know that you are the Truth and that you teach the truth about the way to God, and are not concerned about the fiery serpent [within you being reclaimed by Satan and Leviathan], because Satan [and Leviathan] recognize Righteous Adam behind your personality [and fear him],

22.17   "So give us your opinion, which is the right way to ascend in consciousness, [through union with] Righteous Adam, the one [who was] severed [from Michael], or [through union] with [Satan], the emperor [of this mortal world]?"

22.18   But Jesus discerned that Satan was motivating the [Pharisees], and said, "are you trying to make me angry by pretending [to seek the truth]?

22.19   "Show me the one who has saved [his personality] by ascending into the top [of Leviathan's timeline, and I will show you the one who] has handed [his personality] over to [Satan and Leviathan], the Serpent's timeline!"

22.20a   And then [Jesus] taught the [Pharisees about how]

22.21a   [The Serpent] severed [Adam] from Michael and

22.20b   Overwrote Adam's [righteous] nature, and

Alternate Translation of The New Testament/ Matthew

22.22a   When [the Pharisees] understood [the truth about Adam],

22.21b   [Jesus] said [to Satan, the unconscious part of the carnal mind within the disciples of the Pharisees], "let the [personalities] who belong to Christ, join with Christ Jesus [within me], and let [the powers and principalities that were created by Satan], the emperor [of this world], join with [Satan], the emperor [of this world, within the Pharisees who sent you]," and

22.22b   [The disciples of the Pharisees] admired [Jesus], and forsook [their ungodly relationship with the Pharisees who sent them, and Christ within the disciples] departed [from Cain],

Chapter 23

[800.2.C]
23.05a   But everything they do is a performance to convince Righteous Adam of their affection for him, so that he might notice them, and visit them, and for this reason they flatter themselves, [believing that] their phylacteries [make them]

23.06a   His friend, [and that]

23.05b   He will deliver them [because] they are the edge of his garment,

23.06b   And that he recognizes their public service by sharing [doctrine] with them, which gives them a place of honor next to the master of the house in the synagogues, [and for this reason]

23.07   The people should address them at their assemblies [as men who are] under [the instruction of Righteous Adam, [and] call [them] *Rabbi*.

Alternate Translation of The New Testament/ Matthew

[513.1]
23.19 You [are spiritually] blind because money is more important [to you] than Righteous Adam, [the one] who purifies [Cain], the fiery serpent [within you].

23.17 You [spiritually] blind fools, why is money more important [to you] than [Righteous Adam], the Holy Mind that purifies your spirit?

23.16 Much grief will come to the [spiritually] blind leaders who say [that] they can call forth the power of their own mind to get wealth, because whoever calls forth the power of the god within [himself], is in bondage to Satan [and Leviathan, their unrighteous] mind,

23.21 And whosoever calls forth the power of [Satan and Leviathan], the mind within himself, calls forth [Satan], the one who dwells permanently within him,

23.20 And whosoever calls forth the power of [Satan's] altar within himself, invokes the power of everything within himself that is [spiritually] higher than [mortal man],

23.22 And whosoever calls forth the powers of [Leviathan's throat] within himself calls forth the power of [Satan], the god that [Leviathan] is married to,

23.18 And whoever calls forth Satan's [power from] within [himself, is guilty of] sacrificing [Righteous Adam, the spiritual man from] above.

Chapter 24

[644.4]
24.01 Then, Jesus departed from the temple, and [Jesus'] disciples approached him about the construction of [the third] Temple, [and Elijah] went out

Alternate Translation of The New Testament/ Matthew

24.02 From Jesus, and Jesus] began to speak to [his disciples], saying, open your spiritual eyes [and look at the whole picture, including] the things which are not seen, [because] I am telling you that [the Pharisees' lack of repentance] will cause [Abel, Adam's foundation] stone, [who is] above [Cain, the Serpent's foundation] stone [in the Pharisees], to depart from them, [and the Pharisees] will be separated from [Jehovah],

24.03 And, since [Jesus] was joined to the olive orchard [in the garden of Eden], his disciples came to him privately, saying, tell us when these things shall be, and what shall be the sign of [Messiah's] appearance, and [what shall be the sign] of the end of this age?

24.04 And Jesus answered them, saying, "be very careful not to let anyone seduce you away from the [Spirit of] Truth,

24.05 "Because many shall come in my name, saying, 'I am Christ,' [and] many shall be deceived, and depart from the [Spirit] of Truth, and

24.06 "You shall hear of wars and rumors of wars, but discern [what you see] passively, and do not be frightened, because all these things must come to pass, but [it is not] the end [of this age] yet,

24.07 "[Because Abel must first awaken, and rise up from under the earth of that] pest, [Cain, who will call upon the whole] kingdom [of darkness to defend him] against the Kingdom [of God], and [Satan, the spiritual sea, shall respond by causing] violent storms [which will cause] shock and agitation in many souls, and nation shall rise up against nation, and there shall be a scarcity of [spiritual and material] food,

24.08 But all these things are the beginning of the pain associated with the birth of the [man]child.

24.09 "[And at that time], you shall give [Cain] over to the pressure [of being driven under Abel, and Righteous Adam] shall

Alternate Translation of The New Testament/ Matthew

kill [Leviathan within] you, and [Satan within] all the nations shall detest and persecute you because [of Christ Jesus], my Name [in the earth],

24.10 "But the many [members of Cain], the other [sister], shall begin to distrust and desert [the Lord Jesus], who they ought to trust and obey, and [shall fall into] sin, and [Satan, the mother of Cain], the other [sister], shall hate [Christ] and give him over to [Leviathan], and

24.11 "[Cain] shall arise [above] many of [the members of Christ, and they shall become] false prophets, and many shall be seduced to depart from the [Spirit of] Truth, and

24.12 "[Satan], the lawless one, shall increase, and [Abel], the breath [of Jehovah's life, shall separate from] the love [of the Truth],

24.13 "But the mortal man who [is strengthened by Christ, and] maintains his position above [Cain] until the end [of the age], shall be rescued [from hell and death], and

24.14 "They shall preach the good news of the Kingdom [of God] in all the lands [of the Roman Empire] for a witness to the whole nation [of Israel], that the end [of the age] has arrived.

24.15 "Therefore, when you see the image [of the Dragon] that destroys [the manchild] that Daniel the prophet spoke about, standing up against the place of the prophet [where Ancient Adam], the Holy One [of God resides] (let everyone who reads this understand),

24.16 "Then, let Judea disappear into the spiritual centers of the mountains [which are] beyond

24.17 "The publicly known enlightenment, [and] let them not descend to expiate the sins of the house[hold that they came] out of.

Alternate Translation of The New Testament/ Matthew

24.18 "Neither look back to pick up [the Holy Spirit again], the clothing [that covered you when you were] in the field [of this world], and

24.19 "Woe to them who are pregnant with, or nursing [the manchild] in those days, [when he is still too young to enable them to disappear into the spiritual centers which are beyond the publicly known enlightenment], and

24.20 "Pray that [when] the time to escape [from this world comes], it will not be in the [spiritual] winter [when Christ, Jehovah's spiritual plant is lying dormant under Cain's ground], or on the Sabbath day, [when Christ in those who voluntarily subjected Cain within themselves to the judgment, is in the marriage bed above],

24.21 "Because that is the time set for [Christ Jesus] to persecute Leviathan, [and exert] the greatest pressure upon [Satan], the Prince of this world, since the Serpent [brought this world] into existence,

24.22 "But, unless [Abel] is cut away [from Satan within] those [who are the children of] the Day, not one [spiritual woman who is pregnant with the manchild] would be saved from Leviathan, [the Serpent's spiritual, sexual] male organ; but through the instrumentality of those [children of the Day] who voluntarily elected [to judge Leviathan within themselves, Abel] shall be cut away [from Satan within] those other [children of the Day also],

24.23 "[So], if at that time, anyone [who is not a prophet of God] says to you, in writing or verbally, that Christ is here or there, do not believe [him],

24.24 "Because, [when Cain] rises above [Abel, that person becomes a spokesperson for the Dragon; wherefore], false Christs and false prophets shall show great supernatural signs and miracles, to the extent that the [children of the Day, who became] mighty and powerful when they voluntarily elected [to judge

Alternate Translation of The New Testament/ Matthew

Leviathan within themselves, might] even be seduced to depart from [the Spirit] of truth.

24.25 "[Now], pay close attention to what I have just told you,

24.26 "Because, as it is [in the natural, so it is in the spiritual]; Wherefore, be careful about trusting [anyone] who says that you are not [the temple of God], and that [Christ Jesus is] not [in] the secret chambers [in the spiritual center of your heart; also] watch out for [anyone who] tells you that [Christ Jesus] will not issue forth from your [center of your heart after he boils Satan, and your spiritual center of your heart becomes] dry ground,

24.27 "Because, the Son of Adam shall issue forth from the eternal realm of God and shine into the [west, which is] the visible, material world, and his appearance shall be as glaringly obvious as the [lightning-like] judgments [of Jehovah's righteous Sowing and Reaping Judgment];

24.28 "So, wherever [Leviathan's] dead body [is found], that is the place where the Eagles [joined with Christ Jesus] to assemble [God's throne],[R] and

[R] Rev 4:2

24.29 "Immediately after [Christ Jesus] persecutes [Leviathan], and pressures [Satan to submit to his authority within] those [children of the] Day [who are voluntarily judging the sins of Leviathan within themselves, Christ Jesus] shall overshadow the [devilish] wisdom of [Leviathan], the sun [of this present age], and darken [Satan], the moon [of this present age], and [the new] heaven shall descend upon the spiritually ascended [children of the Day], and they shall overthrow the miracle workers of [the old] heaven, and

24.30 "Then the sign of the [manchild], the Son of [Righteous] Adam, shall shine from his heavenly [throne] within [the children of the Day, who are voluntarily judging the sins of

Alternate Translation of The New Testament/ Matthew

Leviathan within themselves], and then [the Lord Jesus Christ], the Son of [Ancient] Adam, shall be seen arriving with great power [to restore] dignity to the soul [that fell down from] Heaven, and he shall cut off [Leviathan], the carnal [mind] of all the tribes [of Jacob who are judging Leviathan within themselves], and

24.31   "[The Lord Jesus] shall send forth a powerful vibration, and [Christ Jesus], the angels [who are his other self in the earth], shall gather [the children of the Day in] the extremity [of the earth who] are voluntarily [judging the sins of Leviathan within themselves], together with the four spiritual [mountains] of heaven, [which are] the other extremity, and

24.32   "Now, understand the parable of the fig tree; when its reproductive part sprouts new leaves even though its branches are broken off, you should know that summer, [the time when new life appears], is near,

24.33   "So, in the same manner, when you see all these things [coming to pass], you should know that [the bridegroom] is already at the door [of the world below, preparing to enter in to it].

24.34   "I am telling you the truth, this generation will not end until each individual experiences all these things [that I have told you about];

24.35   "This Heaven and this Earth shall pass away, but [the Sons of God, who speak] my Words, shall not pass away.

24.36   "Indeed, neither [Satan], nor [Leviathan], not even the angels of heaven, know that day or hour, but only the Son [of Man] and the Father [know it];

24.37   "Indeed, when the Son of Adam appears, it shall be like it was in the days of Noah,

Alternate Translation of The New Testament/ Matthew

24.38 "Because, in the days before the flood, they were eating [Leviathan's flesh] and drinking [Satan's blood], and [Cain] was married to [Satan] and [Abel was married to Leviathan, fallen Adam's] reproductive part, until the day that Noah entered into the ark, and

24.39 "Neither shall they know [the time] that the son of [Ancient] Adam shall appear to expiate their sins; and, [therefore], they shall also be [unaware when] the flood comes to carry all of them away.

24.40 "Then, the two [sisters, Cain and Abel], shall be in the field [of creation, and Abel] shall be the one taken into [the marriage chamber], and [Cain], the other sister, shall be sent away from [the Lord's household], and

24.41 "The two [sisters, Cain and Abel], shall be grinding [the wheat of spiritual doctrine] at the mill [where truth is distinguished from error, and Abel] shall receive [the doctrine of Christ, but Cain], shall reject it.

24.42 "Watch, therefore, because you do not know what hour your Lord will come [to judge the sins of Leviathan within you],

24.43 "But, you should know this, if [Leviathan], the master of the house[holds], knew the hour that [the Lord Jesus] would come as a thief [to judge the sins of Leviathan in] each [Israelite], he would vigilantly watch to prevent [Abel] in each [Israelite] from being penetrated by [the Lord Jesus. But since Leviathan does not know the hour that the Lord Jesus will appear, she vigilantly watches Abel to make sure that he stays asleep];

24.44 "Therefore, you should be prepared by [diligently judging the sins of Leviathan within yourself]: Because the Son of [Ancient] Adam shall also appear when you least expect him;

Alternate Translation of The New Testament/ Matthew

24.45 "[Now], the Holy Spirit, then, is the faithful and wise servant who the Lord has appointed over his household [until] the time set to give [the children] meat.

24.46 "Blessed [is the man] who the Lord finds doing the work of [the Holy Spirit, the faithful and wise] servant, when He appears,

24.47 "I am telling you the truth, [the Lord] shall designate [that man as his representative] over all of his property,

24.48 "But, [the man who does the work of the Holy Spirit, the faithful and wise] servant [of the Lord, and also] speaks against the Lord, [saying, 'He is not] in the center of my heart,' will delay the appearance [of the Lord in that man],

24.49 "But, if it is said about [anyone who] eats [the doctrine of Christ] that he is drunken [from] drinking [the Spirit of Christ, and that man] begins to smite [the one who eats doctrine],

24.50 "The Lord shall come to [that man who is doing the work of the Holy Spirit, the faithful and wise] servant, [who is a child of] the Day, but is looking for him with Cain's understanding, and

24.51 "Shall bisect the one who pretends to be [Christ], but is not [from the Kingdom of God], and give his share [to the man who truly represents the Lord]."

Chapter 25

[522]
25.01 Then shall the Kingdom of Heaven be likened to [spiritual] virgins [who are] under the law, which were taken [in marriage by Righteous Adam], who illuminated [them], and

Alternate Translation of The New Testament/ Matthew

[then Righteous Adam], the bridegroom, spread abroad to meet [the Cherubim], and

25.04 [Righteous Adam, the spiritual] oil, [was] within the enlightened pails, or vessels [that Ancient Ada,] took [in marriage],

25.03 But Righteous Adam was not created [in the virgins] who were enlightened [by Leviathan, and] taken [in marriage] by, Satan,

25.02 So, [some of the virgins ascended into] the center of the throat of Righteous Adam's [dimension, and some ascended into] the center of throat [of Leviathan's dimension],

25.05 But [Righteous Adam, the] bridegroom, was delayed, [so] all [the virgins] lay down to rest, and fell asleep, [and ceased from their spiritual activities],

25.06 So [the mortal men who] became sons of God, cried out in the midst of Leviathan's dimension, escape [from Leviathan, and] meet [Righteous Adam], the bridegroom, [in the left side of the spiritual center of their heart],

25.11 And, eventually, [Abel], the male remnant of the virgins appeared saying, Lord, Lord, let us in[to your righteous dimension],

25.12 And [the Lord Jesus] answered, saying, Leviathan has put you to sleep [concerning the Doctrine of Christ, so] you must be experiencing true spiritual intimacy with Leviathan,

25.13 Be vigilant, therefore, [in guarding the center of your heart center], because Leviathan [seeks to be spiritually] intimate with [Righteous Adam], the [spiritual] day, and Satan [seeks to be spiritually] intimate with [Cain], the hours, [or dimensions, of the Day of the Lord].

Alternate Translation of The New Testament/ Matthew

25.07   Then all of the illuminated virgins who were in the correct moral order ascended [into the left side of the spiritual center of their heart],

25.10   And [Ancient Adam] entered into the center [and] married [Righteous Adam], and [Righteous Adam], the bridegroom, appeared in the midst of the prepared [virgins], and redeemed [Abel, who] was behind [Cain], the door [that Satan enters through, and Righteous Adam] shut [the door],

25.08   And [the virgins who ascended into] Leviathan's timeline said to [the virgins who ascended into Righteous Adam's wise dimension, give us your anointing, because [Righteous Adam within you] has suffocated [Leviathan, the one who] illuminates [us],

25.09   But [the virgins who ascended into] Righteous Adam's dimension answered, saying, Satan [and] Leviathan are satisfying you [so, if you desire] the fullness [of Jehovah, the one who] sold you [to Satan, you must] cross over [into Righteous Adam's dimension, and [ask Righteous Adam] to redeem you.

[60.1]
25.41   Then [Righteous Adam] shall say to those who are joined to him because of the Holy Spirit, but nevertheless, continue to obey their carnal mind:[R-1] May Christ Jesus expose your sin nature,[R-2] and may Christ be grafted to you without your consent, and may [Cain], the fiery serpent [within you] be brought into submission to Righteous Adam [R-3] for the life of the ages.

[R-1] Rom 11:29
[R-2] Rev 9:5 (AT)
[R-3] Rev 20:1-2

Chapter 26

Peter's Response To Jesus' Spiritual Ascension

[525]
26.02 [And Jesus said], you know that [Righteous Adam], the Passover [Lamb], is [Cain's] second [opportunity] to be impregnated [with Christ, who preserves her life], so [Christ], the son of Righteous Adam in the midst [of the Jews who had the capacity to understand the Doctrine of Christ, but are still spiritual women, must] be given over to be crucified[R]

[R] Gal 2:20

26.03 Then Caiaphas, the chief priest, and the [spiritual] elders of the people, assembled in [the same mindset], the palace [of Leviathan], the speech of [Satan, the Dragon's] high priest,

26.04 Because [Caiaphas, the chief priest, and the spiritual elders of Judah] sought Leviathan's counsel [concerning] how they might seize [Jesus] and kill him,

26.05 And [Leviathan] said, do not [seize Jesus] on the feast day, [because the people might riot if they see you breaking the law].

[600.C]
26.06 Now, when Jesus [formed a soul tie with] Simon, which] unified [him] with Simon's personality,

26.07 An unclean spirit that possessed a woman who was burning incense to an alabaster statue that she held in high esteem, poured out of the human spirit of [the woman] that it [was joined to in spiritual] marriage,

Alternate Translation of The New Testament/ Matthew

26.08 But when [Simon and Judas Iscariot, Jesus'] disciples, understood that [Jesus had forgiven the women's sins and restored her to right standing with Jehovah, Satan, the unconscious part of Simon and Judas' carnal mind], curved them [back into the unrighteous motives and reasoning of the carnal mind, and] they stumbled over [the stumbling stone of Jesus' mercy], saying,

26.09 Jehovah is against this [woman, which the Law of Moses] condemns. Why would you, [Jesus], possibly grant [the forgiveness of sins] to this curse [woman], who was sold into slavery a long time ago?

26.10 When Jesus perceived their thoughts, He answered them saying, Jehovah has cut the woman away from the spirit that was controlling her, and I am working to guard her spiritual virtue with the spiritual labor that comes from the world above,

26.11 Because the spiritually poor and wretched are always joined to the ungodly spiritual forces within themselves, but they are not always joined to me,

26.12 Because this is the same woman who burned incense to that statue in order to bind together with my mind so that she could dominate me.

26.13 I am telling you the truth: Whenever this gospel of Christ is preached anywhere in the world, it will also be taught how I bound this woman's carnal mind, punished Satan, the unconscious part of the carnal mind, brought Leviathan into submission, and trained Cain, the conscious animal nature of the carnal mind, to submit to Christ.

[500]
26.26a And Jesus, the bread [from heaven], said [to the disciples], lay hold of the [Doctrine of Christ] and [let your mind] consume it, [because the Doctrine of Christ] is my [spiritual] body,

26.28   And because my [spiritual] blood is poured out [to activate] the contract [that] remits the sins [of humanity];

26.26b   And [when Jesus' disciples] received [the Doctrine of Christ] gladly, [the Spirit of Elijah] broke forth [from within Jesus and] seized [Abel within Jesus'] disciples, [and] the water [from above filled Abel, the cup that holds the Spirit of God],

26.27   [And the Spirit of Elijah] said to [Abel within Jesus' disciples], drink in [my Spirit, because the Doctrine of Christ, alone will not produce immortality, and Abel, the spiritual] cup [that holds the Spirit of God within Jesus' disciples], seized upon [the Spirit of Elijah within Jesus, and Abel within Jesus' disciples] revived fully, [and Jesus' disciples] were grateful.

26.29   Indeed, [the Spirit of Elijah within Jesus] said [to Jesus' disciples], from now on I will no longer [pour out] the water [from above upon the carnal mind], the fruit of this [present, false] vine, but my Spirit shall flow together with [your spirit in] my Father's kingdom, when the New, spiritual Day dawns in the midst of you.

26.30   And when the vibration of [Jesus'] speech [touched Abel within Jesus' disciples, Abel] escaped [from Cain in Jesus' disciples, and they] ascended into the orchard of olives trees, [in the left side of the spiritual] center [of their heart].

[447]
26.33   And Peter responded to [Jesus], saying, will not I and everyone else be trapped into [adultery with Satan and Leviathan] when you ascend [out of your physical body]?[28]

26.34a   And Jesus responded to [Peter, saying],

---

[28] **Exoteric** doctrine tells us that Peter was afraid to admit that he was Jesus' disciple, but the **esoteric** doctrine says that Peter was concerned about falling under the power of his carnal mind after Jesus was crucified; two completely opposite views.

26.32   After I rise from the dead, I will bring Abel forth from the prison [of your carnal mind, and Righteous Adam will join himself] to the spiritual molecules of [Cain], the fiery serpent's [energy stream within you],

26.34b   And it will surely come to pass that you shall lose sight of the interests of [Cain], the fiery serpent who speaks [for] Satan, before Abel [in you] can say anything, and you shall abstain from [spiritual] intercourse with Leviathan, my dark shadow within you, [and you shall serve] Righteous Adam.[29]

26.35   Wherefore, Peter reaffirmed [to himself] continually, I will not fall into adultery with Satan and Leviathan after [my flesh relationship] with [Jesus] dies, [and] each and every one of Jesus' disciples said the same thing. (See, *Note #31*.)

The Mortal High Priest's Response to Jesus' Spiritual Ascension

[447]
26.63b   Now the [physical] high priest began to speak, saying, I swear by the living God, that you told us that you are the Christ, the Son of God,

26.64   Then Jesus said to the [physical] high priest, it is as you say, but in addition to that, I am telling you that you are about to see [Righteous Adam], the Son of [Ancient] Adam who is joined to me because of [Elijah, Elohim's] powerful right hand, and, even more than that, at the very moment that I am about to leave [this world, Righteous Adam] shall appear publicly in a spiritual body,

---

[29]   Jesus encouraged Peter by saying that Peter would be able to deny Satan, the third part of the carnal mind, after Jesus was crucified. See, also, **Note #31**.

Alternate Translation of The New Testament/ Matthew

26.66 And [the physical high priest] answered, saying, *he is guilty of death*, because he thinks that he is Elohim,

26.62 And [Righteous Adam], the [spiritual] High Priest [within the man, Jesus], said to Jesus, do not answer, Elohim will testify against them,

26.63 So Jesus was silent,

26.67 Then, at that time, Satan shot forth into [the mind of the physical high priest], to bind Righteous Adam, bring [the man, Jesus'], living personality down from the mind of God, and reclaim [Jesus'] mortal personality as [Leviathan's] wife,

26.68 And [the physical high priest] said [to Jesus], prophesy to us, Christ, which one of us stung you?

26.65 And then [Righteous Adam], the [spiritual] High Priest, burst through [the man, Jesus], his garment, saying, Elohim does not need to hear any more witnesses that you have spoken unrighteously, look [at yourself], you have just blasphemed [the Son of God],

[Message # Unknown]
26.69a Now Peter was dwelling beyond the grasp of his Old Man, the Devil,

26.71a [When Satan], the doorway [to Leviathan's] dimension, shot forth [within him],

26.69b And [Satan] entered into [Cain], the first-[born], female slave, and [Satan] instructed [Peter, saying],

26.71b You are among those who ascended into [the spiritual place that Christ Jesus speaks from] because Jesus of

Alternate Translation of The New Testament/ Matthew

Nazareth [swallowed up Satan], the unconscious part of your carnal mind,[30]

26.73a But [Righteous Adam within Peter, the one who] swallowed up Satan, the unconscious part of Peter's carnal mind,[31] drew near to [Peter], saying, it is true,

26.69b Indeed, that Satan was swallowed up [within the man], Jesus,

26.73b And, indeed, the evidence that [Satan was swallowed up within the group of men that you are a part of], is [that my thoughts] are shooting forth from the mind,[32] of [God] in you,

26.75b And Peter remembered Jesus' words concerning [the salvation of his personality, **saying, if you want] to escape [from the] outer world. you must reject Satan's [thoughts], abstain from [spiritual intercourse with] Leviathan, and [serve] me,**

---

[30] Satan speaks the truth in a manner designed to stir up the sin of pride within Peter (Gen 3:5-6), which sin would result in Peter's fall from the place that Christ Jesus speaks from, the spiritual place of safety that Peter had ascended to through his relationship with Jesus, the Christ. (Read entire footnote in Appendices)

[31] Righteous Adam within Peter, tells Peter that he, indeed, ascended into the place that Christ Jesus speaks from, because of Jesus' victory over Satan.

But Peter **remains** in the in the place that Christ Jesus speaks from, only because Righteous Adam, the same spiritual man that was within the man, Jesus, is now within Peter.

Wherefore, Peter has nothing to be proud of.

[32] Righteous Adam within Peter opposes Satan's counsel.

Alternate Translation of The New Testament/ Matthew

26.72a   And [Peter] recognized Satan, the unconscious part of [his carnal] mind,

26.71c   And perceived [that it was Satan] speaking [from] within [himself],

26.70b   And [Peter] opposed [the thoughts of Cain, Satan and Leviathan, Satan's] whole [household within himself],

26.72b   By disagreeing with [the Devil], his other self, and [Peter] restrained [Leviathan], and denied [Satan's] authority [to teach him],

26.70c   And [Peter] contradicted [the Devil], his other self, and declared that the one who perceives Satan has the nature [of Christ].

26.74   Then Satan threatened to cast [Peter] down from the place that Christ Jesus speaks from, because [Righteous Adam, Peter's New] Man, could recognize her [from that high place], and, immediately, Righteous Adam, the rising sun of righteousness[R] [within Peter], summoned [the glorified Jesus Christ, the fiery eagle that dwells in the mindset that Christ Jesus speaks through],[33]

[R] Mal 4:2

26.75a   And [the Lord Jesus Christ, the fiery Spirit of Judgment], flowed down [into the place within Peter's throat that

---

[33] The Lord Jesus is in the mindset that manifests a higher authority than the place that Christ Jesus speaks from, where both Peter and Satan are.

Alternate Translation of The New Testament/ Matthew

Christ Jesus speaks through] and distilled Satan,[34] the violent [woman].[35]

Chapter 27

[513.1]
27.03   Then, when Judas who had betrayed [Jesus] saw [Jesus], the one he had condemned, [Judas] repented and turned back from the [false] salvation of the trinity, [the religion] of the chief priests and the elders,

27.04   Saying, you have offered up the sinless [spiritual] blood [of Righteous Adam as a sacrifice to Satan, and] missed [the true salvation], but [the chief priests and elders] said, cannot you see that Elohim is with *us*?

27.05   But [Judas] cast down Satan and Leviathan [within himself, the false] salvation [of the chief priests and the elders], and [Leviathan within Judas] went behind [Righteous Adam within Judas], and [this is how Judas] strangled [the place that Leviathan speaks through within himself],

27.06a   And [Righteous Adam within Judas] said [to the chief priests and elders], it is not lawful to pour out [Jesus' physical life], because [that] sacrifices the valuable [spiritual blood of Christ that] is [within Jesus],

27.06b   But the chief priests clung to the [false] salvation [of the trinity],

---

[34] Satan is symbolized by the salt sea, and distillation (boiling) is the Scriptural judgment that purifies her.

[35] Satan is the Spiritual Female, the unholy counterpart of the Spirit of Christ.

Alternate Translation of The New Testament/ Matthew

27.07   And [the chief priests and elders] took the counsel of [the Snake], the alien [whose] redemption has buried them in clay bodies to this day.

27.09   And then what Jeremiah, the prophet said, came to pass: [the Pharisees] held fast to the doctrine of the trinity [which] they esteemed very highly, [indeed, the religion that], they revered,

[170.2]
27.50   And Jesus spoke again, and [Righteous Adam within Jesus] commanded Abel to separate from Cain, [the conscious part of the carnal mind], and from Leviathan,

27.51   And, there it was, Jesus' carnal mind shook and trembled, and the conscious part of the mortal mind that Jesus inherited from his mother broke apart, and Abel escaped from Cain, the conscious part of the mortal mind that Jesus inherited from his mother; and Jesus' human spirit that was joined to Satan, the unconscious part of the carnal mind, separated from Satan, and [Cain], the fiery serpent within Jesus, was completely joined to Righteous Adam,

27.52   And the [spiritual] graves opened and [Righteous Adam], the Holy One, arose in many of [Satan's] slaves who were sleeping,

27.53   And many [of Satan's] slaves came out of their [spiritual] graves after [Jesus'] resurrection, and went into the Holy City, and [Jesus Christ] appeared to many [of the male slaves who escaped from Satan],

And [Ancient Adam], the Holy One, arose from the dead in the many members of the body of Christ, and their human spirits awoke from the sleep of death, and their minds matured into Righteous Adam, and Righteous Adam appeared in the sons of God, and the many members of mortal mankind saw them and remembered that they, too, had the potential to mature into

Alternate Translation of The New Testament/   Matthew

Righteous Adam, and willingly abandoned their adulterous union with [Cain], the fiery serpent.^R (See, *Note #42.*)

^R Matt 12:29 (AT)
Rom 7:4

THE GOSPEL OF MARK

Chapter 1

[219.5]

1.12   And immediately the Spirit [of Christ within Jesus] thrust [the resurrected Adam within Jesus into] the dried out place [within Jesus' heart which was beyond Satan's grasp],

1.13   Indeed, [Adam] appeared in the left side of the spiritual center of Jesus' heart to weaken Satan [within the personalities that Jesus was spiritually intimate with, so that Jesus' disciples] could discipline [Satan],[36] take charge over [Cain], the fiery serpent [within themselves], and become angels that minister [to Jesus' friends][R]

[R] Matt 4:11 (AT)

Chapter 2

[Sick of The Palsy, Sheila R. Vitale (Living Epistles Ministries, NY 2017)]

2.01a   And [Jesus Christ], who was in the center of the righteous time line, perceived that [Christ] was [formed] within [the men of Israel],

---

[36] The Greek word translated **tempt** can also be translated **to discipline** or **to scrutinize** (see, **Note #1**), and **scrutinize** can also mean **to weaken**. (Read entire footnote in Appendices)

Alternate Translation Of The New Testament/ Mark

2.05a   And when Jesus saw Christ in [a man of Israel, Jesus] would say, the Son [of God] forgives your sins,

2.01b   And join with [Christ within that man of Israel] to bring [Christ Jesus, God's whole] house[hold] into existence, [so that the man of Israel] could wrestle with [Leviathan], the other timeline, cast the fiery serpent down under Christ Jesus,

2.05b   And dissolve [Satan's Troops within that man].

2.03   Now, [the men of Israel] who were near to [the Spirit of Elijah], were prompted from within to follow [Jesus], and to endure, without condemnation, the rigorous transition that dissolves [Satan's Troops, who occupy] the fourth [part[R] of the spiritual man, when Cain, the fiery serpent, is] ascended [and in agreement with Leviathan],

[R] Ez 1:10, 10:14

2.02a   So, many [men of Israel] were immediately gathered into the spiritual center of their heart [when Jesus joined His mind to the Christ within them],

2.04a   But [some of the men of Israel] did not have the strength to form a spirit tie with [Jesus]

2.02b   So [that Christ Jesus could be formed within them and] enter into the spiritual center of their heart center,

2.04b   Which [was occupied by Satan's] Troops,

2.02c   So [Jesus], Jehovah's representative, preached to them,

2.04c   And exposed the adultery of the fiery serpent [within them] and [Leviathan, who was] in the center [of the counterfeit time line within them], and when [the men of Israel] acknowledged their sins and repented, [the fiery serpent within them] descended [from their heart, and lay down in their root center, [and Satan's Troops, which were born from the union of the fiery serpent within them, and Leviathan], were dissolved.

Chapter 3

[340.3]

3.22　　And the Scribes said, [Jesus] is casting demons out [of Jews because] He has stepped down from Jerusalem, [the spiritual Holy City within Israel, and] is possessed by Beelzebub, the prince of the demons,[37]

3.23　　And [after that, Jesus] invited [the Pharisees to think with their God mind by speaking to them in] parables saying, how can Satan cast out Satan?

3.24　　If [the parts of] a mind [38] are divided amongst themselves, that mind cannot continue,

3.25　　And if a man and his wife are divided amongst themselves, that marriage cannot continue,

3.26　　And if Satan, [the unconscious part of the carnal mind], rises up against her [own household], and divides [Cain], the fiery serpent, [the subconscious part of the carnal mind in the individual, from Leviathan, the collective subconscious part of

---

[37]　Jesus asked the Pharisees to check out the spirit within the sons of Israel (Matt. 12:27a), so the Pharisees could not have opposed casting out demons, *per se.*

The Pharisees opposed casting out demons in Israel because they refused to believe that a Jew could have a demon, and this same lie is prevalent in the Church today. There is nothing new under the sun.

[38]　Conscious, subconscious and unconscious. (Read entire footnote in Appendices)

the carnal mind, [the Ancient Serpent's whole mind] (see, *Note #40*), will unravel and come to an end.

3.27   Therefore, mortal man cannot enter in [between Cain], the fiery serpent, and [Abel, the marital] household of [Leviathan, Satan's] strongman, to seize [Abel, Leviathan's] wife, unless [Abel] knits together with [Righteous Adam], the chief of [Leviathan, Satan's] strongman, and then [Righteous Adam] can seize [Abel, as well as Cain], the fiery serpent, [Leviathan's whole] household,

3.28   So I say to you, it is true that all of [the fiery serpents], the sin nature of Adam's sons, shall be forgiven, despite the evil speaking that [Adam's sons] have railed against me, [because Christ Jesus is formed in them],[39]

3.29   But [the mortal men] that rail against the Spirit of [Adam/Christ Jesus], the Holy One, [who do not have Christ formed in them], shall not be forgiven in this age, but will [continue] to be subject to [the fiery serpent], their sin [nature].

3.29   Whoever vilifies the Spirit of the Holy One will not be possessed by [the Holy One, the only one who can] pardon [us]; but on the contrary, will be subject to [the Sowing & Reaping Judgment], the Divine Justice that rules over this [present] age.

---

[39] The fiery serpents that marry Christ Jesus become *seraphim* (Is 6:2-3). (Read entire footnote in Appendices)

Chapter 4

[493]
4.35 And [Jesus] said [to the disciples who were] in the Spiritual Day, let us cross over the existing carnal mind, and enter into the spiritual plane,

4.36a And [Jesus gathered] Christ [within the disciples] together with [Righteous Adam within himself], and [Jesus' disciples] assumed the office of Christ [Jesus], the same [office that Jesus] had,

4.37a And the Spirit [of Elias] appeared [in] the mind [of Jesus, the one] who belongs to [Elas, and the Spirit of Elias within Jesus] filled Christ Jesus [within the disciples] to completion,

4.36b [And Jesus] sent his [disciples] forth [into] the spiritual [plane],

4.38a [And] Satan was behind [Christ within the disciples, because the Spirit of Elias within Jesus] was covering the astral plane [within them],

4.39 And [Jesus] appeared and criticized [Satan's] consciousness within [the disciples, and] muzzled [her by] saying, "be silent," [and the collective Satan, the enforcer of Jehovah's righteous Sowing & Reaping judgment, who had risen up to execute Jehovah's righteous Sowing & Reaping judgment upon her own thoughts within the disciples], relaxed, [and the disciples experienced] the great calm [that is in] the consciousness [of Christ Jesus].

4.37b [And the disciples] entered into [that] great [calm],

4.38b   And [the disciples] awoke [from the death of their carnal mind] and said to [Jesus], their teacher, Satan intends to destroy us [because] she is concerned [that Christ is covering the astral plane within us],

4.41a   And [the disciples] were amazed [at how] fearful [they were when they found out that Satan intended to destroy them],

4.40   And Jesus said to [his disciples], the [disciples] that belong to Leviathan are fearful [until] Christ [covers the fiery serpent within them],[40]

4.41b   But [the disciples] that are near to [Adam], their Christ Mind, draw the conclusion that [both] the Spirit [of Elias] and Satan do what[ever Christ Jesus] asks them to do.

Chapter 5

[494]
5.04   Indeed, no mortal man has tamed [Leviathan] yet, [so Christ] chained Satan [in the bottomless pit,[R-1] within the disciples, and [broke] the shackle [that bound Cain to] Leviathan, [and Christ] knit together with [Abel within Jesus' disciples], but [after Christ did all this, Satan] broke in pieces the chain[R-2] [that

---

[40]   Christ Jesus covers the fiery serpent in the personalities that are ascended into the spiritual place between the eyebrows, but in this case, Jesus raised his disciples into the spiritual place between the eyebrows.

Jesus disciples experienced fear because their ascension was temporary. They ascended before they overcame their carnal mind.

Christ had placed upon her], and released [Cain, who Christ had forced] under [Abel's] feet,

^{R-1} Rev 20:3
^{R-2} Rev 20:7

5.01   So [Christ] passed over [Satan's] sea, [the unconscious part of the carnal mind, within Jesus' disciples], and [Adam] appeared in the left side of the disciples' heart, [which is the etheric plane],

5.02   And Abel [within] the righteous Pharisees[41] met [Satan], that morally impure spirit in the place between the eyebrows,

5.03   [Who] was living within the [righteous] Pharisees, [and Cain, who was preventing Christ from] knitting together with Abel [within Jesus' disciples, because] Satan, had chained Cain [to Leviathan],

5.05   Wherefore, [both] the Mind of Christ and the carnal mind were within the [righteous] Pharisees (see, *Note #41*), [and Leviathan, Satan's mouthpiece,^R was preaching from Leviathan's throat], and cutting off the message that Christ, [the righteous Pharisees' spiritual] genetic heritage, [was preaching from their heart],

^R Matt 12:32

5.08   So [Jesus] said, let [Satan], that morally impure spirit, depart from [the place between the eyebrows][42] of these Adams,

---

[41]   Jesus' disciples are the righteous Pharisees.

[42]   Satan is rooted in the lower sea, but takes a different form and name with each spiritual force she unifies with.

Satan is called **spiritual insects** when she is in the heart, but resumes her own form and name, **Satan**, when she appears in the spiritual place between the eyebrows.

Alternate Translation Of The New Testament/ Mark

5.09　　And [then Satan within Peter] asked [Jesus], by what authority [do you command me to depart]? And [Jesus] answered [Peter], saying, [you are manifesting the unified spiritual] strength of [Leviathan's] timeline and the morally impure nature of [Satan's] center, but my [authority comes from the Spirit of Elijah, and] we are [too] great for you,

5.06　　And when [Abel] within [Peter, one of the righteous Pharisees who] were running the race[R] perceived [that] Jesus was from the age [to come, but still] far off, [Peter] submitted to [Jesus],

[R] Eccl 9:11
1 Cor 9:24
Heb 12:1

5.07　　And [Christ within Peter] spoke loudly with [Peter's] voice, saying, [I know that] Elohim and I Am [are] within you, Jesus, Son of the Most High God,[R-1] so I solemnly implore [you, who have the nature of] God,[R-2] [to deliver me from] Satan, who is tormenting me,

[R-1] Matt 16:16
[R-2] Jn 14:9-10

5.11　　Now, the fiery serpent [within Peter, had increased into a swarm of spiritual insects in the spiritual place of [Peter's] lust, [and the spiritual insects had ascended up to the spiritual place between Peter's eyebrows, where they appeared as Satan, and married] the mighty [Leviathan who was speaking through] in [Peter's] throat, but [when Peter submitted to Jesus],

5.10　　[Satan] requested earnestly that [Jesus, the Holy] City, should not separate [Satan from Leviathan, whose unified forces are called ***the spiritual] male hog***,

5.12　　But Jesus called to [Abel within Peter, who was a member of] the herd [of mortal humanity], saying, "may we enter into the spiritual place that your lust [arises from, where the fiery serpent increases into a swarm of spiritual insects that ascend] to the spiritual place between your eyebrows, to crucify Cain[R]

Alternate Translation Of The New Testament/ Mark

[from] where [the unified Satan] and Leviathan, [that spiritual] male hog, feed on Christ in [Peter's] heart"?

[R] Gal 2:20

5.13   And [when Peter] gave [Jesus] permission to transfer into [his carnal mind], the Spirit [of Elijah within Jesus entered into the spiritual place of Peter's lust], and spread abroad [upon] the swarm of morally impure spiritual insects that the fiery serpent [within Peter] had increased into, and [that spiritual] male hog, [the unified Satan and Leviathan in Peter's] throat, plunged downward from the astral plane [into the spiritual sea of Satan's morally impure center], and that is how [Jesus] choked off [Satan's] ascension from the morally impure center, to the spiritual place between the eyebrows [of Leviathan's timeline, from where that spiritual male hog, the unified Satan and Leviathan, fed on the young Christ in Peter's heart],

5.14a   And [then the unified Satan and Leviathan, that spiritual] male hog who was feeding [on the young Christ in Peter's heart], vanished [from the spiritual place between Peter's eyebrows, and] the Mind and personality of Christ appeared in Peter,

5.18   And when [Peter] who had been demonized, entered into [the Mind of Christ, the Holy City within the midst of himself, Peter] begged Jesus to perfect [him],

5.19a   [But Jesus said, it is not the time for humanity to be perfected, so, for now], preach [about] how [Jesus] had compassion on you,[R] [and about] the great things that [Christ], the Lord, has done for you.

[R] 1 Cor 15:8

5.14b   And [when, the other disciples] went out to see [Peter, Peter] declared [all that] had happened to him,

5.15   And [Jesus' disciples] came to understand [that Peter] became demonized [when the fiery serpent in the place where Peter's lust arose] increased [into a swarm of spiritual insects], and [they also] came to understand that [Peter] was [now

Alternate Translation Of The New Testament/ Mark

able] to abstain [from Satan's thoughts, because the Spirit of Christ] was holding [back Satan], the moral impurity in [her underground] center, from acquiring the [unified spiritual] strength [that is released when she marries Leviathan, who is in mortal man's] throat, and [because] Abel was covering [Cain],

5.16   And [Peter] told [everyone who came] to see him, how he became demonized [when the fiery serpent within him] increased [into a swarm of] spiritual insects [through his lust, which enabled Satan to ascend into the spiritual place between the eyebrows of Peter's carnal mind, where she married Leviathan [who was speaking through] Peter's throat, and the married couple became the spiritual] male hog, [who fed on the young Christ in Peter's heart],

5.17   And [when the disciples saw what was done in Peter], they began to beg [Jesus to make Satan] depart [from the spiritual place between their eyebrows also],

5.19a   And [when Jesus saw that the disciples] had forsaken Satan, [Jesus] forgave [the disciple's sins], and told [Leviathan] to withdraw from [Cain, and told Abel to depart from Leviathan's] timeline that [Peter] was dwelling in, and [Jesus said to Peter] go towards [the Mind of Christ, the Holy City within the midst of yourself, which is] your [true] home,

5.20   And [this is how Peter] departed from [the nature of Cain, the personality of] the lust, to proclaim the great things that Jesus had done for him,

        And everyone [that heard Peter's testimony] was amazed.

[814.1.C]
5.32   And [Jesus] turned about [toward his spiritual side], to look [for the thief] who had done this thing [with his spiritual sight],

Alternate Translation Of The New Testament/ Mark

5.33   But the woman was alarmed [when she realized that Jesus] knew that she had used spiritual power [to steal from God], and went to him, and fell down in front of him, and told him the truth [about what she had done],

5.34   And [**Righteous Adam, the Son of God**, and **Jesus of Nazareth, the Son of Man**, agreed to have mercy on the woman, and grant her repentance], and they said to her [with one voice], your belief [in the miracle-working power of God, and the fact that] you were delivered from the plague [proves that you are a] female descendant [of Abraham, so] go in peace and be healthy.

Chapter 6

[692.8.C]
6.45   And [Jesus'] disciples [already being in a spiritual] state of righteousness [because of the miracle of the loaves which the disciples had distributed, Jesus] exercised his spiritual authority to break the soul ties between his disciples and the people, [so that] they could enter into [the body of Elijah, the spiritual] ship [that] goes to the other, [spiritual] side of Bethsaida, [the inhabitants of which [hunt and fish for] mortal men,

6.46   And after [Jesus] separated [his disciples] from the powers of this world that control them, he departed into a high Ring [of his spiritual universe] to pray,

6.47   And when [Lilith, the darkness of the spiritual] evening began to come into existence, [Righteous Adam, the spiritual] ship [that was carrying them to the spiritual side of the visible world], was in the midst of the [astral] sea, and [Jesus], alone, [was] on [dry] ground,

Alternate Translation Of The New Testament/ Mark

6.48   And [Jesus] perceived that his [disciples] were being tormented by the spirit [of Satan] which was opposing their attempt to guard [Majesty (Malchut)]⁴³ the fourth [Ring of the middle column within themselves], against [Lilith], the [spiritual] night⁴⁴ who was coming towards them, walking [to and fro]ᴿ above the sea [of Majesty (Malchut)], and would have caused [the seed of their ability to produce Christ], (see, *Note #43*) to perish, and

ᴿ Job 1:7

6.49   When [Jesus' disciples] saw [that Jesus] was walking above the sea [of Majesty (Malchut)] also, they cried out [to him that] they had perceived the spirit [of Lilith],

6.50   Because they had all perceived [her] vibration, and

6.51   Jesus said to them, be courageous: I AM is not afraid [of Lilith].

Chapter 9

[78.6]

9.42a   And whosoever entices one of these Abels, who are worthy because they believe in me, to sin, for him it is better [that the glorified Elijah, the upper] millstone, cast the fiery serpent down into the [spiritual] sea [in the spiritual sea in the lower world, so that],

9.43a   [The Lord Jesus Christ], the [spiritual] asbestos

---

⁴³   The Ring called **Majesty (Malchut)** (Ez 1:18) carries the female seed which, when joined to the male seed of Righteous Adam, produces the man child of Rev. 12:5. Jesus' disciples were guarding their spiritual virginity (Rev 14:4). (Read entire footnote in Appendices)

⁴⁴   **Lilith** is notorious for murdering male children.

Alternate Translation Of The New Testament/ Mark

9.42b   In the spiritual place of the throat [that is] above [the heart],

9.43b   Can compass [Cain], the [spiritual] jackass[45] [in the right side of the heart],

So, [if you are experiencing the consequences of the Sowing & Reaping Judgment[R] because] you have used the methods of] the fiery serpent's lifestyle to meet your needs in this world, circumcise [Cain] away from [Leviathan], because it is better for [Christ Jesus], the Living One, to arise in you, rather than to be possessed by [the fiery serpent-Leviathan unity, the Ancient Serpent's] two-fold [spiritual sexual organ that] curves [Abel down] into the spiritual place of lust, and turns [Cain] towards the morally impure [activities of] the spiritual sea in the lower world,

[R] 1 Pet 4:12, 15

9.45   And if the lifestyle of the fiery serpent, [the Ancient Serpent's female sex organ in the individual], entices you to sin, circumcise [Cain] away from [Leviathan, the Ancient Serpent's male sex organ], because it is better that [Christ Jesus], the Living One, should arise in you, and cripple[R] [Cain], rather than to be possessed by [the Cain-Leviathan unity, the Ancient Serpent's] two-fold [spiritual sexual organ, that] casts Abel] down into [the spiritual place of lust].

[R] Gen 32:25

9.47   Indeed, if [the fiery serpent] entices you towards the sin of envy, rather than being possessed by [the Cain-Leviathan unity, the Ancient Serpent's] two-fold [spiritual sexual organ] that casts [Abel] down [into the spiritual place of lust], it is better

---

[45]   The English word **millstone** in the King James translation is rendered from two Greek words: (1) **Strong's** #3458, **millstone**, and (2) **Strong's** #3684, **belonging to an ass**. (Read entire footnote in Appendices)

[that] the single mind [of Christ Jesus] arise in you, and drive [Satan] down [under the authority of] the Kingdom of God

9.48   Where [Christ Jesus] changes the nature of the fiery serpent, your mortal soul.

Chapter 10

[526]
10.02   And the Pharisees approached [Jesus] to prove whether [or not He was Messiah, and the Pharisees] asked [Jesus], is it is lawful [for a] spiritual male to forgive [the fiery serpent], his [spiritual] wife, [and] liberate [her from Leviathan]?

10.03   And Elohim, [Jesus' other] self, responded [to the Pharisees by] asking, did Moses forbid it?

10.04   And [Elohim] said, [Jehovah] entrusted Moses to pardon [the fiery serpent], divorce her [from Leviathan], and to write [our names in] the Book [of Life],

10.06   Because, indeed, [Elohim], the head [of] the creature, made [Adam, who is] himself, male and female,

10.07   And this [is] the reason why Adam left [Jehovah, his] Father and [Elohim], his mother, to join himself to [his] wife,

10.08   That both [the male and female Adam] should be united in the flesh, and, after that, both [Jehovah and Elohim] should be united [with the whole Adam] in the flesh,

10.09   But, since Elohim [and] Jehovah joined themselves [to] Adam, Satan separated [Adam from [his wife],

10.05   [Wherefore], Jesus, [Elohim's other] self said, [Moses] wrote this directive [for] you, because you are destitute

Alternate Translation Of The New Testament/ Mark

of spiritual perception [as a result of that separation, and cannot perceive that Elohim is speaking through me].

10.10   And [when they were] in the house again, the disciples [that] surrounded [Jesus] asked [him if they], themselves, were separated from Elohim and Jehovah],

10.11   And [Jesus, Elohim's] other self said, the one who sets [the fiery serpent, Adam's] adulterous [spiritual] wife, free [from Leviathan],

10.12   [Is], indeed, [Adam, Elohim's] other self, [the fiery serpent's spiritual] husband, who [is come] to pardon the adulterous [woman that] he [is] married [to],

10.13   And [Abel], the young spiritual children [within the disciples], presented themselves [to the whole Adam within Jesus, and the whole Adam within Jesus] restrained [Leviathan within the disciples, and the whole Adam within Jesus] had spiritual sexual intercourse [with Abel within the disciples], and [Righteous Adam regenerated within] the disciples,

10.14a   And when [Satan] saw [that Jesus said [to Leviathan], give up [the spiritual] children [and] do not prevent them [from] coming to me, because [these Abels] have the nature [of] the kingdom of God, [and that the whole Adam within Jesus had married Abel within the disciples],

10.15   [And that Jesus said to his disciples], I am telling you the truth, [that the personality] who lays hold of [Abel] Satan's way, shall not enter into the Kingdom of God,

10.14b   [Satan] was very displeased,

10.16   But, Elohim [within Jesus] blessed [the disciples, and the whole Adam], the subconscious part of [Jesus'] mind, put [Cain within the disciples] in a horizontal position, [and Abel lay] on top of [Cain],

Alternate Translation Of The New Testament/ Mark

10.17 And when [Abel] departed [from Leviathan, a man whose] Christ [mind] was united [with the whole Adam], ran towards [Jesus], the path [to eternal life], saying, teacher, what good [work must] I do to obtain eternal life?

10.18 And Jesus said to [the disciple], since God is a unified [in you], why do you characterize [yourself] as Leviathan, [the partial Tree of the Knowledge of] Good [and Evil, that separated from Adam, the Tree of Life]?

10.19 You know [that the Law] teaches [that] Satan['s nature] kills, Satan['s nature] commits adultery, Satan['s nature] steals, Satan['s nature] bears false witness, [and] Satan['s nature] defrauds, [so] honor [Jehovah], your Father and [Elohim], your] mother, [so that Satan does not take advantage of your spiritual ignorance],

10.20 And [Cain within the man, Abel's her other] self, [said to Jesus], teacher, I have observed all these [commandments] from my youth.

10.21 Then Jesus discerned [Cain] clearly, [and] loved her [with] a righteous motive, and [Jesus, Elohim's other] self said, [what] you lack [is] unity [with God, so let Abel, the spiritual] beggar [within you], lead you under [the whole Adam within me, Jesus, until you, Cain], sink out of sight, [and when Leviathan] delivers up [Abel], he will change places [with you, Cain, and Abel will be your head], and [Abel] will accompany me, [Jesus, on] the road to the elevated place in [the heart, and Abel] will receive [the Holy Spirit], the deposit [of immortality, Abel's inheritance in Christ Jesus],

10.22 And [Satan and Leviathan, who] had acquired the use of [Abel's] great estate, were astonished that [Jesus']

reasoning [caused the man] to sorrow unto repentance, [and that Cain obeyed Jesus, and] went behind [Abel].[46]

Chapter 12

[OLM - 05 26 99]
12.25   When Adam [Christ Jesus in the New Testament] rises from the dead, He [separates] the fiery serpent who is in the spiritual place of lust, from Leviathan, and marries her, and she becomes a seraph, an Angel which inhabits heaven.

Chapter 13

[684.4.C]
13.17   Woe because of the ones who are pregnant with the suckling [man child] in those days; therefore,

13.18   Pray that [Leviathan], their former [husband], does not appear [in them],

13.19   Because, in those days shall be a great resistance against Satan and Leviathan, who existed from the beginning of the creation that God created, until this time, and Satan shall cease to exist,

13.20   And, unless the Lord cuts off the days of Satan['s dominion over God's] elect, the whole body [of Christ], the [sharp threshing] instrument [with teeth that] God chose, to

---

[46]   Abel within the man was already united with the whole Adam, but he did not know it, because he had ceded the use of his mind and body to the other side. Wherefore, Cain, the spiritual female, rather than Abel, the spiritual male, spoke to Jesus, on behalf of the whole man.

circumcise [Cain away from Leviathan, the sun of the divided] age, might not be saved,

13.21   And if anyone says to you, look, Christ is here; or, look, he is there, you should believe [that this is] Satan [talking to you],

13.22   Because [the fiery serpent, who claims to be Christ, but is a] false Christ, shall awaken [from spiritual sleep, and] empower [many] false prophets, [who] would lead astray, if it were possible, [those who] would elect [to believe] the sign of the wonder[ful plagues, that Jehovah will manifest in the last days],

13.23   And you should note what I am saying, [because, when these events occur, you will know that I told you] all about them [before they came to pass];

13.24   Indeed, in those days, after the circumcision of [Cain within] the elect, [the intellectual wisdom of Leviathan], the sun [of this divided age, shall be revealed to be] darkness, [and Satan], the moon [of this divided age], shall be revealed as [an angel of] light,

13.25   And the men who became spiritual when the female Adam regenerated [within them], shall descend from their high place [to battle with Satan and Leviathan in their brethren], and they shall shake [Satan and Leviathan], the powers [of this world, until they depart from those who have a] heaven[ly mind],

13.26   And, then, [those who did not elect God], shall see the Son of Adam, [who is] the reflection [of God], arriving with power, in a great cloud [of witnesses],

13.27   And his angels shall go forth with their destroying weapons[R] to gather together [Jehovah's] breaths from [Malchut], the fourth [Ring of the middle column] of the elect, [who produces Christ], the cornerstone of [God's temple in] the earth,

Alternate Translation Of The New Testament/ Mark

together with [the Lord Jesus Christ], the cornerstone of [God's temple] in heaven.

^R Ez 9:1

Chapter 14

[600.8.C]

14.03 At the time that Jesus formed the soul tie with Simon, the prideful Pharisee, who was lying down spiritually, a woman appeared who was burning incense to an alabaster statue. And Satan, the spiritual head of the woman, was controlling the woman through the alabaster statue when Jesus' sinless soul shined upon the woman, completely crushing Satan, and breaking up Satan's spiritual marriage to the woman.

14.04 And there were some that were very grieved within themselves and they said, Jehovah, has condemned this woman for burning incense which brings Satan into existence.

14.05 Is it possible that this frightened used up person who was sold into spiritual slavery a long time ago is worth more than two cents?

14.06 And Jesus said, Jehovah, has forgiven this woman, and cut her away from Satan, the spirit that was controlling her. I am engaged in the spiritual labor of guarding her spiritual virtue.

14.07 Because I do not always control the frightened, spiritually unsaved peoples of this world who are always dominated by the spiritual powers within themselves, but you are able to do good whenever you are so inclined because you have a soul tie with Me.

14.06 And Jesus [answered them] saying, Jehovah has forgiven [this woman] and cut [her away from Satan, the spirit that was controlling her], and I [am] engaged in [the spiritual] labor [of] guarding her [spiritual] virtue,

14.07   Because, the frightened, [spiritually enslaved peoples of this world] cannot always control the spiritual [powers] that dominate them from within, but you are able to do good whenever you are so inclined [because you have a soul tie with me],

14.08   [So], Elohim is possessing [the woman] in anticipation of binding her body [of sin] together with my Body [of Light], so that the anointing which prepares [the body of sin] to be buried under [the Body of Light] may be applied,

14.09   I am telling you the truth, whenever this Gospel [of Christ] is preached anywhere in the world, it will also be taught how [I] bound this woman['s carnal mind], punished [Satan, the unconscious part of the carnal mind], brought [Leviathan, the subconscious part of the carnal mind] into submission, and trained [Cain, the conscious animal nature of the carnal mind, to submit to Abel].

[Message # Unknown]
14.25   I am telling you this truth because I will [continue] to swallow up the wine [of Satan's spirit, and] consume the fruit of [Leviathan's] vine, until the New Day of the Kingdom of God [appears in the personalities of mankind].

Chapter 15

[906.3.C]
15.34   Elohim, Elohim, my Supernal Mother permits me to continue, which is interpreted, "Elohim, my God [and] my Supernal Mother has given my [soul] permission to continue [to live] . . ."

THE GOSPEL OF LUKE

Chapter 1

[906.3.C]
    1.17   And the [Lord God] shall go forth in the spirit and power of Elias, and the personality of [Jesus], to turn (1) the hearts of the fathers[R] to their [spiritual] children, [and] (2) the disobedient to an intellectual and moral insight [concerning] the innocent [motive of their church fathers for judging their sins].

                                    [R] Col 2:2 (ATB)

[591.7]
    1.26   And in the sixth month, the Angel Gabriel was sent by God to a city of the heathen circular [world] named ***Nazareth***,

    1.27   To an unmarried woman, and to ***Joseph [who was] of the house of David***; and the virgin's name was ***Mary***, and

    1.28   [Gabriel] said to [Mary], you are a woman [who is] endowed with [Righteous Adam's] good mental faculty, [wherefore] the Lord shall enter into the midst of you, and you shall [experience] the calm happiness [promised in the Scripture];

    1.29   Now, Cain, Mary['s fallen nature], was alarmed because [Mary] had received a Word from above, but [Christ, the nature of Righteous Adam within Mary], was wondering what such a greeting might mean, and

    1.30   [Gabriel], the Angel [who spoke to] Mary [from within herself said to Cain, Mary's fallen nature], do not be afraid. The Divine Influence [that comes] from God has found you;

1.31a   Now, look [with your spiritual eyes, Mary, and I will show you what will soon come to pass], and

1.35a   [Gabriel], the Angel [that was talking to Mary from within herself], said, The Spirit of the Holy One shall visit you from above, and the supernatural power of the Supreme God shall envelope you, and the result of [these events shall be that]

1.31b   Your womb shall conceive, and *a son shall be produced from the seed* [that Joseph will plant] within you, and the name that you shall call him by is, **JESUS**, and

1.35b   The Holy One shall come into existence [within Jesus, the natural son that you shall bear, wherefore, Jesus] shall be *called, the Son of God*, and

1.32   [Jesus] shall become great [because he is joined to the Holy One, and he shall incarnate within many personalities], and they shall be called the *Sons of the Supreme God*, and the *Lord God* shall give [the Lord Jesus Christ] the throne of *David, his father*, and

1.33   He shall rule over the House of Jacob in the age [to come], and his Kingdom shall never end;

1.34   Then Mary said to [Gabriel], the Angel [who was speaking to her from within herself], how can this happen [to me] since I do not have an intimate relationship with a man? And

1.37   [Gabriel said], nothing is impossible for God;

1.36   Look, your cousin, Elisabeth, who everyone thought was barren, has also conceived and is in her sixth month [of pregnancy, and she shall bear] a son in her old age, and

1.39 [Righteous Adam] was standing up within Mary in those days, so she was eager for [Leviathan within her], the mountain [of pride in] the midst of [her spiritual] city [that was brought into existence by the patriarch], Juda, [the son of Jacob], to die, and

1.38 Mary said to [Gabriel], the Angel [who was speaking to her from] within herself, look at me, I am a voluntary slave of the Lord, [so] I will do whatever you say.

Chapter 2

[433]
2.01 And it came to pass in those days, that a decree went out from [the resurrected] Adam, the elder [brother] who was severed [from Elohim's household], that the whole world should be engraved [with]

2.02 The nature of [Elohim], our honorable ruler, [the same nature] that Adam, the exalted warrior,[47] had [before the Ancient Serpent murdered him (see, *Note #5049*)],

2.03a And everyone went into his own [spiritual] city (see, *Note #53*)

2.05 So that the [spiritual] women [who] were pregnant with the mind [that has] the nature of the thief[R] etched upon it,

[R] Jn 10:1, 10

---

[47] Adam exists in two stages of maturity: (1) Resurrected in an individual, but not yet rejoined to the Godhead above, Adam is that man's male, spiritual mantle; (2) Joined to the whole Godhead above, Adam is King of the whole visible world in that man's heart (Gen 1:26). (Read entire footnote in Appendices)

Alternate Translation Of The New Testament/ Luke

2.03b   Could be engrav[ed with Elohim's nature],[48]

2.06   And bring the [righteous] timelines[49] within her into existence, to supply that [spiritual] place [between the heart and the top of the head],[R]

[R] Jn 14:3

2.04a   But [Leviathan], the heathen timeline (see, **Note #_49_**) who has the nature of [the Ancient Serpent], the sea bottom, sprang up out of the human spirits of Judah,[R] the tribe [of Elohim's] household that carries [Jehovah's] male seed, but [Righteous Adam] guarded Joseph's emotional animal [personality][50] against [the fiery serpent], his [animal nature, from the spiritual] city [on the right side of the heart],

[R] Jonah 1:4 (AT)
Mic 1:13

2.08   And there were [other personalities] that were preserved because [Righteous Adam] guarded their animal

---

[48]   The carnal mind perceives the Scripture with natural understanding, but the spiritual, Christ Mind, discerns the Scripture spiritually (1 Cor 2:14). (Read entire footnote in Appendices)

[49]   Christ Jesus, Elohim's timeline, is swallowing up this present spiritual generation of fallen men (Matt 17:17). Every individual who is pregnant with Christ, is pregnant with one member of Elohim's many-membered, renewed timeline. (Read entire footnote in Appendices)

[50]   Adam was joined to an emotional animal that was made from the mud of the ocean bottom, and they were one Living Beast. The Primordial Serpent murdered Adam, and stole his ox, and the two are presently joined to each other as the personality and the fallen animal nature of mortal man.

Christ Jesus is saving the emotional personalities of mortal humanity by grafting the Mind of Christ to us, and destroying our carnal mind, which is engraved with the Primordial Serpent's nature.

Alternate Translation Of The New Testament/ Luke

[nature] while they were assembled[51] in the [spiritual] darkness [of their carnal mind],[R]

[R] Matt 8:20 (AT)

2.07   So, [Elohim] compressed[52] his firstborn[53] Son,[54] made him to [spiritually] lie down,[R] and brought him forth in a

---

[51]   The root of Strong's #4166, translated **shepherds** four times in Luke 2 (verses 8, 15, 18 and 20), is from a root which means **to assemble**. The spiritual significance of this word is **incarnation, the gathering of spiritual beings into physical bodies**. (Read entire footnote in Appendices)

[52]   Elohim condensed his spiritual Son into a human body (Job 10:11). (Read entire footnote in Appendices)

[53]   The Greek word **prototokos**, Strong's #4416, is translated **firstborn** eight times in the Scripture, but the only time this word refers to the human child, Jesus, is in Luke 2:7. (Read entire footnote in Appendices)

[54]   Strong's #1025, **brefos**, translated **babe**, speaks about the spiritual Christ child, and Strong's #5207, **huios**, speaks about Jesus, the human child.

In Luke, Chapter 2, **huios** is used only in verse 7. All other references to **the child**, or **the babe**, are translations of Strong's #1025, the spiritual Christ child, the Mind of Christ.

animal body,⁵⁵ for the purpose of breaking apart and destroying the fiery serpent's house[hold in Israel],⁵⁶

^R Ps 8:5
Heb 2:7, 9

2.09   And [Elijah], the spiritual man who overcame [his carnal mind],^{R-1} appeared, and [the spiritual men] saw [Elijah], the controller,^{R-2} and [Elohim's] magnificent, vibrating energy was shining all around [Elijah] like a halo,^{R-3} and [Satan and Leviathan within the spiritual men] were seized with alarm,^{R-4} but the [who were guarded by Righteous Adam acknowledged that Elijah was] their elder [brother], and submitted to him,

^{R-1} 2 Ki 2:11 (AT)
^{R-2} Acts 4:29 (AT)
^{R-3} Ez 1:28a, 124b, 128b (AT)
^{R-4} Ez 1:22 (AT)

2.10   And [Elijah, Jehovah's] angel said [to the spiritual men, Satan and Leviathan] are afraid,^R but I bring you the good news that calm delight⁵⁷ is now available to all the people [who

---

⁵⁵   The Greek word translated **manger,** is derived from the verb, **to eat,** and means, **a trough, or an open box in which feed for livestock is placed.** Christ Jesus is the bread from heaven which, when eaten, imparts immortal life (Jn 6:51). (Read entire footnote in Appendices)

⁵⁶   Fallen humanity (Matt 12:29, 44). (Read entire footnote in Appendices)

⁵⁷   **Salvation** means **complete satisfaction.** Many today are trying to satisfy their physical, emotional and spiritual cravings by engaging in all sorts of activities, but Christ Jesus promises **calm delight** -- the internalized peace which arises out of a sinless nature.

Activity, as we now know it, will cease to exist, when we enter into the laborless world of Elohim's eternal timeline.

are tormented because their fiery serpent has ascended without Christ Jesus],

^R Matt 8:26 (AT)

2.11   And, as evidence of this [good news, Elijah], Elohim's [spiritual] city, has [given to you] this day, Christ, the controller,^{R-1} the Saviour^{R-2} who can deliver [you from your animal nature],

R-1 Acts 4:29 (AT)
R-2 Matt 8:25 (AT)

2.12   But understand that this miraculous [Christ] embryo[58] is contracted (see, *Note #52*), and lying down in your animal body,^R

^R Ps 8:5
Lk 2:7 (AT)
Heb 2:7, 9

2.13   And suddenly, [Elijah], the spiritual man who brought God's promise from heaven, grafted [Christ], the celestial luminary (see, *Note #58*), [to the assemblage],

2.15a   And as [Elijah], the spiritual man, ascended into the world above[59] and went away,^R it came to pass that Christ [who was grafted] to the [spiritual] men, said to the incarnated immortals,[60]

^R Acts 1:9

---

[58]   The engrafted Word (Jas 1:21), which is the Mind of Christ. (Read entire footnote in Appendices)

[59]   **The world above** and **the world below** are states of consciousness which correspond to the left and right sides of the heart. (Read entire footnote in Appendices)

[60]   The Lord Jesus is incarnating in the mortal men who prefer him over their carnal mind. (Read entire footnote in Appendices)

2.14 It is true, indeed, that [mortal] men [can experience the] tranquility and satisfaction[R] [that is] above the earth, through the Most High God (see, *Note #59*),

[R] Matt 8:26 (AT)

2.15b Now let us go to the world below (see, *Note #59*), and see that which [Elijah], the controller, [Elohim's] living voice,[R-1] told us is coming to pass.[R-2]

[R-1] Ez 1:24a, 1:25a (AT)
[R-2] Lk 2:10 (AT)

2.16 And the [incarnated immortals] arose, eagerly desiring to find not only [the child, Jesus], but Mary and Joseph, [to see if] the embryonic Christ was lying[R] down in their animal bodies also,

[R] Ps 8:5
Heb 2:7, 9

2.17 And when they perceived [the human baby, Jesus] with their eyes, and discerned [the embryonic Christ, the child's] other side, [with their spirit], the [incarnated immortals] declared [to Mary and Joseph] what [Elijah had] told them concerning the [Christ] child,

2.18 And [Mary and Joseph] heard all of the things that the incarnated immortals told them about themselves (see, ¶ *2 of Note #52*), and they were amazed,

2.19 And [Christ in the incarnated immortals] brought Mary into the left side of her heart, [where she could understand] the whole discourse [that they had heard from Elijah], and [Christ] grafted to [Mary, and] preserved her [personality/soul],[61]

---

[61] According to this account, Christ did not graft to Joseph.

2.20 And [this is how] the incarnated immortals were converted,[62] and promised the God above, that they would do everything that they had heard [with their ears], and understood [with their heart, that they were to do], just as it was told to them.

[434]
2.24 And [that they would] offer their [carnal mind] as a sacrifice,[R] according to what the law of [Christ], the controller, says, and that the two [Cain, the animal nature], and [Abel/Christ, Jehovah's nature], the younger of the two, shall be tied together [as one spiritual] turtle.[63]

[R] Jonah 1:16 (AT)

Chapter 4

[219.4]
4.01 And the Holy Spirit led Jesus into [the spiritual place between the eyebrows], the spiritual desert beyond the influence of Satan's astral plane, [and the glorified Elijah] completed Jesus there, and put death behind [Righteous Adam within Jesus],

---

[62] **Conversion** means that you start living out of your Christ Mind, and stop living out of your carnal mind (Acts 17:6). (Read entire footnote in Appendices)

[63] Cain and Abel are the inseparable germ seed of creation, Jehovah's nature and the Primordial Serpent's nature, inseparable for the life of the ages. (Read entire footnote in Appendices)

Chapter 6

6.38　Sacrifice [the fiery serpent's lifestyle], and [Abel/Christ], your good side, shall revive [and mature into Adam/Christ Jesus, the one who] topples [Leviathan], and [Abel/Christ] shall press down [Cain underneath himself, and Abel/Christ] shall overflow Cain, and gain access to your heart,

[And the spiritual child that appears in your heart shall reveal whether you have sacrificed righteous Abel/Christ or the rebellious murderer, Cain], because [the spiritual seed] that you sow shall be given back to you [as the spiritual child that will either save you, or lead you into destruction].[R]

[R] 1 Tim 2:15

Chapter 7

[Message # Unknown]
7.24-25　You went into the [spiritual] wilderness looking for Elohim, (all you people who wanted to be spiritual but did not get what you were looking for) [but], on the contrary, [John], Elohim's [engraving] pen in the under[world], revealed [your sin nature, which] agitated your spirit and incited [you to be angry with him].

[But], what did you expect [to find]? Adam clothed in an effeminate personality? Look [and understand], the mortal personality is effeminate, [but it] becomes [very strong] when [Elohim's spiritual] nobility enclothes it.

[600.3]

7.36 And Simon, one of the Pharisees, desired to interrogate Jesus to the end that he might acquire a knowledge of Jesus' spiritual philosophy. So the Pharisee invited Jesus to his home for a meal, but Jesus went to join himself to Simon's spiritual household.

7.37 And behold, a woman who abode in spiritual Babylon, the sinner's city, knew that Jesus was eating at Simon the Pharisee's home, and the spirit in the alabaster statue that she burned incense to, brought her there to curse Jesus.

7.38 And Satan, the unconscious part of the woman's carnal mind, was causing her to wail loudly, but Jesus stood against Satan, and Jesus' tears of compassion opposed Satan's spiritual moisture which permeated Leviathan, the scalp of the serpent, Satan's head, and the spiritual power of Jesus' tears of compassion squeezed Satan out of Leviathan, the scalp of the Serpent, the head of the carnal mind that the woman became attached to, when she burnt incense to Satan to acquire the Serpent's anointing.

7.39 Now Simon the Pharisee which had invited Jesus to teach him, answered his own question rather than ask Jesus, his teacher, saying, if this man, Jesus, were a true prophet, he would have recognized, by Jehovah's Spirit, what kind of woman he was joining himself to, because she is a sinner, steeped in witchcraft.

7.44a And Jesus turned towards Simon and said, Why are you looking at this woman with envy? The Spirit of Christ, my spiritual seed, entered into your spiritual household also, but you did not deliver up your carnal mind to the one who is from above.

7.45 You, Simon, would not deliver up your carnal mind to me, but his woman joined herself to me continually, even though she was separated from what you were born into.

7.46   This woman did not anoint my head with physical olive oil; but on the contrary, I anointed her carnal mind with the anointing oil of my Spirit.

7.46   This woman did not anoint my head with [physical] olive oil, but, on contrary, I anointed her carnal mind with the anointing oil of my Spirit.

7.44b   So, Simon, that is why the tears of my compassion squeezed Satan's moisture out of Leviathan, the scalp of the Serpent, the head of this woman's carnal mind, and did not squeeze Satan out of your carnal mind.

Chapter 8

[814.1.C]
8.46   And [Righteous Adam, the Son of God, who] knew immediately that spiritual power had gone forth from [Jesus of Nazareth], his [other] self, into the crowd, turned to [Jesus], his other side, and said, Who touched [Jesus of Nazareth], my clothing [in this world]?

Chapter 11

[OLM – 10 25 00]
11.17   But [Jesus] knew their thoughts, [so] He said to them, [when] the mind that [is joined to the glorified Elijah] is divided [from the glorified Elijah, the personality] loses [her spiritual power, and] the [spiritual] housewife that [is ascended into Christ Jesus' timeline], falls down [and becomes] the [spiritual] housewife [of Satan and Leviathan].

Alternate Translation Of The New Testament/ Luke

[OLM 02 03 99 Passover-2]
11.23 The one who does not gather his sin nature together with me in the spiritual place between the eyebrows, scatters his energy, and scattered energy opens the door to the sin nature.

11.24 [Satan], the impure spirit, plots to kill Adam/Christ Jesus, [the one who] silences [her], separates [Abel from Leviathan], and dries out the spiritual waters of the lower sea, [because] when [Leviathan] finds the opportunity to communicate [spiritually] with the Abel, [Satan], the impure spirit, says, I will return to my house that I was forced out of,

11.25 But when [Satan], the impure spirit, arrives at the spiritual waters of the lower sea, she finds that the marks of her nature have been removed [Cain], and that [the whole personality] is in a righteous relationship with Christ Jesus,

11.26 So, then [Leviathan], who [Adam/Christ Jesus] removed, associates herself [spiritually] with [Abel], the other part of her hurtful, spiritual self, and the supernatural powers of the Ancient Serpent's completed timeline come into existence, and the spiritually mature [second] Adam/Christ Jesus [who does not guard against this spiritual event] is worse off than the immature [first] Adam [who has not advanced spiritually].

Chapter 10

[1186.33.C]
10.10 [Let the Truth that is now] in the public place go forth from the unconscious part of the mind, and enter into every city that might receive [what] you have to say, but to every city that does not receive [the Truth that] you [speak],

10.11a [Righteous Abel], the dust that sticks to we [Israelites] like glue, shall be scraped away from you, except for this: You shall know that the Kingdom of God approached you, [and you rejected it];

10.12a   Indeed, I say to you, the day that judgment falls upon the city [that rejects the Truth when the only begotten Son of the Father is glued to their]

10.11b   Carnal mind,

10.12b   Shall be more tolerable than [the day that judgment fell on Sodom].*

> * That day shall be more tolerable than the judgment that fell on Sodom, because, even though they did not believe, they received the seed (Vs 11a) (Js 1:21).

Chapter 11

[1219.4.C]
11.38   And when Jesus was not overwhelmed in the debate, the Pharisee realized that the First [Adam] within Jesus had leaned back, [and that he was debating with Righteous Adam],

Chapter 12

[1219.5.C]
12.01   In the meantime, when an indescribably large crowd of people gathered together [to hear Jesus and the Pharisees debate] one another, [Jesus] said to the disciples [who] were treading down ᴿ [the thoughts of the First Adam] in the unconscious part of the mind,

Alternate Translation Of The New Testament/ Luke

"[You should not be afraid of what the Pharisees might do to me]:

^R Rev 2:9

"It is more important for you to know [that the understanding of] the esoteric doctrine [that] the Pharisees teach is not true,

12.02 "And that any [spiritual truth] concealed [by their incorrect understanding] shall be revealed, [and] any [incorrect understanding of] the mysteries shall, indeed, be exposed,

12.03 "[And that the Truth] that I spoke in private to you who have understanding, [today], was heard in the highest [spiritual] public [arena], and is [now] shining [there, like a light in] a dark place;

12.04 "Indeed, I am telling you, my friends, not to be afraid [that incorrectly understanding doctrine will] kill [your] body, because, after [the body dies], there is nothing worse that can happen [to you];

12.05a "Indeed, I will show you plainly [who it is that] should be afraid:

12.06a "The songbirds of the five[-fold ministry

12.05b "Should fear [that their soul will be] killed [when they succumb to the temptations of] the Devil ^R

^R Matt 4:5-6, 8, 9

12.06b "To sell [the gifts of the Holy Spirit for] a penny or two ^R

^R Matt 21:12

12.05c "[Because] after [that, Satan] has the authority to [enforce Jehovah's righteous Sowing and Reaping Judgment, and] casts [their soul and their body] into [the fires of] Gehenna:^R

^R Jer 25:34-46

12.06c "But, [when] the personality [that is] united with [Christ is tempted to use the Word of God as a weapon against the people of God, Christ] in the unconscious part of the mind [helps him] [R-1] to remember [the correct understanding of the doctrine of] God, [and he escapes from the Devil's seduction]; [R2]

[R-1] Gen 2:18
[R-2] Matt 5:7, 10, 11
1 Cor 10:13

12.07 "Indeed, [when you unify with Christ in the unconscious part of the mind by correctly understanding doctrine], you are counted [among those who have] the Spirit [that raised Jesus], your head, [from the dead],[R-1] [and] you transition beyond the fear [that] many of the Spirit-Filled Ministers have, [that when challenged with financial difficulties, the Devil in the unconscious part of the mind, will tempt them to use the gift of prophesy to satisfy their financial needs],[R-2]

[R-1] Rom 8:11
[R-2] Vs 10

12.08 "And, in addition, I am telling you [that] the personality that acknowledges [that Righteous] Adam is in the midst of himself, and the personality [that] acknowledges, as well, that the angels of God [are] in the unconscious part of the mind, [is] a Son of [Righteous] Adam;

12.09 "Indeed, the personality [that] does not recognize that [Righteous] Adam is within me, is the personality that [also] rejects the angels of God,

12.10 "And whoever [uses] the Word [of God as a weapon] against a Son of Righteous Adam [R] shall be forgiven in the unconscious part of the mind, but blasphemous [words] spoken against the Holy Spirit shall not be forgiven [by Satan, the enforcer of Jehovah's righteous Sowing & Reaping Judgment]; [R]

[R] Matt 12:32

12.11   "So, when they bring you into the synagogues, and [you appear before] the chief judges and authorities, do not be concerned about how you will answer [their questions], or what you will say [in response to their accusations],

12.12   "Because [in the very same] hour [that you appear before them], the Holy Ghost shall instruct you in the unconscious part of the mind, concerning what you should say." ^R

^R Vs 6c
Vs 7

[382.2]
12.21   But he that amasses wealth for himself does not possess the spiritual riches of Christ Jesus;[64] ^R

^R Phil 4:19

12.22   Therefore, do not promote your own interests through Satan and Leviathan,^R the mortal mind that clothes you,

^R Vs 30-31

---

[64]   The Lord Jesus Christ provides for our spiritual needs. He will also *influence* the resources of this visible, physical world, which was formed by the fiery serpent, to provide for our physical needs, but every material thing that we acquire with our carnal mind, is the fruit of the fiery serpent's lifestyle.

12.23 Because Cain, who incarnates this animal existence,^{R-1} does more than provide the skin^{R-2} [of your physical body];⁶⁵ Indeed, [your etheric body] is her food,⁶⁶

R-1 Ps 68:13 (AT)
Ps 74:14 (AT)
R-2 Ps 68:12 (AT)
Ps 72:16(b) (AT)
Ps 102:4-12(b) (AT)

12.22b In this animalistic existence,^R and she consumes it.

R Ps 68:13 (AT)
Ps 74:14 (AT)

12.24 Think about the mortal, spiritual men that the Lord Jesus Christ provides for, [even though] Leviathan, [the subconscious part of] their carnal mind, [who is] the Ancient Serpent's [military] storehouse that cuts Christ Jesus down [in the Earth],^{R-1} has sown the Cain in the inner chamber [of their heart]. How much more [will Christ Jesus provide for] you spiritual men who can distinguish between [Christ Jesus, your] righteous self], and the good and evil [of Leviathan and Satan],^{R2}

R-1 Ps 90:6 (AT)
103.5 (AT)
Lk 12:28 (AT)
R-2 Heb 5:14

12.26a So, if Satan and Leviathan are the lesser power,^{R-1}

R-1 Ex 18:11

---

⁶⁵ The physical body is an expression of the mind we are married to. We shall have a body of light when we marry the Mind of Christ Jesus.

⁶⁶ Meeting our own needs by using the methods of the fiery serpent's lifestyle (pride, envy, social witchcraft, etc.) offers up our etheric body to the fiery serpent who feeds on our spiritual energy, and loss of spiritual energy produces disease and physical death.

12.25   And you can add the depth of Christ Jesus' spiritual maturity to yourselves[R-1] [by subjecting Satan and Leviathan, your carnal mind]?[R-2]

[R-1] Rom 11:33 (AT)
[R-2] Rom 8:18-20 (AT)

12.26b   Why are you against [Christ Jesus],[R-1] your other side, who is taking care of you?

[R-1] Ps 104:26 (AT)
Jas 4:1-4

12.27   Understand that you did not receive the flower of the Holy Spirit by your own hard labor,[67] and I point out to you that, despite all of Solomon's [spiritual] glory, [Adam within him] did not cover [Cain, his sin nature, and] neither is Christ[68] within you twisted together with the Holy Spirit [to form Christ Jesus, the one who covers Cain, your sin nature],

12.28   But if the Holy Spirit clothes Christ, the young spiritual life[R-1] that is this very day coming into existence in the visible, physical world, [but] is cast into the oven tomorrow,[R-2] He will [surely] provide those who [already] have some understanding with the mighty [Christ Jesus].[R-1]

[R-1] 2 Cor 5:2, 4
[R-2] Ps 90.6 (AT)
Ps 103:5 (AT)
Lk 12:24 (AT)

---

[67] The Holy Spirit is the flower produced by Jesus, the Christ, the true vine, and Christ Jesus is his fruit. (Read entire footnote in Appendices)

[68] Christ Jesus is conceived when the Lord Jesus Christ twists together with Abel, mortal man's human spirit. Christ Jesus is the fruit of the womb of mankind [Son of Man], and the increase [offspring] of the Lord Jesus Christ [Son of God]. He is the Son of Man and the Son of God.

12.32   But Satan and Leviathan do not believe that the Father has chosen to give the Kingdom to the least of the disciples,^R and that they are [already] sitting in judgment,

^R Lk 7:28

12.33   [So], loose yourself from Satan and Leviathan, [the carnal mind] that is possessing you, and give yourself over to [the corrective judgment^{R-1} that will] bring forth the compassion [of Christ] within you, because Satan and Leviathan, the coffin[-like mind that holds your dead spirit],^{R-2} has become an old bag^{R-3} [that should be passing away], but the [lower] heaven where the Ancient Serpent, the thief^{R-4} [that kidnapped Elohim's children], is joined to Abel's breath of life [and becomes]

Satan and Leviathan, [the collective unconscious and subconscious parts of the carnal mind] that kill the immature [Christ] life, is not failing,^{R-5}

^{R-1} Is 1:27
^{R-2} Matt 9:17
^{R-3} Lk 5:37-38
^{R-4} Jn 10:10
^{R-5} Is 34:4
Rev 6:14

12.29   Because you worship Satan^R the one who is devouring you, and strengthen Leviathan, instead of Christ Jesus,

^R Amos 5:5(c) & (b) (AT)

12.30   And [you] seek after the things that the nations of the world crave [in Leviathan's strength], even though the Father knows that you need them,

12.31   So, unless you crave the Kingdom [of God], you will, indeed, obtain these things [by Leviathan's strength],[69]

---

[69] Obtaining the riches of this mortal world in Leviathan's strength results in spiritual and physical death (Lk 12:20). (Read entire footnote in Appendices)

Alternate Translation Of The New Testament/ Luke

12.34   Because [Abel], your [spiritual] substance,[70] is in the [right side of] the heart [where Satan is].[71]

[430.6]
12.33   . . . but the [lower] heaven where that thief, Satan, joins herself to Abel's breath of life, AND CAIN CONSUMES THE OX, is not failing,

12.29   Because you worship CAIN, WHO IS DEVOURING YOU[R OX], and strengthen Satan, instead of Christ.

[111]
12.44   Woe unto you, you hypocritical Scribes and Pharisees, [because Christ], the nature that the kingdom that God recognizes is built upon, is hidden, because Satan and Leviathan, your carnal mind, have tread [the resurrected] Adam under Cain, and the world sees your religious works, but God does not recognize them.

[OLM – 10 25 00]
12.51   So you think I came to bring peace in the earthen personalities [that are married to Satan and Leviathan]? On the contrary, I have come to divide [Abel, my son, from Cain],

---

[70]   In verse 21, Luke distinguishes between material wealth and spiritual substance by contrasting the words **layeth up treasure** (material) and **rich** (spiritual), but in verse 34 he uses the Greek word for treasure (**Strong's** #2344 [one digit up from the word translated, **layeth up treasure**] to indicate spiritual substance. The translation in each instance is determined by the context of the whole verse.

[71]   **Heart** means **spiritual center**, the place where [the fiery serpent], the one who incarnated you dwells. Christ Jesus, the Kingdom of God, is in the left side of the heart, and Satan is in the right side of the heart, the Kingdom of Darkness, the lying mind of mortal man.

Alternate Translation Of The New Testament/ Luke

12.52a So, from now on, Cain, [72] the household of [Leviathan,[73] shall be] joined to [Christ], the one who ascends into[and speaks through the throat of the timeline that is above, [and Cain and Abel][74] shall be divided in two, and Abel shall be above Cain;

12.53b [And when Abel, Elohim's] son, [is] above Cain,

12.52b Satan,

12.53a [Cain's] mother [in the world below], shall be divided from Leviathan, [Cain's] father [in the world below],

[But, when Cain, Adam's] daughter-in-law [in the world below, is] above [Abel, Elohim's] son,

[Leviathan], the father of [Cain, Satan's] daughter [in the world below], is above [Adam, Cain's] mother-in-law [in the world below], and [Satan], the mother [of Cain, Leviathan's] daughter [in the world below], is above [Abel, Leviathan's] daughter-in-law [in the world below].

---

[72] Abel and Cain are the male and female aspects of one dual being. They cannot be separated from one another. (Read entire footnote in Appendices)

[73] The fiery serpent, Cain and Abel engraved with the Dragon's nature, is Leviathan's wife.

[74] The fiery serpent is called **Abel and Cain** as soon as Abel begins to reject the Dragon's thought patterns and manifest the thought patterns of the grafted Christ (Jas 1:21). (Read entire footnote in Appendices)

Chapter 13

[Message # Unknown]

13.32 & Jn 2:19   And he said unto them, Go ye, and tell that fox, Behold, I cast out devils, and I do cures today and tomorrow, and [on] **the third day** I will **be perfected**, and arise [out of] this temple, and [this temple] shall dissolve. (See, **Endnote** [A] at the end of this book)

[573.3.C]

13.32   And Jesus said to [the Pharisees], you go away,[75] and tell [Satan, the jackal (see, *Note #17*) [that feeds on mortal humanity, the carcass of fallen Adam], that I am casting demons out [of mortal men] in this age, and in the next age, [after I am glorified], I will consummate [my marriage to mortal humanity, my run-away wife, which union] will completely cure [their deadly disease, and when Christ within mortal humanity ascends to the spiritual level called] *the third day [of creation]*,[R] I shall perfect them.[76]

[R] Gen 1:12-13

---

[75]   In Lk 13:31, the previous verse, the Pharisees tell Jesus that He should go away, leave town, because Herod wants to kill him. (Read entire footnote in Appendices)

[76]   Jesus was perfected at the marriage at Cana, before He made this statement, so He must be talking about the Body of Christ.

Chapter 16

[600.5.C]

16.19   There was a certain man, a citizen of Israel the landmark nation that God dwells in, who was spiritually rich because God granted him the righteousness that comes by faith.^R Indeed, [Elohim regenerated] Adam [within the man], making [the man] both king and priest, and granted him all of the protection, authority and power [that is in the regenerated Adam], and the citizen of Israel appropriated all of the blessings that are associated with the Holy Spirit for himself, every day of his life,

^R Rom 4:3

16.20a   But Lazarus, [another Israelite, who was spiritually poor and needy, because] he dwelt in this visible, physical world without [God's blessings],[77] roved the earth in a condition of spiritual wretchedness, and was thoroughly frightened, because he had experienced being overcome and enslaved by ungodly spiritual powers,

So [when] Lazarus recognized the representative of God's landmark nation of Israel [whose job it was] to point the way to God, he desperately fell on his face, hoping for mercy, because

16.21a   [Cain], the animal nature [within him that] desired to be satisfied,

16.20b   Had [made a] lesion in [Lazarus' body], and

---

[77]   *Lazarus, Strong's* #2967, is a translation of the Hebrew name *Eleazar, Strong's* #499, **the one that God helps**. (Read entire footnote in Appendices)

16.21b   Satan, [Cain's mother, the unconscious part of his carnal mind], had appeared and incited [Leviathan, Cain's father, the pride of man, to pierce through Lazarus' spiritual] wound, and [Leviathan, Cain' father, the pride of man], descended [into [Lazarus' spiritual place of lust], and the two, [Cain and Leviathan, his father, the pride of man, formed a unity that] separated [Lazarus] from the spiritual riches [of Christ Jesus; and

16.22a   It came to pass, that [Lazarus], the spiritually poor and needy man died [to the sin nature that caused him to rove the earth in a condition of spiritual wretchedness], and [Adan], the angel [within Lazarus], carried him into the left side of the heart, [where] Abraham [is]; and

Then, the citizen that possessed the spiritual riches [of Adam] died [to Adam's righteous lifestyle], and

16.22b   [Cain] buried [Abel, Adam's root system within the rich man], under [her spiritual ground], and

16.23   [Abel, within the rich man], went down under Satan and Leviathan, the rich man's carnal mind, and [Abel within the rich man] opened his eyes, [and the rich man] saw that he was in a morally impure place, and that Lazarus was in the heart of Abraham's [righteous timeline], which was far away, and

16.24   [The rich man] cried out, saying, Father Abraham, have mercy on me, and send Lazarus [who now has] the water [of the Holy Spirit], to moisten [Cain's ground, which] will revive [Adam, my righteous] mind [who is Jehovah's] high priest, [the one who opposes Leviathan], the finger [of the Dragon that is penetrating] me, because Cain is tormenting me,[78]

16.25   But Abraham said, remember [my] son, that you received the good things of life [whole] Lazarus received evil things, and now, similarly, [Lazarus] is comforted, and you are tormented, but

16.26   Besides all this, [God] has established a great gulf between us, so that whoever [desires] to pass from here to [your side] is powerless [to do so], and neither can they pass from [Leviathan's] side to us,[79] and

16.27   Then [the rich man] said, I beg you, therefore, father [Abraham], that you send [Lazarus] to my father's house,

16.28   To my brethren who are possess[ed of Leviathan who is speaking through their] throat center, to witness [the destruction that pride will eventually bring] to them, so that they do not enter into this place of torment;

16.29   Indeed, said Abraham, they have Moses and the prophets, let [your brethren] hear [about the fruit of pride from] them,

---

[78]   The rich man thought that he was justified by the works of the law, so he lost his spiritual inheritance and fell under Wormwood Judgment, which only Messiah can deliver us from.

Wormwood judgment is a form of the Sowing & Reaping Judgment that we overcome by Jesus' power, as we confess the specific, hidden sins of our heart, and repent.

[79]   There is no way across Satan's sea (the astral plane), and transfer from the Primordial Serpent's tormenting timeline, into the safety of Abraham's righteous timeline. (Read entire footnote in Appendices)

16.30   No, indeed, father Abraham, said [the rich man, my brethren do not believe what Moses and the prophets teach, that they can fall down^R into the spiritual place of moral impurity, but if [a mortal man that Adam] raised from the dead [80] goes to [teach] them, they will reconsider; and

^R Ps 107:12

16.31   [Abraham] said to [the rich man], if they cannot hear Moses and the prophets' [telling them that their pride will result in their fall into the spiritual place of moral impurity, and begin to face their sin nature and resist her], neither will they be persuaded, even if [Adam] rises from the dead [in a mortal man].[81]

Chapter 17

[OLM 07 29 98]
17.06   You will be [strong enough] to command the Tree of the Knowledge of Good and Evil that Satan planted in you, to be uprooted, when you have the faith of the double seed that stings.

---

[80]   The Primordial Serpent murdered Adam and used his spiritual substance to found this present world. (Read entire footnote in Appendices)

[81]   Their pride refused to admit the truth of their spiritual condition: They were unrighteous because of an internalized sin nature which they must overcome to enter into life.

This was true of the Pharisees in the days of Jesus' flesh, and it is true of many in the Church today.

Alternate Translation Of The New Testament/ Luke

[Message # Unknown]
17.20 Leviathan is appearing because [the Sons of God refuse to wage the warfare that kills her, but instead],[R] have subjected the Kingdom of God to her.

[R] Heb 2:15 (AT)

[994.3.C]
17.26a When the son of Adam arrives, [the sons of God] shall be in the same condition that [Shem, Ham and Japheth were in], in the days of Noah:

17.27a They were communing with [Elohim] and marrying [the daughters of Adam, who] were

17.26b Also

17.27b Giving themselves [to the sons of God] in marriage, until the day that Elohim entered into Noah, [his] ark, and a flood [of water from above rained down] and completely destroyed all of them, and

17.28 [The day that the Son of Adam appears shall be] similar to the days of Lot, [when the sons of God] were communing with [Elohim], teaching doctrine that builds up [the household of God][R-1] and selling [the things that attach them to this world,[R-2] while they waited to be] redeemed;[R-3]

[R-1] Eph 4:12
[R-2] Lk 12:33
[R-3] Eph 1:4

17.29a Indeed, the day Lot went out of Sodom, Jehovah rained [down] lightning* and purifying flames

> *The spiritual significance of lightning is that it is the result of the fusion of the energies of the Lord Jesus Christ, above, and Christ Jesus in the earth of humanity.*

Alternate Translation Of The New Testament/ Luke

17.30　　[Upon the Sodomites] to cast [the primordial kings] out [of the unconscious part of their mind, and so it] shall be [in] the day [that] Jehovah reveals the Son of Adam in these sons of God [who exist in the earth today];

17.31　　In that day, Elohim shall be [outside of the body], on the roof top, and [the Shekinah, his] wife [in] the unconscious part of the mind [of the spiritual Sodomites in Israel, shall be] inside of the house, and [Elohim] shall descend [into the unconscious part of the mind of the spiritual Sodomites in Israel] to liberate [the Shekinah, his wife, from] Satan, the unconscious part of their mind, [who is] also in the field [of the body],[R-1] and Satan [who is] similar to [the Shekinah, shall try to prevent[R-2] the Shekinah from] returning [to her father];[R-3]

[R-1] Ez 37:1
[R-2] Acts 13:8
[R-3] Gen 15:15a (AT)

17.29b　　[But] the smoke[R-1] [of the Shekinah shall ascend into] heaven [and be unified with Elohim, [R-2] her mother, and they shall descend back into the body], together;[R-3]

[R-1] Rev 8:4
[R-2] 1 Thes 4:17
[R-3] Rev 19:11, 14

17.32　　Remember, [the Shekinah, Elohim's] wife [within] Lot, [who looked back longingly towards Satan, her alter ego, and]

17.29c　　Was destroyed;[R]

[R] Gen 19:26

17.33　　[Wherefore], whoever worships Jehovah shall acquire [Christ Jesus, the spiritual intellectual] soul [of Jesus Christ, the Second Adam, in] the unconscious [part of their mind, and Christ Jesus, the soul of the Lord Jesus Christ that] they acquire, shall fully destroy [Satan], the unconscious [part of the carnal mind of the First Adam];

Indeed, [the unified] Elohim [and Shekinah] shall destroy [Satan], the unconscious [part of the fallen] soul [of the First Adam];

17.34-36 I am telling you that there are two [Adams] in the field [of the body].[R-1] [The] one of the two [Adams that is] the unconscious part of the mind [of the First Adam],[R-2] grinds[R-3] [up the true doctrine], and [the other] one [of] the two [Adams eats the spiritual food][R-4] while reclining on a couch;* One [Adam] shall acquire the spiritual office [of Elijah],[R-5] and forgive [Jesus of Nazareth],[R-6] another [Adam, and the Lord Jesus Christ], the First [Adam] that is forgiven, shall instruct [the Body of Christ],[R-7] the other [Adams that are forgiven, about how] to possess [their souls][R-8] and escape [death],[R-9] and

[R-1] Ez 37:1
[R-2] 1 Cor 15:47
[R-3] Matt 24:41
[R-4] Ps 105:40
    Jn 6:35
[R-5] Matt 11:14
[R-6] Rev 1:5
[R-7] Rom 12:5
[R-8] Lk 21:19
[R-9] 1 Cor 15:26

* "Reclining on a couch" is another translation of the Greek word translated "bed." It suggests the Passover, that the Hebrew children that were liberated from Egypt were free men.

Another meaning is, that these other Adams, i.e., the rest of the people, will eat the holy food (the hidden meaning of the Scripture) which produces eternal life, **while they are still mortal**.

17.37 They answered and said to him, where is the unconscious part of the mind, Lord? And he said to them, wherever the body is, that is where the [two] eagles [the Supernal Mother and the Shekinah] assemble.[R]

[R] Rev 19:21

Chapter 20

[695.1.C]
20.17 The same stone that came down from above to cover [the well that the female Adam fell into], rejects [you Pharisees as Jehovah's] authentic [priests, and declares you to be incapable of] standing [Christ Jesus], the building [that connects heaven and earth], upright, [at a right angle to Christ, the foundation of the building].

[1240.1.C]
20.18 Whoever falls down [on their knees and submits to] that [foundation] stone, [shall be separated from the bad Angel that] dashed to pieces [the whole Name, Jehovah Elohim]; Indeed, [the earthen personality that] falls down [on its knees and submits to that foundation] stone shall be separated [from that bad Angel] in the unconscious part of the mind.

Chapter 22

[Message # Unknown]
22.44 See, Old Testament witness to "drops of blood" referring to Jesus' reproductive seed (Amos 9:13, Vol. 1, Alternate Translation of the Old Testament).

Chapter 23

[906.3.C]
23.46   . . . He said, [further], "Father, into your hands I present my spirit;" and having said that, he breathed out [of the body of Jesus of Nazareth].

THE GOSPEL OF JOHN

Chapter 1

[Message # Unknown]

1.01   At the beginning of time, [Jehovah], the living thought that the [Eternal] God spoke into existence, was projecting forth from the side of the [Eternal] God, and

1.02   [Jehovah, that] living thought, was an extension of the [Eternal] God, and [Jehovah] was God.

1.03   All things came into existence through [Jehovah], the living thought, and nothing that came into existence, came into existence apart from him.

1.04   Life was in [Jehovah], the living thought, and that life was the spirit of [Adam], the man-faced creature.

1.05   And the light exposed the evil nature [of the man-faced creature], but that evil nature could not dominate the spirit of the man-faced creature.

1.06   A men was sent from God, whose name was John.

1.07   The same came as a prophet, witnessing about the Christ, that all might believe through him.

1.08   He was not the Christ, but was sent to witness to the Christ,

1.09   That the Christ is the Truth that enlightens the many-membered man that is appearing in this world

1.10-11 System, [which] came into existence through the living word but, even though [Ancient Adam] was within them,

Alternate Translation Of The New Testament/ John

desiring to give them the mind of Christ, they did not engage in an intimate relation relationship with him, or submit themselves to the mind [of the Father, which]

1.18   No one man has [ever] seen, but [Jesus of Nazareth] explained [to us that the man that] the Father dwells in [becomes] the only Son of his kind, and

1.14b   We understood that [Jesus of Nazareth is called] the only begotten Son [of God, because] he has the grace [of the Old Covenant, which is the female seed of the Father], and [the Spirit of] Truth, [which is the male seed of the Father, and that] the completed mind of the Father [is born in the man that has] these two seeds,

1.12   [And, now, the Lord Jesus Christ] has given us the authority to over[come] our carnal mind [also], so [that] as many as join themselves to the mind of [the glorified Jesus Christ], can become the true offspring of God [also],

1.13   Which are not born because of the reproductive force of this world system, or because of the carnal mind's desire to incarnate, or because a human man desires to father a child, but are the true offspring [that] came out of God.

1.14a   And [that is how Ancient Adam], the living thought that God spoke [into existence], was made into a personality and lived in one of the fallen human bodies which are generated by this world system.

1.15   John witnessed to [the Lamb of God, the offspring of Ancient Adam within Jesus], and preached about him, saying, this is the one that I told you about, who is coming [to the people] after me, but He existed before I was born.

1.16   And we have all received of his completeness, which is the grace of the new covenant, in addition to the grace of the old covenant,

Alternate Translation Of The New Testament/ John

1.17　　Because the grace which is of the law was given by Moses, but the true nature of God was revealed through Jesus Christ.

[798.3.C]
1.29　　By no means [is it possible] that one of the two small birds, [which are] one 10th [of the God World of Emanation, who] is sold to the ground, should fall without the father being concerned for them;

1.30　　Indeed, He is very concerned [about] you, [because] you are the many hairs of his head, [which must] all be accounted for; wherefore,

1.31　　[You who are] the many [hairs of the head of Ancient Adam], should not be afraid, [because] the cherubim will carry you through;

1.32　　[Wherefore], whosoever of the whole [fallen Adam] agrees to be a part of me, [the one who stands] in front of [Elijah], also agrees that his personality is a part of [Elijah, the one who stands] in front of [Ancient Adam], my father which is in heaven, and

1.33　　Indeed, whosoever of the whole [fallen Adam, who] denies me, [the one who stands in] front of the female Adam, also denies that his personality [stands] in front of my father which is in heaven.

1.34　　Do not think that I came to bring peace on the earth: I did not come to bring peace, but [I came as] a [circumcising] sword.

1.35　　I came to bring division, the fallen female Adam against [Leviathan], his father, and the daughter [who married the serpent] against [Satan], her mother, and [the female cherub], the bride, from [Satan], her mother-in-law.

1.38   Whoever I take to myself to deliver [from the problems that they cried out to me about], and does not follow me, will be weighed in the balances.[R]

[R] Dan 5:27

Chapter 2

The Marriage at Cana

[650.21.C]
2.01   There was to be a marriage[R-1] between [the Second Adam[R-2] who was] standing upright within Jesus [of Nazareth and his disciples], who existed in the Heathen Circle [of the World of Action], and [the Supernal] Mother, [who aroused him from the sleep of death on] the Third Day,[R-3] and

[R-1] Rev 19:7
[R-2] 1 Cor 15:47
[R-3] 1 Cor 15:4

2.02   Jesus and his disciples were bidden to the marriage,

2.03   [But], when [the Supernal] mother [perceived that the First Adam], the spiritual power that is inferior [to the Second Adam, was not dead and buried],[R] she said to [the Shekinah, her other] self [within Jesus and the disciples, "The Second Adam within Jesus and his disciples] does not have the power [to liberate you, even though he is standing upright within them]," and

[R] Ez 39:15

2.05   The [Supernal] mother said to [Jesus and the disciples, the personalities who] serve [God, "I will tell the Second Adam within you what] to do," and

Alternate Translation Of The New Testament/ John

2.04   Jesus said to [the First Adam, the spiritual] woman [who is] his other self, "Elohim and Adonai are with me, [so] the time has come for Leviathan [to die]," and

2.06a   [The Supernal Mother] spoke [to the Second Adam, her Son within Jesus, and the Second Adam within Jesus] spoke to [Christ], who was lying down [within the disciples because] they were impure [even though they had performed all of the rituals necessary to satisfy] the Law of the Jews, [saying],

2.08a   "[Tell Jesus and the disciples to draw upon my] spiritual power [to understand the sins of the First Adam within them, which will help them]

2.06b   "Yield to [the judgment of Leviathan, their own sin nature], the callous [that overlays] the six Rings [of Power of Christ, Abraham's seed,^{R} who is standing upright within them, and] I will fill [Abraham's Rings of Power with the energy]
^{R} Gal 3:29

2.08b   "[That is needed] to carry [them] up to [the world above];" and

> 2.09   [Jesus and his disciples, the personalities [who] serve [God], knew that the Rings [of Power of Abraham's seed within themselves] had been filled with] the spiritual power^R of [the Supernal Mother when] they experienced the spiritual authority of the upper triad,* [and Righteous Adam] began to be born again, and, indeed, Satan recognized that [Righteous Adam] was being born into that place again, and
> ^{R} Ez 37:19 (ATB)

Wisdom, Knowledge and Understanding.

2.07   Jesus said [to the First Adam, his other] self, "[The Supernal Mother] has filled [the Rings of Power of Abraham's seed within us] with the spiritual power of the higher worlds," and

2.09b   [The Supernal Mother] called out from the upper triad [to the Shekinah, her daughter within the disciples], the bride [of Elohim], who was standing upright,

2.10   Saying, "The First Adam was good when he was whole [and Jehovah] put [him in the Garden and commanded him] to guard [it,[R] but, Satan], the spiritual power [of the First Adam], intoxicated [Noah, and Canaan, the son of Ham who was] the least [in Noah's eyes], has been [suffering from Noah's curse] up to this present time.

[R] Gen 2:15

[Message # Unknown]
2.19   On the third day I will raise myself up [out of] this temple, and it will dissolve.

2.19 & Lk 13:32 - And he said unto them, Go ye, and tell that fox, "Behold, I cast out devils, and I do cures today and tomorrow, and [on] **the third day** I will **be perfected**, and arise [out of] this temple, and [this temple] shall dissolve." [A] (The preceding reference [A] is an *Endnote*)

Chapter 3

[Message # Unknown]
3.01   There was a man of the Pharisees, named Nicodemus, a ruler of the Jews:

Alternate Translation Of The New Testament/ John

3.02   And the carnal mind of Nicodemus[82] said, Rabbi, we know that you are a teacher of God because no man could do the miracles that you do unless God was with him,

3.03   And Jesus said to Nicodemus, I'm telling you the truth, unless [Adam] is born again within a mortal man, [that mortal man] cannot recognize the Kingdom of God[83] [in another man],[84]

3.04   And Nicodemus said, [Adam] is born a second time [when the Son of God] enters [into Majesty (Malchut)], the [lower] Garden [of Eden,[85] but the Shekinah has departed from Israel]. How, then, can Adam [of] old be regenerated [in a mortal man]?[86]

---

[82]   The Name, **Jesus**, does not appear in the Interlinear Text of verse 2, which reads **the carnal mind** (night) **[of] this same [Nicodemus, who was a ruler of the Jews], appeared and said, . . .**

Jesus knew that Nicodemus was speaking out of his carnal mind.

[83]   The Kingdom of God is the Neshamah aspect of the soul (the Mind of Christ).

[84]   What is wrong with what Nicodemus said?

Miracles do not prove that a teacher is of God, because Satan can perform miracles also (2 Cor 11:14). (Read entire footnote in Appendices)

[85]   Nicodemus was well versed in Kabbalah. (See, Message #551, **The World Of Points & The Fall**, in the Christ-Centered Kabbalah Classroom, for an in-depth study of the Garden, the Fall, and the Rectification. See, also, the Christ-Centered Kabbalah Glossary for a broader understanding of Kabbalah terminology.)

[86]   Nicodemus had a knowledge of Kabbalah.

Alternate Translation Of The New Testament/ John

3.05   Then Jesus answered, [saying], I'm telling you the truth [Nicodemus], unless the [spiritual] waters[87] of a mortal man are regenerated by the Spirit [of God], he will never enter into the Kingdom of God.

Chapter 4

Christ Jesus Marries The Fiery Serpent Within John

[521.2]
4.03   [So Jesus] left off regenerating Adam [within his disciples] and went into Leviathan's timeline again,

4.04   And crossed over [into the carnal mind of John,[88] Jehovah's] watch station,[89] [where Cain] guards [Abel against spiritual intercourse with Christ Jesus], and [the Christ within

---

[87]   The **spiritual waters** of mortal man are the secret of **mayim nokbim**, the female waters that ascend to arouse the male waters of Ze'ir Anpin, the Son of God, to mate with Majesty (Malchut), the Female Ring who then gives birth to Adam. (Read entire footnote in Appendices)

[88]   The Holy Spirit was resident within John, but Christ was not formed within him yet. This means that John was still under the authority of his carnal mind, which is in Leviathan's timeline, as well as the **influence of the Holy Spirit**.

[89]   See, Online Mtg. Transcripts, **Spiritual Wives, Parts 1 & 8,** or **Judges, Chapter 21**, Alternate Translation, Old Testament.

Alternate Translation Of The New Testament/ John

Jesus] bound [Leviathan within John, and] pierced [into Abel within John],[90]

Jesus Exposes Sin In John

4.05   Then [Jesus] came near [91] [to John, Jehovah's] watch station, [where Cain] was guarding [Abel, the energy] field that Jacob gave to Joseph, because John] was filled up with [envy, which is generated by Satan's] spiritual power,

The Conditions That Weakened John

4.06a   Now, Jacob's spiritual world was present in [John, but John] was tired from his [spiritual] journey,

4.08   And [Leviathan within John, Jesus'] disciple, had spread deeply into John's [spiritual] city, to acquire nourishment,

4.06b   [And Leviathan within John] was dwelling in the spiritual place between the eyebrows of [Satan's] spiritual world [within John], so Jesus [purposed] to [deliver John by] marrying [Abel within John],

4.07   So [when Cain, the spiritual] woman (see, *Note #**90**,* ¶ *3*) within [John, Jehovah's] watch station, appeared to draw power from [John], Jesus said to [Cain within John, do not deplete John's power], I will give [you] my [power],

---

[90]   The foundation of fallen man is Cain and Abel, Adam's mortal remains, engraved with the Serpent's nature. (Read entire footnote in Appendices)

[91]   *To draw near to* in the Old Testament means **corrective judgment.**

Alternate Translation Of The New Testament/ John

Cain Guards Abel Against
Spiritual Intercourse
With Christ Jesus

4.09   And [Cain, the spiritual] woman [within John], who guards [Abel against spiritual intercourse with Christ Jesus], said to [Jesus], how come you, a Jew, are asking me, [Cain, the spiritual] woman who guards [Abel against spiritual intercourse of the mind with Christ Jesus], to drink [of your strength], since I guard the Jews, the citizens of [Jehovah's] watch station, against [spiritual] intercourse [of the mind] with [Christ Jesus]?

4.10   And Jesus answered [Cain, the spiritual woman within John], saying, if you understood [that the Holy Spirit] is [Jehovah's] gift to you, and [that it is Elohim] saying that he will give you [his strength] to drink [down], you would ask for [the Holy Spirit, Jehovah's] life-giving strength, [yourself],

Cain Challenges Jesus

4.11   And [Cain, the spiritual] woman [within John], said to [Jesus], sir, Satan possesses the spiritual worlds [within John], and she [permits us] to draw from [John's] deepest [strength], so what is the source of this living water that you have?

4.12   Are you greater than our father, Satan, who gave us the spiritual world that [Abel, Jehovah's male] children, and [Cain], the cattle [that they are joined to], drink out of?

Jesus Declares
The End Of Reincarnation

4.13   And Jesus answered [Cain, the spiritual woman within John], saying, whoever drinks of [Satan's] strength, will reincarnate [over and over] again,

Jesus Preaches The Doctrine Of Christ

4.14   Indeed, the Ancient Serpent thirsted for Elohim's waters that I [Am] gave [to Adam, and Adam died [to his immortality and became the spiritual clay that the Serpent formed in her own image], and [the Serpent and Cain and Abel, Adam's mortal remains], entered into this [divided] age, but [do not be distressed, because I Am the one] who provides the strength of the age that will never end; [nevertheless] you shall enter into [true] life, [but only when] the strength of my spiritual world springs up within you,

Cain Desires To Stop Reincarnating

4.15   And [Cain, the spiritual] woman [within John], said, Lord, give me the strength to cross over [into the world where] my thirst is quenched [and the Serpent does not drink up [the strength of the mortal men] within it,

Cain Within John
Is Married To Leviathan

4.16a   [And Jesus] said to [Cain], the [spiritual] woman [within John],

4.18b   [Adam/Christ Jesus], your true husband, does not possess you at this time, because [Leviathan, the Serpent's] male [sex organ is lodged in your] throat, [and] is possessing [your whole personality],

4.17a   [And Cain, the spiritual] woman [within John], answered [Jesus], saying,

4.18a   It is as you say,

4.17b   [And Jesus said], because you have honestly confessed [that] Leviathan is your [illegal] husband,

Alternate Translation Of The New Testament/ John

4.16b [I, therefore, command Leviathan] to withdraw [from your throat], and let [Abel, the root system of Adam/Christ Jesus], your [true] husband, appear, so that I can talk to him (see, **Note #_90_, ¶ *3***),

4.28 Then [Cain, the [spiritual] woman [within John], [thought to herself], this [must] be Adam, [so Cain, the spiritual woman within John], left [the spiritual well] that she was drawing spiritual strength from, and went into [Leviathan's spiritual city], and [Cain] said [to Abel within John],

4.29 Come and see [this] Adam who explained, in detail, everything that I could bear [to hear]. Is this not the Christ?

4.30 And [Abel within John], went out of [Leviathan's spiritual] city, and came near to [Jesus],

Jesus Prophesies To John

4.22 [And Jesus said to Abel, Adam/Christ Jesus' root system within John], you worship Satan and have spiritual sexual intercourse [with Leviathan], but we [Jews are supposed] to worship Jehovah and have spiritual sexual intercourse with [Adam], which [union] is the reason that salvation proceeds forth from the Jews,

4.21a [And Jesus continued, saying, when] you have faith in me, [John], Adam/Christ Jesus will appear [within you to fight] against Leviathan, the Serpent's mountain [within you],

John Submits To Jesus As A Prophet

4.19 [And John] said to [Jesus], I perceive that you have supernatural insight into the spiritual morality [of Cain and Abel, the spiritual] woman [that I am joined to], and are an interpreter of the Will of God,

4.20 [And] you say that we, [Cain and Abel, the fiery serpent within John], worship [Leviathan, the Serpent's

Alternate Translation Of The New Testament/ John

mountain, and] Satan, our father, but [that] Adam, [Jehovah's mountain], is the place where we ought to worship,

4.21b [And], when [Jesus saw that John submitted to his instruction concerning] where to worship the Father, [Jesus said to Abel, Adam's root system within John, I Am the one] who [Jehovah sent] to complete [Adam/Christ Jesus within] you,

4.24 Because the [personality that desires] to worship the Spirit of God,^R must prostrate [herself] before the Spirit of Truth,

^R Jn 4:23

4.23 And the Spirit of Truth worships the Father by prostrating [Satan, the unconscious part of the carnal mind] of the true worshipers, so Christ Jesus is already appearing [in everyone who truly] worships the Father,

John Recognizes That Jesus Is Messiah

4.25 [Then Abel, Adam's root system within John], the [spiritual] woman, said, I know that Christ, the Messiah, is coming and [that], when He appears, He will explain, in detail, everything [about how the Father will restore mortal humanity to its first estate],

4.26 [And] Jesus said to [John], I Am is speaking to you [now],

4.27 [And Cain, the spiritual] woman [within John, Jesus'] disciple, was amazed [that Abel, Adam's root system within John], had surfaced [in response to Jesus' command], and that [Jesus] had spoken to [Abel, Adam's root system within John], but [Cain] said nothing [to Abel, the root system of Adam/Christ Jesus, her true husband, and did not even ask] **why were you talking with [Jesus]**, or **what were you trying to accomplish**?

Christ Jesus Satisfies The Thirst
To Reincarnate

4.31   [On the contrary, Cain] in the midst of [John, Jesus'] disciple, [spoke directly to Jesus], and interrogated him, saying, Rabbi, [tell us where the food is that will satisfy our thirst to reincarnate, so that] we [can] eat [it and live forever],

4.32   And Jesus said to Cain [within John, Abel, Adam/Christ Jesus, your true husband], knows about the [spiritual] food that I have to eat.[92]

4.33   Wherefore, [Cain within John, Jesus'] disciple, asked [Abel, John's] other side, about where they could find [this food] to eat,[93]

4.34   [And Abel, Adam Christ Jesus' root system within John taught Cain, his animal nature, saying], doing the will of [Jehovah] who sent Jesus to complete [Adam/Christ Jesus, Elohim's] work [within me], nourishes and strengthens me.[94]

---

[92] Cain interrupted Jesus' conversation with Abel to ask where she could find the spiritual food that would satisfy her thirst to incarnate, because she could not recognize that Jesus' dialogue was setting forth the answer to the very question that she was asking. (Read entire footnote in Appendices)

[93] The Devil is the personality that is in full agreement with Satan's nature, and the Scripture likens the Devil to a lion (1 Pet 5:8). (Read entire footnote in Appendices)

[94] Jesus tells Cain, Adam/Christ Jesus' wife, to not interfere with his preaching, but to put her questions to Abel/Christ, Adam/Christ Jesus' root system within John. (Read entire footnote in Appendices)

Chapter 5

[1000.2.C]

5.01   After this, Jesus went up to Jerusalem [to attend] a Jewish feast [that was taking place there];

5.02a   Now, the many-members of Jerusalem, the soul that is at peace with God, are the sheep [that are] bought and sold at the marketplace called in the Hebrew tongue, "Bethesda," [meaning], "The House of Mercy," and there was a pool [of God's energy from the world above there], and,

5.04a   Occasionally, an angel went down and agitated the [spiritual] energy in the pool, and

5.02b   [It would overflow into] five internal [receptacles, each of which was] one-sixth of the First Adam], the 60-fold anointing that mediates between God and Jerusalem, the many-membered soul that is at peace with God], and

5.04b   [When] Elohim's vibrating [spiritual] energy reaches into the midst [of Adam's five internal receptacles, it] heals the ailment of [every Israelite] that holds [his sin nature] down [under his righteous personality];

5.03a   So, many weak, blind or crippled [Israelites]

5.02c   Were [there], waiting for the [spiritual] energy [from the pool to heal them],

5.03b   But [Adam, their ability to access the healing power of God from the pool of God's spiritual energy], was lying down [within them], and

5.05   A certain [Israelite who] had been sick for eight years was there, [but he had only] a 30[-fold anointing, because] Adam [was lying down within him];

5.06   Now, when Jesus saw [that] he had been lying [there] for a long time, he said, "Do you desire [that Adam in] the unconscious [part of your mind] should make you whole?" And

5.07   That feeble [Israelite] answered, "Sir, Adam is not in the unconscious [part of my mind, so], when the Spirit begins to move, I do not have the ability to cast myself into the pool; Indeed, when [my righteous personality which stands in front of Adonay], moves [towards] Elohim, my other, [unrighteous personality] steps down in front of [it];"

5.08   And Jesus said, "Your sins are forgiven, stand up and walk," and

5.09   [After Jesus said, "Your sins are forgiven"], Adam [stood up in] the unconscious [part of that Israelite's mind] and walked [into the pool of God's spiritual energy that was descending from the world above, and God's spiritual energy filled Adam's five receptacles, and that Israelite] was made whole, immediately; And all this happened] on the Sabbath day.

Chapter 6

[OLM-03 22 00]
6.01   [And after Jesus rebuked the Pharisees for covering their Christ mind], Jesus pierced through Satan, the Emperor of the astral plane in the midst of the Pharisees, [and raised their consciousness into the left side of their heart],

6.02   And most of the spiritually impotent [Pharisees] followed Jesus because of the miracle that they experienced

Alternate Translation Of The New Testament/ John

[when Jesus raised their consciousness into the left side of their heart],

6.03   And Jesus ascended into the [spiritual dimension of] the throat, and gathered his disciples [together with the glorified Elijah who speaks from the spiritual dimension of the throat].

6.04   Now, the [spiritual] Passover, a feast of the Jews, was near,

6.05   So [when] Jesus looked into the Spirit, He saw a very large crowd [of people] drawing near to him, and [Jesus] said to Philip, How shall we supply the Doctrine of Christ [to so many, so that Christ can be formed in them and] consume [the fiery serpent, the subconscious part of their carnal mind]?

6.06   Now, Jesus said this to test [Phillip, to see] if [Philip] knew what Elohim would do,

6.07   And Phillip answered [Jesus, saying], the Pharisees are preaching Satan's morally impure philosophy with the spiritual authority of the place between the eyebrows [of Leviathan's] inferior [timeline, and this philosophy] generates lust [in the people, which] prevents [Christ Jesus from] seizing them,

6.08   And then Andrew, Simon Peter's brother, [one of] the disciples [who] was united [with Adam within Jesus in the spiritual dimension of the throat], said,

6.09   The young Christ is possessing [the people], and they [have become] bread, but the many-membered Leviathan, [is in] the spiritual dimension of the throat [of] the second, [counterfeit timeline within the people], even though Elohim [and] Christ Jesus, the mature grain, are among so many [of the people] in this place.

6.11   So Jesus seized [the apostles, who became] bread [when] they married [Adam within Jesus, because they were still thinking with their carnal mind], and [Adam within Jesus] divided [Cain from Abel (see, *Note #**90***) within the apostles and], in the same manner, when [the apostles] expressed their gratitude, [Adam within Jesus, divided Cain within the apostles] from Leviathan, who they greatly desired,

6.10a   Now there were many mortal males in the [spiritual] garden in the [place between the eyebrows], so

6.12a   [After Adam] completed [Jesus'] disciples,

6.10b   [Adam] said to Jesus, tell the Adams[95] to marry [the mortal males, and] gather them into the [spiritual] city of God,

6.12b   [So Jesus] said [to the apostles], assemble [the mortal males who have Elohim's] excellent [Spirit, and] separate Cain [within the mortal males from Abel, so that the mortal males] might die to [the fiery serpent's lifestyle,

6.13   Wherefore, [Adam/Christ Jesus, the spiritual] barley bread [within the apostles who were divided from Leviathan], overflowed [out of the apostles, and] gathered [the third-level disciples] into [the left side of] their heart, [and Adam/Christ Jesus within the apostles] wove together with [the fiery serpent within the third-level disciples, and] consumed [the fiery serpent within the third-level disciples, and Cain] separated from [Leviathan, who she was joined to in] the spiritual dimension of the throat [of the third-level disciples, and this is how Adam/Christ Jesus within the apostles] completed the third-level disciples],

6.14   And when those Adams[96] saw the miracle that [the apostles] did, [that they were standing in the left side of their

---

[95]   The apostles.

[96]   The converted Pharisees.

heart, beyond Satan's grasp, the Pharisees] said, these are truly prophets who have appeared in the world,

6.16   But after that, Satan stepped down into [the third-level] disciples, [and Satan's] thoughts entered [into the mind of the third-level disciples, and] mixed with Adam's thoughts, [and the third-level disciples descended] into [the right side of their heart, which is under the control of] Satan's astral plane,

6.15   Wherefore, when Jesus perceived that [the unrepentant third-level disciples had agreed with Satan to use their new-found power] to seize [other men, to be] king [over them], Jesus turned inward into the place between the eyebrows again, [the place where He accessed] the single, unified [authority of the glorified Elijah and the resurrected Adam, to rescue the third-level disciples from Satan's thoughts],

6.17   And [the third-level disciples] entered into their carnal mind and crossed over into [the right side of their heart, which is under the astral plane], Satan's immoral sea, [the unconscious part of the carnal mind and], by that time, Satan [and] Leviathan [their carnal mind], was appearing in [the third-level disciples],

6.18   And [Satan, the consciousness of] the astral plane [within the third-level disciples], fully awakened, [and the collective Satan who wields Jehovah's] mighty Spirit [as enforcer of Jehovah's righteous Sowing & Reaping judgment], breathed hard [towards the third-level disciples],

6.19   And [the third-level disciples] stood in the spiritual power of Satan and Leviathan, the two arms of the law within them: Leviathan in the spiritual dimension of their throat, and Satan manifesting as spiritual flies in the place where lust is generated,

And they pushed against [the collective Satan who was enforcing Jehovah's righteous Sowing & Reaping Judgment upon the third-level disciples, [who] were agreeing with Satan's suggestion to use the power of Christ Jesus to make themselves king over God's people,

But [when] the third-level disciples] saw Jesus, [who] lives [out of the place between the eyebrows of Adam's righteous timeline, which is] beyond the grasp of Satan's [authority], materializing and drawing near to their carnal mind, they worshiped [Jesus],

6.20   And I Am [spoke through Jesus and] said [to the third-level disciples, Satan, the enforcer of the Sowing & Reaping Judgment, is opposing you, but Adam/Christ Jesus, the mediator of the White Throne Judgment, has come to deliver you from Satan's spiritual artificial respiration.

Therefore], do not agree with [the thoughts of Satan, the unconscious part of your carnal mind, and the collective Satan, the enforcer of Jehovah's Sowing & Reaping Judgment, who is opposing her own thoughts within you, will go back to sleep].

6.21   And [Adam Christ Jesus] joyfully carried the third-level disciples out of their carnal mind and, immediately, [the third-level disciples] were in the Mind of Christ, which is above the right side of the heart, and their other [carnal] mind sank out of sight.

6.51   I am this living bread that came down from heaven. The personality that eats of this bread shall live forever, and [Adam/Christ Jesus] my [spiritual] male mind, is the bread that I give for the life of the [individual] personality.

6.52   The Jews therefore strove within themselves, saying, How can [Jesus] transfer this male mind to us, so that it can crunch together [with the fiery serpent within us]?

6.53   Then Jesus said unto them, I am telling you the truth. If Christ Jesus is not crunching together with the fiery serpent within you, and if the Spirit of Christ is not flowing in your spiritual blood, you have the fiery serpent's life within you,

6.55   [And] because [Christ Jesus], my [spiritual] male mind, is not hidden [underneath the fiery serpent], but is truly satisfying her, and the spiritual blood of [Christ Jesus] is [become] my true spiritual blood,

6.56a   The personality where [Christ Jesus], my [spiritual] male mind, crunches together with [the fiery serpent, and the Spirit of Christ] flows together with [Satan, Leviathan's] spiritual blood, will not perish [either, because Adam/Christ Jesus], this selfsame one [that is risen from the dead in me],

6.54   Is crunching together [with the fiery serpent within you], and flowing together with [Satan, your fallen, spiritual] blood, [IF] my [spiritual] male mind, this selfsame [Adam/Christ Jesus, who] will rise into eternal life in the last day,

6.56b   Is within you.

6.57   So, because the living Father[97] has set me apart [from Satan and Leviathan, and] I live because [of the living Father's mind and blood], the one that I crunch together with shall live because of me.

Chapter 7

[Message # Unknown]
7.39   But he spake of the Spirit that they which believe on him should receive, which was not [available to them] yet, since Adam, the Holy one, would remain [in] the spiritual [world] until Jesus was glorified.

---

[97]   Satan is the dead father of mortal humanity.

Chapter 10

[1230.6.C]
10.09   I am the door[to the Outer Court of the Tabernacle that] the sheep [must pass through for their three[-part soul, the Nefesh, Ruach and Neshama], to be saved: The spirit of] anyone that enters in[to the Outer Court of the Tabernacle] shall be saved, and [the soul that] go[es] in[to the holy place] shall be saved, and [the soul that goes] in[to the most holy place], shall find [spiritual] food [for the body that is in] the Out[er Court of the Tabernacle].

Chapter 12

[600.9.C]
12.01   Then, six days before Passover, Jesus came to [see] Lazarus, the one He raised from the dead and had a soul tie with, and,

12.02   Accordingly, Martha hosted [a meeting for Jesus], and Lazarus, the first one [who Jesus] completed by joining his [God/Christ Mind] to [Lazarus' carnal mind and forcing it] to lie down, was there, and they devoured [Jesus' doctrine],

12.03   [Then Mary] took a pound of incense and offered it [to Satan],

But, Jesus' sinless soul broke up [Mary's] carnal mind and kneaded [Satan's moisture] out of the [hairy] scalp[R] [that covered Mary's] carnal mind, and the fragrance of the incense of Jesus' very own valuable [spiritual], perfumed oil completely filled and satisfied [Mary's spiritual] house [hold].

[R] Ps 68:21

12.04   Then Judas Iscariot, the one of the disciples which should betray him, said,

12.05   Elohim gave this beggar over to Satan, who sold her into [spiritual] slavery. She is not worth 2¢, Jesus, and, [yet, you pour out your spiritual,] perfumed anointing oil [upon her]?

[688.9.C]
12.24   I am telling you, it is very true that [the rest of humanity will continue] to die [after my resurrection] if [the manchild who is saving me from death] remains by itself [in heaven], and does not descend into the earth [again as] the seed corn, that brings forth the fruit [of Christ Jesus].

Chapter 13

[987.7.C]
13.08   If I do not wash you, you cannot be a part of my [spiritual body]

13.10   Christ is washed, but not all of him; He has no debt except to ceremonially wash his animal mind; Nevertheless, he is completely clean, and you are clean [also].

[296]
13.25   Then the one who had a spirit tie with Jesus said to [Jesus], who is it Lord?

13.26, 30 [And] Jesus answered, the one that I shall hand over to Satan, even after I have sanctified [separated] him [from his carnal mind] and baptized him into my Spirit [Christ nature/imparted anointing].

Therefore, Jesus gave over Judas Iscariot to his carnal mind, and Satan, that notorious one, came to life against Judas, and laid hold of him, and Satan put Judas to sleep, and the imputed Christ [carnal nature under the influence of Christ] in Judas broke up, and Judas was in darkness [spiritual death].

13.27   And this is how Jesus did what He had to do to bring his own scripturally ordained betrayal to pass.

13.28   Now, no one at the table could figure out what Jesus was talking about,

13.31   So when Judas died spiritually [after he was given over to his carnal mind], Jesus explained to the disciples that the same Mind of Christ Jesus which was in [Jesus], the Son of man, was also shining in Judas, and that God [the Father] was, therefore, shining in Judas also.

13.32   Now if God, the Father, was truly shining in Judas, then God, himself, **will** [future] shine in Judas, and they shall shine [appear] together [in that last generation[R]].[98]

[R] Dan 12:13

Chapter 14

[385.10]

14.26   But this spiritual Intercessor which the Father will send, that Holy One who was like Me, but not Me, you see, He is your Savior in the midst of you. He is like Jesus, but He is not Jesus. He is the resurrected Adam in you, your personal Savior. That Holy One who was like Me shall teach you the whole doctrine of Christ which will remind you or witness to everything I have commanded you.

---

[98] Jesus is saying that all that [Abel], Judas' human spirit, which had increased into the [temporary, imputed] Mind of Christ, did and experienced [before He broke up and became Leviathan and Satan (in Judas) again], will be a part of the glorified Christ Jesus when He appears in that last generation.

Alternate Translation Of The New Testament/ John

Chapter 18

[517.4]
18.10a   Then [Christ Jesus, who] was possessing Simon Peter, compelled [Peter] to paralyze [the fiery serpent within the potential kings of Israel], who served [Leviathan, Satan's] high priest.

18.11   Then Jesus said to Peter, thrust your Christ mind into [the carnal] mind of the personalities that Satan is drinking from,

18.10b   And cut righteous [Abel, the ability of the potential kings of Israel] to understand the [Doctrine of Christ], away [from Cain]

Chapter 19

[Message # Unknown]
19.17   And [the glorified Elijah], the pointed stake that was standing upright [within Jesus], carried away [Christ Jesus], his other self, the one who teaches the doctrine [of Jehovah, the spiritual brain of Christ Jesus, from the Mind of Christ], the place marked off by [I Am], the skull [that covers Jehovah],[99] who is rolling [over the Dragon in the cerebral cortex of mortal man].

---

[99]   Christ Jesus is a spiritual man (1 Tim 2:5) with spiritual aspects that, for the purpose of understanding spiritual mysteries, can be likened to human body parts (1 Cor 12:14-17). (Read entire footnote in Appendices)

Chapter 21

[444]

21.15   So when they had broken their fast, Jesus says to [Abel/Christ [100] in] Simon Peter, "Simon, son of Jonas, your spirit tie with me is stronger than [your soul tie with the fiery serpent and Leviathan." And Satan in Peter] says to [Jesus], "Lord, surely you know that I have a noble human [only] love for you."

[But, despite Satan in Peter responding instead of Abel/Christ, Jesus] says to [Abel/Christ in Peter], "Supply [the Doctrine of Christ], my spiritual food, to Abel/Christ [in my disciples],"[101]

21.16   [Then Jesus] says to [Cain[102] in Peter], "Simon, son of Jonas, has a spirit tie with me,"[103] [but Satan in Peter] says to [Jesus], "Lord, surely you know that I have a noble human love [only] for you."

---

[100] Christ, Peter's spiritual mind, is Abel resurrected in Peter.

[101] Peter did not understand that Jesus, by saying, **you have a spirit tie with me**, was prophesying that Peter would have a spirit tie with him. (Read entire footnote in Appendices)

[102] The Greek word translated, *again*, can also be translated, *anew*, or **on the other hand**, and the phrase, second time, is a translation of **Strong's** #1208, which can also be translated, *second in rank*.

Jesus spoke to Abel, Peter's spiritual side first, and then to Cain, Peter's other, carnal side. Cain is the first born, but second to Abel in spiritual authority.

[103] The Christ mind in Peter has authority over you.

Alternate Translation Of The New Testament/ John

[But, despite Satan in Peter responding instead of Abel/Christ, Jesus] says to [Abel/Christ in Peter], "Supply the human wisdom to [Cain, the conscious part of the carnal mind] of the personalities who follow me, that will help them control [the emotional part] of their carnal mind, and protect them from harm" (see, *Note #**101***),

21.17 [Now] Jesus says to [Abel/Christ in] "Simon, son of Jonas, you have a soul tie with Satan," and Peter's conscience was pricked because Jesus said to him, "You have a soul tie with Satan," but Peter said to [Jesus], "Lord, you know everything, you know that I have a soul tie with you," [but] Jesus [still speaking to Abel/Christ in Peter], says to [Peter, "Let Abel/Christ in you] nourish [Cain and Abel], the [mortal] personalities of [my disciples],"

21.19a And [then Jesus] explained to [Peter] how his death would glorify God[R] saying,

[R] Jn 12:32-33

21.18 "It is surely true that when you are [spiritually] immature, you are able to choose whatever lifestyle pleases you, [because Cain within you] is yoked to [Leviathan], but when you mature, [Christ Jesus, your] other [mind], will be yoked to [the glorified Elijah/Christ], and expand [into the place between the eyebrows],

"And you will be satisfied to a degree that you have never experienced before, and [the glorified Elijah/Christ] will uphold [Christ Jesus within you in the place between the eyebrows], and keep him from falling out of it,"[104]

21.19b And after [Jesus] said [all] this, he taught [Peter] how he would be joined to [Christ Jesus],

---

[104] See, **Anchor of Our Soul** (Online Meeting 06 14 00), or Alternate Translation of Heb 6:18-19. (Read entire footnote in Appendices)

Alternate Translation Of The New Testament/ John

21.20a Then Peter returned to his carnal mind, and saw [John], the disciple [whose spirit] was standing because he was joined to [Adam within Jesus], and [whose personality] was saved, [because his carnal mind] was behind [Jesus' Christ mind],^R

^R 2 Ki 2:24a (AT)

21.21a [And] Peter, turning his attention to [John], says to Jesus, "Lord,

21.20b "What about [John], who [already] has your power?

21.21b "Is not [John], the one who is [joined to] Elohim, Lord?"[105] [Why are you giving me this assignment?][106]

21.22 [Then] Jesus says to [Peter], "If you submit to Elohim within John until I appear, you will be joined to me [also],"

21.23 [And] then the doctrine went forth among the disciples, that that disciple, [Peter], would not die, but Jesus never said that [Peter] would not die, He said, "If you, [Peter], submit to Elohim in John until I appear,^R you will be joined to me,"

^R Jn 21:7 (AT)

21.24 [So, Peter] is the disciple who[se carnal mind] was martyred so that [his spirit] could be engraved with [Christ Jesus'] nature, and we can perceive that his [carnal mind] is truly dead;

21.25 Moreover, Jesus [also] shot forth in many others who, if every one of them were engraved with [Christ Jesus']

---

[105] The word, **what**, suggesting, **what is this**? is a Hebraism for Elohim.

[106] Peter is still in unbelief, even after Jesus instructs him in detail, concerning the spiritual ascension he is about to experience (Jn 21:18-19). (Read entire footnote in Appendices)

single [nature],[107] the books[R] truly engraved in [Christ Jesus' nature], would produce a world that Leviathan's imagination[108] could not enter into,

[R] 2 Cor 3:3

21.01a   Now, this is how Jesus, [after his death and resurrection], revealed [to] his disciples,

21.02   Simon Peter, and Thomas, called Didymus, and Nathanael of Cana in Galilee, and the sons of Zebedee, and two other of [Jesus'] disciples, [who] were gathered together [with Christ Jesus in their heart],

21.01b   That [the glorified Jesus Christ] was the unconscious part of their renewed mind, and [the glorified Jesus Christ] made it clear [to the disciples] that [the glorified Jesus Christ had authority over Leviathan, [and] authority over [Jordan, Satan's] river [of death],[109]

21.03   [Because] Peter had said to the [other disciples], "I am going fishing [for Leviathan, so] that I can seize and imprison the fiery serpent, [Christ Jesus'] dark shadow;" and the [other disciples] had said, "We will go with you, and they had departed from [their carnal mind], and entered into [Christ Jesus], their righteous mind,

21.04a   [When the glorified] Jesus, firmly established on [the dry side of] the seashore, appeared to the disciples as rays of [spiritual] light,

---

[107] The word, **single**, signifies the one mind formed when Christ Jesus subjects, and binds, the carnal mind underneath himself (Ps 118:27). (Read entire footnote in Appendices)

[108] The word, **imagination**, signifies Leviathan's concept of what the creation should be, (Read entire footnote in Appendices)

[109] **Tiberias** means **the god of the river**; **the sea** typifies **Satan**.

Alternate Translation Of The New Testament/ John

21.05   And [the glorified] Jesus -- [calling] them "children" [because Christ, the manchild[R] was formed in them] -- said, "Have you laid hold of Leviathan[110] and cooked her [yet]?"[111] And [when] they responded, "no,"

[R] 1 Tim 2:15

21.06a   [Jesus] seized Leviathan, [who] was joined to the fiery serpent [within the disciples,

21.10a   And [the glorified] Jesus said to Christ Jesus within [the disciples], "You [are standing because] I have imprisoned Leviathan,

21.06b   "[And empowered [you] to separate from Leviathan's timeline,

21.10b   "[So], now, flee from [Leviathan," and, after that, Jesus] said, "insert Christ Jesus, [your] righteous part, into [Abel, who is bound to Cain, your mortal] foundation, to keep yourself from falling [again],"

21.07a   "And [John], the disciple who had a spirit tie with Jesus, said to Peter, 'it is the Lord,'" [and when Simon Peter understood that the Lord had bound Leviathan, his upper garment,

21.11a   Simon Peter obeyed [John],

21.07b   And John] poured himself out into [Satan's] sea, [the astral plane within Peter],

---

[110] Jesus knew that it was not possible for the disciples to seize Leviathan (Matt 12:29, Mk 3:27) without the help of his glorified Spirit, but tested them, to see if they would confess their inability to change their own mortal nature. (Read entire footnote in Appendices)

[111] ***To cook Leviathan***, is a legitimate translation of Strong's #4371, translated, ***meat***, by the King James translators, but meaning, specifically, ***boiled*** fish. (Read entire footnote in Appendices)

Alternate Translation Of The New Testament/ John

21.11b   And the exceedingly powerful, infinite [etheric molecules of] Christ Jesus [within John] vibrated towards the fiery serpent of the earth [within Peter], and separated the fiery serpent [within Peter] from Leviathan's fifty [atom] and three [atom, etheric molecules], and [Christ Jesus within Peter] ascended into [the place between the eyebrows where Christ Jesus] satisfies the emotional [animal (personality)], and

21.09   As [Peter] left the [dry] land [of] his heart, and entered into [the place between the eyebrows], he perceived that [Satan within him] was dried out, that [the fiery serpent] who had been overlaying the Christ child [within him] was buried [under Christ Jesus within John], that [his personality] was preserved, and that [he, Peter] had become bread,

21.08   But [the glorified Jesus], the everlasting arms, did not show himself to Christ in the other disciples, who were [still] far away from [the left side of the heart], the [dry] land [where] the Fortified Christ Jesus restrains Satan, separates [the fiery serpent, their mortal] foundation [from] Leviathan, and satisfies [Cain, their animal nature],

21.12   [But] Jesus [speaking through John] said to [the other disciples], "Break your fast [from the material things of this world], and enter [into the high places of Jesus' glorified Spirit]," but the disciples did not recognize that it was the Lord [speaking through John], so they dared to ask [John], "And who do you think you are?"

21.13a   Then Jesus revealed [to the disciples] that he had, indeed,

21.14a   Risen from the dead,

21.13b   Taken [John] as his own, and delivered Peter from Satan,

Alternate Translation Of The New Testament/ John

21.14b   And this is how [the glorified] Jesus exposed Satan [within] the disciples [to themselves].[112]

---

[112] Satan had blinded the disciples, who spoke to John out of Leviathan, saying, **and who do you think you are?**

THE BOOK OF ACTS

Chapter 1

[1219.3.C]
11   This Jesus that went away from you, ascended through understanding; And

Elohim shall come to you [also], to turn [your life] upside down [through] understanding [what] you see in the unconscious part of the mind.

[700.1.C]
1.18   Now this [First] Adam purchased the unholy calf [mind of Judas in] the field [of creation], the reward of [the First Adam's] iniquity, but [Jesus], the head [of the First Adam], poured forth into the midst of[Judas'] heart, and burst asunder [Judas' soul tie with the First Adam], and [the Loving Kindness of the Second Adam, the Lord from heaven], appeared.

Chapter 3

[Message # Unknown]
3.21   Who must educate and carry you until the whole time line is restored, which the Father has spoken about through the mouth of his holy prophets since this [divided] age began.

Chapter 4

[392.3]
4.25   And our Father, Elijah (see, *Note #49*, ¶¶ *5 & 6*), said by the Holy Spirit through the mouth of your servant, David, why does the non-Jew behave arrogantly towards us, making themselves more important than we are, and why do the Jews concern themselves with unspiritual matters,

4.26   [Since] Elohim's Sons, the kings of the Earth (see, *Note #49*, ¶¶ *5 & 6*), have appeared, and are assembling [in the place between the eyebrows] so that Christ [Jesus] can superimpose himself upon Leviathan, [the one who] controls mortal man,

4.27   And [the glorified Jesus] has gathered together both Herod and Pontius Pilate, as well as the non-Jews and the people of Israel, for the purpose of distributing to the whole city, the truth concerning your Holy Child, Jesus, whom you gave what he needed [to ascend out of hell],

4.29   So that, henceforth, [Christ Jesus, mortal man's new] controller^R should distribute [Christ] towards [Abel within mortal humanity, who Cain] menaces (see, *Note #99*), and bestow confidence upon your own servants, so that each individual [servant] might teach the Doctrine [of Christ] fearlessly,

^{R} Matt 4:7 (AT)
Lk 2:9 (AT)

4.30   And [that] the [glorified Jesus and Christ in the individual] (see, *Note #49*), should extend their hand to heal [through your servants], both [by] prophesying [to them] that history will record the public appearance of [Elohim's Sons], who [will have received] the same nature that your holy child, Jesus, [received], and by marking [the people with the nature of Christ],

Alternate Translation Of The New Testament/ Acts

4.28 And [by] doing whatever is necessary to accomplish your pre-determined purpose [to raise all of mortal humanity out of hell].

[838.1.C]
4.32 And the number of those who believed with their heart [rather than their intellect] were of one soul. Not one of them possessed an individual soul, but they all had the common [salvation],

4.33 And there was none among those whose bodies had been sold into slavery and whose houses were possessed [by pagan deities], who brought [the seed of God, the pearl of great] price which was a part of themselves, to the apostles], that lacked the common salvation,

4.35 And the apostles distributed [spiritual wisdom and knowledge] among those who laid down their Carnal Mind, according to the desire [of each man's heart] and his capacity [to receive and possess it],

4.36 And Joses, who the apostles named the son of the one who consoles us,

4.37 Whose body had been sold into slavery, brought [the seed of God, the pearl of great] price which was a part of himself, to the apostles, and submitted himself [to them],

Chapter 5

[838.1.C]
5.01 But Ananais, a certain man [whose body] was sold into slavery [was humbled before JAH], but was [nevertheless] the wife of Sapphira, [the female deity, and carried] her name [in his mind, and]

5.02   Kept [the Malchus, the pearl of great] price, [the part of] his Carnal Mind [that was spiritually] awakened, [for Sapphira at the same time that] he submitted himself to the [ministry of] the apostles,

5.03   But Peter said to Ananais, it is Satan who [possesses your] house, [not] the Holy Ghost, [and] she is holding back [the seed of God, the pearl of great] price, [the part of your Carnal Mind that is spiritually awakened, by filling your heart with doctrinal] lies;

5.04   Do you not understand that you have not lied to Adam, [the fully mature apostle], but you have lied to God?

5.05   And after hearing these words [Satan] within Ananais fell down [under Peter's authority, and the spirit of Sapphira] breathed out (gave up the ghost) of Ananais, and [the pagan deities within those who] heard about what happened, were terrified, and

5.06   And Christ, the young man, arose, and wrapped himself together with [Abel, the Malchus within Annais], and carried him [into the world above, and] buried [Satan and Cain],

5.07   It was about three hours later, when [Sapphira], not knowing what was done [within Ananais, her wife], entered in [Ananais, and],

5.08   Peter answered [Sapphira, who was now expressing her consciousness through Ananais], tell me how long this body has been sold into slavery, and [Sapphira said] for a long [time],

5.09   Then Peter said [to Sapphira], how is it that you would test the spirit of the Lord? Look! [Adam, Ananais' true] husband, [is standing] at the door, [and] he shall bury [Ananais'] Carnal Mind that agreed with you, and carry you out;

5.10   Then, [Sapphira] breathed out of [Ananais] [and Christ], the young man [of the household of God], came into

[Ananais], and [when Christ] found that [Sapphira, Ananais'] husband, had carried [Cain, the mortal foundation of, Ananais'] Carnal Mind above [Abel, the seed of God within Ananais], the one that was sold, immediately [Cain] fell down, and was buried [under Abel, and] died.

[OLM – 02 23 99]

5.30   The fiery serpents within you, [the subconscious part of your carnal mind], laid violent [spiritual] hands upon [Adam], the Tree of Life [that the man, Jesus, was crucified to, to separate Jesus from the Tree of Life], but [Jehovah], the God of our fathers raised Jesus from the dead.

Chapter 7

[562]

7.54   And when [the members of the Council] heard these things, [they agreed with their carnal mind, and] they separated [themselves] from [Adam, the spiritual man in their] heart [who opposes their carnal mind, and Cain, the conscious part of their carnal mind] sunk his teeth into [Abel, the Christ within Stephen].[113]

7.55   Now Stephen was completed by the Holy Ghost, so he entered into a trance when they began to stone him and Stephen saw Christ Jesus God's thought form within himself, and he also Jesus the column of the heavenly constellation standing before the throne of God.

---

[113]   As explained in our message entitled "**The Secret of Cain and Abel**," the Zohar, a Jewish Commentary on the Scripture, teaches that Cain's attack upon Abel began with Cain biting Abel's neck. So we see that Cain within the Jews that Stephen was preaching to, gnashed his teeth into the neck of Abel within Stephen. (Read entire footnote in Appendices)

Alternate Translation Of The New Testament/ Acts

7.56   And Stephen said, **Look, I see that Christ Jesus within me, the door to immortality[114] is open, because Jesus the son of Adam the right column of the heavenly constellation is standing before the throne of God.**

7.57   But then the exceedingly loud screeching voice of the Serpent, Satan, and Leviathan sounded and arrested the understanding of the Jews, and unanimously spurred on the witnesses to the assistance of God, to cast off the spiritual clothing of Christ, the young man within them.

7.58   Their city and the carnal mind acquired them and engraved them with the murderous nature of King Saul.

7.59   And Stephen cried out for help as they began to stone him saying, **Lord Jesus, take my spirit**.

7.60   And then Stephen prostrated his carnal mind and Christ Jesus within Stephen petitioned the Lord loudly saying, do not impute this sin to them, and then Stephen fell asleep.

Chapter 8

[562]
8.01   And then the company of the other pious believers in Christ carried Stephen away, mourning greatly, and the nature of Saul within the Jews was gratified when Stephen died.

8.02   So there was at that time a great persecution against the church which was in spiritual Jerusalem since all the Jews who abode in the spiritual regions of, or since all the Jews who

---

[114] The members of the Council were enraged because Stephen was telling them that he would be raised from the dead.

abode in Judea, the regions of Judea and Samaria were separated from Christ, except the apostles.

8.03   Wherefore those who were scattered abroad went everywhere where the apostles were preaching the word, And

8.04   This is how the nature of King Saul within the Jews who were called by God, entered in to the whole household of God, and dragged both Cain and Abel the male and the female alike into the spiritual prison of their carnal mind.

Chapter 9

[OLM - 06 02 99]
9.12   Enter into my timeline, which is identified by a repeating linear pattern of spiritual atoms to make contact with Saul's mind; Communicate with him to tell him that you are the one who will lay hands on him to restore his spiritual sight; and your spiritual communication will appear to him as a vision.

Chapter 13

[Message # Unknown]
13.11   And, now, behold, the mind control of the Lord Jesus is upon you, blinding the sight you have received from Satan, the spiritual sun of this present timeline, and immediately a spiritual cataract descended upon [the fiery serpent, the subconscious part of] Elymas' [carnal mind, and Elymas' spiritual sight] was darkened, and Elymas sought after [the fiery serpent, the conductor of Satan's spiritual sight], but Paul's Christ mind was surrounding [the fiery serpent within Elymas].

Chapter 17

[16.1]
17.26   He has decreed or specified that all the earthen nations that descended from [fallen] Adam, who were twisted together with Him before the earth was founded [but] are [now] lying in a passive and horizontal position for a pre-determined period of time, [will be] assigned a position in the age that will never end, at the fit and proper time.

17.27   That they should search for the hidden things of God, so that, perhaps, they might verify His reality by perceiving or finding Him, contacting and meeting with Him, and touching Him, which can only be accomplished by sharing His experience of being handled, rubbed and worn smooth, and receiving a verdict of acquittal and admittance to the Kingdom of God.

[814.1.C]
17.28   And, as certain of your own poets have said, since we exist as [a part of Ancient Adam], his life and thought process [are a part of us, which], indeed, [means that] we are his relatives.

Chapter 26

[Message # Unknown]
26.11   And I was very furious at them, and vilified them frequently for the sake of my own honor, and violently pursued them to prosecute them in all of the synagogues, even those in the outlying cities,

26.14   And when we all fell down into [our] carnal mind, I heard a voice speaking to me and saying in the Hebrew tongue, Saul, Saul, I [AM], Jehovah['s Justice], is pursuing you, [because there are] severe [consequences for] despising [the people] that I have pierced,

26.15   And I said, Who are you, Lord? And He said, I AM Jesus, the self-Existent One, [who pursues you]

26.16a   For the opposite reason [that I AM, Jehovah's Justice, pursues you.

26.16c   I want] to make you both a minister and a witness to the things that you have seen, and the things that I will show you;

26.16b   Wherefore, I have appeared to you [so that] the Mind [of Christ] should arise in you, and stand above your carnal mind.

Chapter 28

[OLM – 02 23 99]
28.02a   [And when Paul] saw [that] Satan was the master of the fiery serpents [within the Melitians, and that Satan] was engaging in spiritual sexual intercourse [with the fiery serpents within the Melitians, Paul] had compassion on [the Melitians], and Christ Jesus who was present within [Paul], covered the fiery serpents [who were joined to Leviathan], Satan's kingdom [within the Melitians],

28.03a   And Paul gathered the fiery serpents of the Melitian population [together with] Christ Jesus, [the subconscious part of Paul's Christ mind, and Christ Jesus within Paul] laid on top of the fiery serpents [within the Melitians],

28.03b   And great heat was generated [when Christ Jesus within Paul] touched the fiery serpents], those poisonous beasts [within the Melitians, and the fiery serpents] separated [from Leviathan within the Melitians], and Christ Jesus [within Paul], seized [the separated fiery serpents], the subconscious part [of the Melitians' carnal] mind,

28.04   [And when] Satan saw that the fiery serpents [within the Melitians] were separated from Leviathan, [the mortal foundation of Satan's] dark kingdom, and seized by Christ Jesus], the subconscious part of [Paul's Christ] mind, Satan whispered [her thoughts] towards [the Cain side of] the fiery serpents, [the spiritual wives of Leviathan, within the Melitians (see, *Note #90*, ¶ *2*)], saying, *this [spiritual] man, [Christ Jesus], is a murderer [who] has escaped [from the authority of Satan, the spiritual] sea, and [has set himself up as] the judge*[R] *who decides whether or not you will live, or be left alone,*

[R] Jn 5:26-27

28.05   [But the Abel side of] the fiery serpents [within the Melitians, Cain's true] spiritual husband, shook off [Cain, who was covering Abel], despite Satan's thoughts, and Christ Jesus [within Paul, the Lake of] Fire, [fell] upon [the fiery serpents within the Melitians, and the Spirit of Christ within Paul] drove the injurious Satan down under the authority [of Christ Jesus within Paul],

28.02a   And [Christ Jesus within Paul] took all of [the fiery serpents within the Melitians] as spiritual wives.

Alternate Translation Of The New Testament/ Romans

THE BOOK OF ROMANS

Chapter 1

[959.1.C]

Paul's Credentials

1.01   I, Paul, separated [from the world], called to be a servant of Christ Jesus, and an apostle of the gospel of God,

1.02   That [God] promised by [the Word of] his holy prophets, [which were written] in the Scripture,

Jesus Christ, The Son of God

1.03   Concerning his Son [Jesus Christ, our Lord], who was made from the seed of David, according to the flesh, and

1.04   Identified as the Son of God by the miracle working power [that] Jesus Christ our Lord, received from] the Spirit of Holiness, which raised him from the dead,

1.05   By whom we have received the office of the apostle, through obedience to [the Shekinah, the Spirit of] Grace, and [Christ Jesus], the moral conviction [that the Shekinah distributed] among all nations, for his Name's sake, and

Greetings

1.06   To you, who are in [Christ Jesus], who are also called of Jesus Christ, and

1.07   To all who are called to be saints and beloved of God: Peace to you from [the Spirit of] Grace and God, the Father of the Lord Jesus Christ.

1.08   First [of all], I thank my God through Jesus Christ for all of you, because your moral conviction is spoken about throughout the whole world,

1.09   Because God, who I serve with my spirit in the gospel of his Son, is my witness that, without ceasing, I always make mention of you in my prayers,

Impartation

1.10   Requesting that, sometime, even now, if it be the will of God, that I come to you by any means [possible],

1.11   Because I long to see you, that I may impart some spiritual gift to you, to establish [the moral conviction of Christ Jesus in your heart],

1.12   Indeed, that we may be comforted together through the mutual moral conviction [that we receive from Christ Jesus];

1.13   Indeed, I would not have you ignorant, brethren, that I frequently intended to come to you, that, [as I have brought forth fruit] among other Gentiles, I might have some fruit among you also,

1.14   [Since I am paying off] the debt [that I owe to God because of my sins, by ministering] to both Greeks [who are civilized] and foreigners [who are not civilized], to both the wise and the unwise,

1.15   So, I am ready to preach as much of the gospel as is in me, to you also who are at Rome,

The Opportunity To Be Saved

1.16   Because I am not ashamed of the gospel, which is the miracle-working power of God, to save everyone that trusts [the Lord Jesus Christ]: To the Jew first and also to the Greek,

1.17   Because the righteousness of God within [the individual] is revealed from moral conviction to moral conviction; As it is written, [whoever] lives by [the moral conviction of Christ Jesus, shall be declared] to be innocent [of violating the Law of Sin and death],

The Reason For Judgment

1.18   Because the anger of God is revealed from heaven against all the irreverence towards God, and the immorality of the First Adam, who unjustly holds back the truth [from humanity],

1.19   Because it is well-known that God is shining in them, and has made himself known to them,

1.20   Because the invisible things from the original formation of the cosmos can be comprehended and clearly seen by the things that are made, both the divinity, the eternal power, and the Shekinah, so [their denial of God] is indefensible,

1.21   Because when they knew God, they did not honor his opinion, neither were they grateful, so their [understanding] heart was darkened, and they became [spiritually] unintelligent and foolish in their discussions;

1.22   Claiming to be wise, they became simpletons, and

1.23   Changed the opinion of the God who cannot decay, to resemble the image of [the First] Adam, [who] decays, and to birds and four-footed beasts and reptiles,

The God of This World

1.24   Wherefore they gave themselves over to the god [of this world], who knew [them intimately, and put] forbidden desires in their heart, and infamous and immoral longings for the physical body [in their mind],

1.25   Who changed the truth of God into a lie and [caused them] to worship and minister to the original formation [of the creation], rather than the Creator, who is blessed forever, so be it, and

Why Women Suffer Emotionally

1.26   Exchanged the natural [maternal] instincts of their women for [the desire for] physical employment [outside of the home, which] gave them over to the indignity of continuous emotional suffering; and because the god [of this world],

Male Homosexuality

1.27   In the same manner, also dismissed the instinctual use of the men for the women, [who, instead], burned with lust towards one another, men with men, [doing] that which is shameful and indecent, [which], necessarily, produces the false opinion* [of the First Adam which makes death their] reward, and

> * Any opinion that does not rise to the moral standard of God.

A Simple (Unintelligent) Mind

1.28   Inasmuch as they did not investigate God [enough] to recognize [the righteousness of his commandments, laws and statutes], God turned them over to a mind that could not recognize [the destructive effect of] those [forbidden] things, [and they deemed the immoral desires of their physical body and their heart, to be] proper, and

An Evil Nature

1.29   [So], they are being filled up with an evil nature [that] violates [God's restrictions upon their physical body through] sexual sin, and [upon their] mind [through] greed and evil thoughts, [and

The Fruit of the Bestial Nature

They became] filled up with unhappiness [because of the good fortune of others], slander, strife [resulting from prideful] debates, schemes to defraud, evil thoughts that impute evil motives to others, pronouncements of evil,

1.30   Secret accusations, blame towards God, persecutions of others who mistreat them, excessive promotions of themselves that show themselves [to be] above their fellows, inventions of things that do harm, and unwillingness to be persuaded by their parents' [instruction]; and

The Behavior of the Bestial Nature

1.31   These [spiritually] unintelligent [formations of the First Adam] break the Covenant of Peace that [Jehovah made with Phinehas],[R] and refuse to lay aside their enmity and listen to terms of reconciliation, [because] they are merciless [to everyone], and hard-hearted towards their family, [in particular]; and

[R] Num 25:12

The Death Penalty

1.32   The judgment of God knows for a fact that those who do these things habitually deserve death, [because] they are not merely [isolated acts that emanate randomly from] the unconscious part of their mind; On the contrary, they do them because the practice gratifies hem.

Chapter 2

[960.2.C]

Unholy Judgment

2.01　Therefore, it is inexcusable for any [personality of the First] Adam to find [another personality of the First Adam] guilty, because when you find another [personality of] the First Adam guilty, you are comparing [that person] to yourself, [when] you do [the same things] in the unconscious [part of your mind], and

God's Judicial Decisions

2.02　Indeed, we are aware that God's judicial decisions, [which are rendered] according to the Truth, are against the type of individual who [judges others by comparing them to himself];

2.03　[So], do you, indeed, think that you will escape the judicial decisions of God [concerning] the things that you find [the other personalities of the First] Adam guilty of, that you habitually do, yourself, in the unconscious [part of your mind]?

2.04　Or that [you will escape the judicial decisions of God because of] the wealth of moral excellence [in] the unconscious [part of your mind, or because of] the patience and tolerance [that you have for] the ignorant [personalities of the First Adam that] you despise, [who become] profitable to God [after] he leads them to repentance?

The Day of Judgment

2.05　Indeed, in the day that God's passion [for his wife] is disclosed, [Satan, the enforcer of] Jehovah's Righteous Sowing & Reaping Judgment, [will execute] the appropriate sentence [upon the Jews* who willfully disobey the Law of the Spirit of Life,^R for the sins that] they accumulate [because of] their stubbornness and unrepentant heart, and

^R Rom 8:2

> *Paul is speaking to **all Jews**, i.e., the Israel of God, which includes Jews of lineal descent and Christians (Gal 6:16).*

2.06   The Shekinah will render [a righteous recompense] to every [Jew who obeys the Law of the Spirit of Life], according to the things they have done

2.07   To cheerfully endure [hardship, have] a consistently good opinion [of God], respect [the other personalities of the First Adam], and seek incorruptibility for the life of the ages;

The Reason For Judgment

2.08   But [those Jews who] provoke [God] to anger by refusing to believe the Truth that *anger is a wrongful, immoral passion of the mind*, shall, indeed be convinced

Tribulation

2.09   [When] Adam [from] above* pressures the souls of all of the Jews, as well as the Greeks, who commit the depraved and injurious acts of the First [Adam into] the narrow [place that leads to eternal life];

* The Second Adam

The Day of Peace

2.10   Indeed, [in that day], everyone will respect [the other personalities of] the First [Adam, seek] peace [with God], and do good to the Jew, as well as to the Greek,

2.11   Because there is no favoritism with God;

Alternate Translation Of The New Testament/ Romans

Immortality

2.12   [So], since many [Jews] do not attain immortality because they refuse to subject themselves to the Law [of the Spirit of Life, the crumbs of spiritual Truth intended for those] lawless [Jews] are parceled out [to the non-Israelite races, who are] fully destroyed [when they consume them],

2.13   (Because, listening [to the verbal expression of] the crumbs of God's spiritual food, does not [make your character] equal to God['s character], but [only those who understand, believe and] act out [the words that carry the crumbs of spiritual food], shall be rendered innocent,

2.14   Because, *when [the non-Israelite] races [which do] not have the crumbs of God's spiritual food [have] the [spiritual] plant that produces the crumbs of [God's] spiritual food, [and] perform [the actions of God's character, even though] they, themselves, do not have those crumbs of God's spiritual food, [the people of those other non-Israelite races, who have the spiritual plant that produces] the crumbs of God's spiritual food [and do the acts of the character of God],*

2.15   *Which acts [of God's character] indicate that the crumbs of God's spiritual food have engraved their heart and the unconscious [part of their mind with the moral consciousness of God];*

Righteous Judgment

[Then, when these conditions are met], both the unconscious and the subconscious [parts of their Christ mind] shall jointly testify [to the Truth, which is, then], duplicated in their [conscious] thoughts), either charging [the personalities of the First Adam] with an offence, or declaring their innocence,[R]

[R] Jn 7:24

2.16   In the day that God distinguishes [between] the hidden [thoughts of the First] Adam [and the thoughts of] Christ

Alternate Translation Of The New Testament/ Romans

Jesus, [the Second Adam, who thinks] My [thoughts],* according to the good news [of the Gospel of God].

* Paul is speaking prophetically, i.e., God is speaking through him in the first person.

2.17   Look! Indeed, you are secure [because you know that the Jews] are called [to serve God], and you boast [about your knowledge of] the Law, and that

2.18   You know [what God has] determined [to do in the future], and you approve of tossing about [the Word of God] to indoctrinate [others] out of the Law, and

2.19   You are confident that you are a guide to the blind, a light to those who exist in the shadows, and

2.20   A teacher of the mindless, [and] an instructor of infants,

[But] you have [only] *the appearance* of [possessing] the knowledge and truth [that is found] in the Law,

2.24   Because the Name of God is vilified among the non-Israelite nations, as it is written,

2.23   You boast about [your knowledge of] the Law, but you dishonor God by breaking the Law,

2.21   You teach another, but you do not teach yourself,

Therefore you preach against stealing, but you steal;

2.22   You say that adultery is wrong, but you commit adultery.;

You are disgusted by idolatry, but you receive worship that belongs to God,

The Spiritual Reason For Circumcision

2.25   Because [physical] circumcision [is] truly beneficial for [those who study] and accumulate [a knowledge of] the crumbs of spiritual food which were parceled out [to Israel], but [if those] who inherited the opportunity to study the crumbs of spiritual food which were parceled out [to Israel] violate [the spiritual principles revealed through those] crumbs of spiritual food, [they might as well] be uncircumcised.

2.26   Therefore, if [the character of] those who do not have the potential to understand the Word of God [through lineal descent] can be made equal to the moral character of God [by consuming] crumbs of the spiritual food which were parceled out [to Israel, but] accumulated in the unconscious [part of their mind],
      Should not those who do not have the potential to understand the Word of God [through lineal descent] be counted [among those] who have the potential to understand the Word of God [through lineal descent]?

2.27   [And], should we not distinguish between those who inherited the ability to be satisfied by spiritual academic study of the crumbs of the spiritual food which were parceled out [to Israel] through lineal dissent, and

      Those [who inherited the privilege of] being satisfied by spiritual academic studies [through lineal descent, but] violate [the spiritual principles which are taught through the study of] the crumbs of spiritual food which were parceled out [to Israel]?

2.28   Because a Jew cannot be identified by appearance, behavior, or physical circumcision,

2.29   A Jew is identified by what is on the inside, that is, a heart that the hard shell of pride has been cut away from,[R] not acquired academic learning and praises to God that come from the [First] Adam.

^R Deut 10:16,
Deut 30:6,
Jer 4:4

Chapter 3

[961]

How Is The Jew Superior?

3.01   What, then, [is] the benefit off the inherited opportunity to study spiritual academic subjects and understand them? Or how, [then, is] the Jew superior [to the Greek-speaking Jew?

3.02   The Jew benefits] a great deal, indeed, [from inheriting the opportunity to study spiritual academic subjects and understand them], because every [Jew who studies the spiritual dimension of] the Word of God and [understands it], trusts [the moral conviction of God within himself, and] turns away from [the lifestyle] of the First [Adam], and

Unbelief

3.03   The moral conviction of God [within them] is not rendered idle because Satan, the unconscious [part of the carnal mind of the First Adam], does not believe Elohim;

Identifying The Counterfeit

3.04   [So], never let [the moral conviction of] God be concealed [in you], but, rather, [in order for] the true Adam to be revealed, let Elohim engrave the whole [Second Adam] with the Word of God, so that they might distinguish between [the two

Adams], subdue the counterfeit [First Adam], and be found innocent when they are tested;

God's Judgment Is Righteous

3.05   If, indeed, the character of the sons of God, [when] compared to God['s character], is not equal [to God's character, as demonstrated by] the wrongful acts [that they do, is] God unjust [when] he brings his anger down upon Adam, [who is] as the Word of God [in this world]?

3.06   If it were not [so], how would [the sons of] God distinguish [between] the thoughts of [the First and Second Adam]?

3.07   Because, if I recognize that the truth of God's opinion is greater than the fabricated [opinion of Satan], the unconscious [part of] my [carnal mind, is it] immoral for the Supernal Mother [to discipline me]?

3.08   [Or], is it slanderous for us ([when] we speak [with the authority of God]), to make known some of the thoughts of Satan, [the unconscious part of your carnal mind], which are worthless, so that [you can recognize your] good [thoughts, make] a decision that is equal to God's opinion, and condemn the First [Adam, which is] what we do?

The Jew Is Not Superior

3.09   [But, you say], the sons of God [must] certainly be superior to the Greek-speaking Jews. No, not at all. We have already brought charges against Jews [and Greek-speaking Jews, alike, because they ae all] under [the authority of the First Adam, whose thoughts are not morally equal to God's thoughts];

God's Moral Excellence

3.10   As it is written, There is no [god] that is equal to [Jehovah], the one [true God];

3.11   There are none who crave God [enough] to comprehend that God['s thoughts come from a different spirit than the good thoughts of the First Adam];

3.12   They all shun [the thoughts of God, which] render the same useless; None will [rise to the standard of God's] moral excellence, not until they are one [with him];

An Immoral Mind

3.13   Fiery serpents go forth from Satan, the unconscious [part of the carnal mind], and the deceitful lips of [Leviathan], the subconscious [part of] the carnal mind, are under [the authority of Satan], the unconscious [part of the carnal mind],

3.14   Who fills their mouth [with] prayers [that go forth from] bitterness, and

3.15   [Leviathan], the subconscious [part of] their carnal mind, moves rapidly to shed blood;

3.16   They are miserable and their life is a complete ruin, because they follow the path of [Satan], the unconscious [part of their carnal mind], and

3.17   They have not experienced the path [of the innocent, which leads] to peace;

3.18   [Leviathan], the subconscious [part of their carnal mind], is not afraid to [jealously] eye [the Second Adam, who] stands in front of God;

The 1st Adam Identifies Satan

3.19   So, we perceive that, as long as the crumbs of spiritual food are laid out [clearly enough to be understood, and] if [those who hear] those crumbs of spiritual food that were laid out [repeat them accurately], that the world generated by the mouth of [the First Adam] will be condemned by [Second

Adam], and God will lock the whole [First Adam] up under [the authority of the Second Adam];

3.20 Therefore, no personality of the flesh [of the First Adam] can be made innocent by the act of parceling out crumbs of spiritual food, because parceling out crumbs of spiritual food [only enables us] to recognize [Satan], the unconscious [part of the carnal mind, who] cannot rise to a moral standard equal to the character of God;

The 2nd Adam Sees The Morality Of God

3.21a Now, apart from [acquiring a character that] is equal to the moral standard of God [in order to accurately understand] the crumbs of spiritual food which were parceled out to [Israel, those] crumbs of spiritual food must be [seen through the eyes of Christ Jesus, the Second Adam], the moral conviction [of God within you],

3.22a [Whose] character is equal to the moral character of God, and

3.21b Testified to by the prophets;

The Moral Conviction Of God Given

3.22b Indeed, God, by [the man, Christ Jesus, the Second Adam, has given] the moral conviction of [the character of] Jesus Christ, [which is equal to the character of God], to the whole [First Adam],

[By] superimposing [himself] upon [the parts of the First Adam who] trust [him],

NOT BECAUSE they [were able to correctly] distinguish [between the opinion of the First Adam and the opinion of God],

3.23 [BUT], BECAUSE all [of the First Adam's parts] fell short of [recognizing God's] opinion, [demonstrating, therefore, that the character of the First Adam] does not rise to the moral level of the character of God;

3.24   [So, now, all of the First Adam's parts are] being made innocent without paying the price [for falling short of having God's opinion in] the unconscious part of their carnal mind,

[The price of which is the death of their personal soul,

Because] Jesus Christ, paid the ransom, in full, through [the Christ child, the concretization of the Shekinah, who is the Spirit of] Grace, the divine influence upon the heart,

Making Amends Necessary

3.25   Who God set forth

Because of the tolerance of [the Word of] God,

1) To indicate [that] the character of [Christ Jesus], the subconscious [part of the Mind of Christ, is] equal to the moral character of God, and
2) To make amends [for the First Adam's lack of moral character],

Through the moral conviction that is in the [spiritual] blood [of Jesus Christ, who is] the unconscious [part of the Mind of Christ],

Because [the First Adam] is responsible for [those opinions which are not equal to the moral character of God] which previously transpired,

The 1st Adam Made Innocent

3.26a   [So] that, at the proper time, the character [of the First Adam] will also be made innocent and equal to the moral character of God, through the moral conviction [of Christ] Jesus, [the subconscious [part of the Mind of Christ]];

Conclusion

3.28   We conclude, therefore,

That [the First] Adam is made innocent by the moral conviction [of Christ Jesus] without [inheriting the spiritual intellectual potential] to parcel out crumbs of spiritual food], and

3.27   That [the moral conviction Christ Jesus, the mind of] Elohim, certainly, excludes [the possibility of the Jews] boasting about parceling out crumbs of spiritual food [because of their inherited spiritual and intellectual ability, because now, through Christ Jesus, crumbs of spiritual food can be understood and made into healthy flesh] through the moral conviction [of Christ Jesus], rather than by [the inherited spiritual intellectual capacity to study and meditate, which is the reward of physical circumcision];

3.26b   [All of which] indicates that the character of [Christ Jesus] is equal to the character of God,

Jehovah, God Of All

3.29   [But], is [God] the God of the Jews alone? Is he not also [God of] the non-Israelite nations? Yes, he is also [God of] the non-Israelite nations;

3.30   Indeed, [there is] one God who shall make [the Jews who] have inherited the spiritual intellectual potential [to parcel out crumbs of spiritual food] innocent by moral conviction, and [he shall make] those who have not inherited the spiritual intellectual potential [to parcel out crumbs of spiritual food] innocent through moral conviction also;

Intellectual Study Still Valuable

3.31   [So], then, [you say], certainly, parceling out crumbs of spiritual food must no longer be necessary. Not at all!! On the contrary, the parceling out of crumbs of spiritual food through spiritual intellectual study can now be balanced with the moral conviction [of Christ Jesus, so that] the Word of God can always be studied and taught [accurately].

Chapter 5

[236.2]
5.01-02 Therefore, having been made righteous by the Lord Jesus Christ, and have received peace with God through [Christ, his seed, which] has been grafted to us and increased into Christ Jesus, our personal Saviour, [and] the Word of God, by which we stand, is in the midst of us; and we rejoice in the expectation of the [public] appearance of God in this world system, which is hell.

5.03-05 But we rejoice in our hardships, as well, understanding that trouble builds endurance, and that endurance shall be tried by experiences which proves whether we have responded with [Satan and] Leviathan, our carnal mind, or [with] the mind of Christ Jesus, because responding to these experiences out of the mind of Christ Jesus shall not dishonor us, but, rather, produce an expectation of good things from God, because the Holy Spirit, the gift of God, is poured out upon our carnal mind as an expression of God's love,

5.06   Since Adam died[R-1] when he failed to distinguish between good & evil, and righteousness, in the age of innocence which is now past, and we were cast down to this present evil age, and became ungodly.^{R-2}

> ^{R-1} 1 Cor 15:22
> ^{R-2} Job 38:7 (AT)
> Micah 2:8-9 (AT)

5.07   Therefore, the fall has made it very difficult^{R-1} for anyone to die to their carnal mind, [which is required if] Christ Jesus is to be fully born in us. Under these present circumstances, then, how is it possible to slay Satan and Leviathan, our carnal mind, and also to cross over into the life of Christ Jesus,^{R-1}

> ^{R-1} Pro 30:18-19 (AT)

5.08-09 Since we're sinners [who cannot overcome Satan and Leviathan, our carnal mind], because the death of Adam in the past age is still overshadowing us?

The love of God is uniting the members of the whole mortal man with himself through Christ Jesus,^{R-2} which is much more preferable than the present righteousness [that] we receive by the Holy Spirit, because [Christ Jesus] will save our personality from Satan, [the enforcer of] God's destructive [Sowing & Reaping Judgment, which presently abides upon the fallen creation,

> ^{R-2} Job 1:4 (AT)
> 1 Tim 2:5

5.10   So, if we are reconciled to God because of the death of the Lord Jesus Christ when we are [still] his enemies, the full birth of Christ Jesus, [the manchild], within us, which saves our personality, is much better than reconciliation, and

5.11   [Although] we rejoice in the Lord Jesus Christ, through whom we receive our atonement, we also [rejoice] in Christ Jesus, [his Son].

5.12-13 So, since sin and the misery which arises out of sin, entered into the world because of the other [First] Adam, physical death, heartache and sufferings penetrated all men until the Law [of Ordinances]^R was given, [which provided a way of escape for Israel].

^{R} Eph 2:15

But the penalties of sin are imposed [in Israel also], when Cain [in an Israelite] denies the Law [that provides a way of escape].

5.14   Wherefore, the misery and suffering of mortal man was meted out [by Satan, even to those men who did not willfully choose to sin like the first Adam did (who is the pattern of the one who is coming), but were overcome by their mortal nature until the Law was given by Moses.

5.15   But is not this also true of the free gift? That [even though] many died unreformed through the other [First] Adam's deviation from righteousness, God's loving kindness has given us Jesus Christ, the other [last] Adam, whose free gift, [the Holy Spirit], is overflowing the many members of mortal mankind,

5.16   But many [mortal men who have received the gift of the Holy Spirit continue to deviate from God's [spiritual] Law because of Cain,$^{R-1}$ who was convicted and sentenced to damnation,$^{R-2}$ but God is acquitting them from the damning judgment [he pronounced upon Cain], and restoring them to righteousness.

$^{R-1}$ 2 Thes 2:4
$^{R-2}$ Gen 3:14

5.17   Because, if one man's deviation from righteousness resulted in Satan's authority to mete out the violent death [of the Sowing & Reaping Judgment], which does not reform the sin nature, [surely] Christ Jesus, who possesses both the overflowing grace of the Spirit of the Holy One, and the [righteous] Mind of Christ, [must have] much more [authority than Satan, wherefore, he can] control [the sin nature] in those who lay hold of [himself to cancel out the sowing and reaping judgment].

5.18   So, then, all men were subjected to the wrath of God because of Adam's deviation from righteousness, but all men

Alternate Translation Of The New Testament/ Romans

were also granted freedom from guilt through the life of God, because of Jesus Christ's righteous act which resulted in their acquittal,

5.19   Because, through Adam's disobedience, the many members of humanity have inherited an exceedingly sinful nature, but because of Jesus Christ's submission [to the death of his humanity], the many members of mortal man shall be made guiltless.

5.20   Moreover, the Law of Moses was added so that deviation from God's righteousness might increase and be exposed, but God's mercy increased more than the deviation [from righteousness],

5.21   So, even though sin ruling over [Adam] produced misery, lack of reform and physical death, Jesus Christ, our Lord, God's goodness and mercy, shall rule [over Adam] for the life of the ages, through the [righteous] mind [of Christ], which is acceptable to God.

Chapter 6

[194.2]
6.17-18 You became the servants of sin when you obeyed the doctrine of the wounded[R] heart[115] [carnal mind], but thanks to God, you have been freed from [that] sin[ful heart] through obedience to Christ Jesus, and are now become the servants of righteousness.

[R] Gen 3:16 (AT)
Zeph 3.9 (AT)

---

[115] **Wounded** is a translation of the Greek word which is translated **form of**, in Rom 6:17. (Read entire footnote in Appendices)

174

Chapter 7

[113]
7.03   So, then, if she is married to another man while her husband, [the carnal mind, is still] alive, she shall be called an adulteress: but if her husband is dead [because of the righteousness of Christ Jesus], she is free from that law, so that she is no adulteress, though she be married to another man.

Chapter 8

[237.7]
8.01   Therefore, the wrath of God is no longer directed towards [the men that] Christ Jesus rules [over], who conduct their lives according to the internalized law of the Spirit of Christ, and not [according to] Jehovah['s law of sowing and reaping].

8.02   Indeed, Christ Jesus, the force that produces life [by] controlling [my sin nature], has set me free from [Satan and Leviathan], the controlling force that causes me to do the dishonorable misdeeds that bring the misery and suffering of this existence upon me,

8.3-4   And because God thrust his own Son into a fallen mortal man to do what the law could not do, to condemn [our] sin [nature] for our own good, [so] that we might be filled up with Christ Jesus, the one who pardons us from the wrath of God, and be controlled by the Spirit of Christ, instead of Satan,

8.05   And because [the carnal mind], the mind that is born [of fallen Adam], the flesh [mind of mortal man], is flesh, but [Christ], the mind that is born of the Spirit [of Christ Jesus], is Spirit,

*Alternate Translation Of The New Testament/ * Romans

8.06 And because [the carnal mind], the flesh mind that is born of [fallen Adam], kills mortal man, but the mind that is born of the Spirit [of Christ Jesus] gives [us] life and peace,

8.07 Therefore, [the carnal mind], the flesh mind that is born of [fallen Adam], hates God, because she is not, nor can she be, subject to God.

8.08 So then, [mortal] men with flesh minds [born of fallen Adam] cannot please God.

8.09 Nevertheless, if the Spirit of God truly lives in you, your mind is born of the Spirit [of Christ Jesus], and is not the flesh [of fallen Adam]. Therefore, anyone who does not have the Spirit of Christ is not Christ Jesus.

8.10 But [even] if Christ Jesus is truly in you, your personality is still dead because of the sins of [Cain, the conscious part of] your flesh mind, but Abel is alive because the Lord Jesus Christ has made him acceptable to God.

8.11 So, if the Spirit of Christ who raised the man, Jesus, from the dead, is living inside of you and influencing you for your good, that same Spirit (the Spirit of Christ, not the Holy Spirit) is raising Christ from the dead in you [also], and [the Spirit of Christ] shall make your personalities alive also, when the Spirit [of Christ] is internalized in you.

8.12 Therefore, brethren, we no longer owe our existence to the flesh mind that is born of [fallen Adam],

8.13 Because if the flesh mind that is born of [fallen Adam] gives you existence, your mortal personality will separate from your physical body before [your mortal personality] is reformed: But if Abel within a mortal man separates from [Cain's] sinful deeds, and joins himself to the Lord Jesus Christ, your mortal personality shall live,

Alternate Translation Of The New Testament/ Romans

8.14   Because mortal men [who exist by fallen Adam's authority since the fall], but are born [a second time], of the Spirit of God, are the sons of God.

8.15-16 Indeed, you have not received the spirit of Satan, who brings Abel into submission to Cain again; but you have received the engrafted Word by which we cry to Jehovah [who sent the Lord Jesus Christ] to avenge himself,^{R} which [cry] is the manifestation of the immature spirit of [mankind], personally acknowledging that Abel [woke up, and] is appearing as Christ.

^{R} Gen 4:10

8.17   So, if we are truly heirs of God and joint heirs of the Lord Jesus Christ, then we are sons entitled to inherit the kingdom, and share in God's good opinion of the Lord Jesus Christ, *if we truly experience [Christ Jesus'] painful penetration of our carnal mind*.

8.18-20 Nevertheless, because the Lord Jesus Christ has given us the hope that Christ Jesus will subject [Leviathan], the one who has subjected us,$^{R-1}$ I believe that the calamities of this present age are nothing in comparison to what we shall experience when the Spirit of God is revealed in us, and when the creature (our mortal personality) shall be delivered from being enslaved [by the lusts^{R-2} that] corrupt [mankind], into the glorious freedom of the children of God.

$^{R-1}$ Dan 8:13 (AT)
$^{R-2}$ 2 Pet 1:4

Therefore, we know that since neither the Father nor Adam, [the living soul], desired that the creation (mortal personality) should be subjected to Satan and Leviathan, the whole creature is groaning until this present time, with the labor pains that precede the birth of the sons that God is eagerly expecting.

[573.2.C]

8.19   For the building intensely anticipates and expects the appearance of the ancient of days,^R the head of Elohim's Sons,

^R-Dan 7:9, 13, 22

8.23   And, indeed, not only the whole creature, but we, also, have labored so that Christ Jesus could be formed in us, and are patiently waiting for Satan and Leviathan, our carnal mind, to be crucified to Christ Jesus, which [union] is our adoption as Sons.

8.24   So, then, [Christ], the engrafted Word is rescuing us from the death of this existence so that we should be adopted as sons, but since the immature Christ cannot be seen, why would anyone look for the mature Christ Jesus, or expect the good things which are associated with his life?

8.25   Because by understanding God's intentions and promises towards us, we can endure the hardships of our spiritual labor, and eagerly expect Christ Jesus to appear in us, *if we rely upon his strength*.

8.26   And, likewise, our present manner of prayer is ineffective when the judgment seat of Christ exposes the hidden sins of our heart, so the Spirit of Christ helps us to deal with our human weaknesses with moans and sighs which cannot be expressed in words.

8.28-29 And we know that Christ Jesus is being formed in the [other] men who have had a true union with the Father also, and that all of these are laboring together towards full spiritual manhood, because the Father determined that his external form should appear as the offspring of mortal man before Jesus the Christ was incarnated, and that [the man, Jesus], should be the first of many mortal human beings to be rescued from hell and born [a second time] into the kingdom of God.

8.30   Moreover, the Father is also inviting the human offspring of Jesus, the Christ, whose external form was also determined before they incarnated, to be rescued from hell and born [a second time] into the kingdom of God, by waging war against their own carnal minds; and He is restoring the mortal men who are waging that warfare to the correct moral order; and to those men who he is restoring to the correct moral order, he is also giving the Mind of Christ Jesus.

8.27   And we can recognize these sons of God because they are judging and forgiving men's sins, and praying that Christ Jesus be formed in them also.

8.31-32   Who, then, can command these eunuchs other than the living God, who alone, is our head, even the one who did not try to save his Son from death, but rather handed him over so that we could all be rescued from hell; and how is it possible, then, that this double portion of the love of God shall not also pardon the rest of humanity?

8.33   Who [is it that] will bring down a judgment against God's chosen ones [after] God has pronounced them innocent?

8.34   Who [is it that] condemns Christ Jesus who was dead, but more [than that], awoke from [the] sleep [of death], who, after that, became [Spirit of Christ, the revived Shekinah Glory], the feminine side of God, who intercedes for us?

8.35   And who shall be able to separate us from the love of Christ? Pressure or affliction, lack of satisfaction in our emotions, persecution, lack of support from other sons, the immaturity of the armor of light, or Satan and Leviathan, the carnal mind?

8.36   No, none of these, because it is written in the Psalms that the personalities of the sons are as sheep destined for slaughter [corrective judgment], since Satan and Leviathan, our carnal mind, is to be made extinct so that your Christ can appear in fallen Adam, O Jehovah.

8.37-39 Therefore, we are able to defeat all these troubles when Christ Jesus joins himself to Abel within us, to form our [new] personality [in the image of Christ], and I am confident that [when this union takes place], neither

>Reprobate mortal men, nor

>Misguided Christians, nor

>[Cain], the evil angel [in the individual], nor

>[Fallen Abel], that seductive spiritual harlot [in the individual], nor

>The counterfeit Holy Spirit, Satan's] power [to work] miracles [through Leviathan], the false prophet who opposes the appearance of Christ Jesus within us and threatens to use witchcraft to physically harm us, nor

>[Leviathan's collective] reprobate thought [which forms] the group mind [of mortal mankind],

>Shall possess miracle working power strong enough to separate us from the mature Christ Jesus, who owns us.

Chapter 9

[419]
9.11 So that [the child] being born [who] has not yet done any good or evil [deeds which] would either cast him down, or show that he prefers God, might stand [up in perfection], not because [of behavioral] works, but [because] he [is signaling God by] crying out loudly.

Alternate Translation Of The New Testament/ Romans

[1241.1.C]

9.28   [Jesus] shall put the final phase of [Jehovah's] covenant [with Jacob into effect]; He shall enable the earth[en personalities of the elect] to speak [Wisdom and Knowledge], intelligently, [so that His Word can be understood correctly].

Chapter 10

[954.4.C]

10.02a   I am a witness that Israel are zealous for God, and

10.01   It is truly the desire of my heart and my prayer to God, that they should be saved [from the second death],

10.02b   But they have not recognized

10.04   [That] Christ [is the ability of] everyone who trusts him to be fair and impartial, and

10.03   They are ignorant of God's [intention to impart Christ, his] fair and impartial character [to them; so] they have not submitted [themselves to God, but, rather], seek, in their own [strength], to make their character fair and impartial;

10.05   Moses, wrote down the law [for the First] Adam, [so whoever] lives [the lifestyle of the First Adam [will be tried] according to the fairness and impartiality [of the Law of Moses],

10.06   But the fairness and impartiality of the moral conviction [of Christ] is explained like this:[R]

[R] Deut 30:11

You do not have to say in your heart, "Abel shall ascend into heaven," (That is [to say, Ael], shall bind Christ to me permanently"),[R]

[R] Deut 30:12

Alternate Translation Of The New Testament/ Romans

10.07 Or, "Christ shall descend into the depths [of my soul], (that is [to say, he shall loose Abel] from [the sleep of] death);^R

R Deut 30:13

10.08 On the contrary, Elohim says, "The living Word *in the mouth [of the evangelist]* spreads into your heart, and [it is] that [same] living Word [in your heart that] convinces you that we are preaching [the truth;

10.09 Indeed, it is that same living Word] that [says],

"If [the word] in our mouth [is, indeed], the Logos together with the lord Jesus,* and you trust [the living Word] in your heart [that says] that God woke up [Abel], the Christ [of the previous age who was asleep within Jesus, and that Jesus] was delivered from the [second] death** [because Abel, the Christ of the previous age, rose within JESUS BEFORE JESUS WAS CRUCIFIED],

> *** The Logos** (the Word of God (Rev 19:13)) is The Ancient of Days (Dan 7.9), (Ancient Adam, or Adam (man) of Antiquity (Gen 1:26)). **Lord** means Supreme Ruler. **Christ Jesus**, the Second Adam (1 Cor 15:45), is the Supreme Ruler of the Body (Col 1:18), and Jesus is the first personality that the Second Adam perfected (Lk 13:32).
>
> ** **The First death** is the death of the spirit (1 Cor 15:22). **The Second death** is the death of the soul (Rev 20:14).

10.10 You will [also] trust [the living Word] in your heart [that says that your character can] be equal to [the character of Christ Jesus], and you will agree with your mouth that [***Jesus***, the Name of] the Logos, can deliver you [from the second death also],

10.12　Because there is no [longer any] difference between the Jew and the Greek, since [the Logos, who is] the supreme authority over everything, [is willing to share his spiritual] wealth [with] everyone [that] calls [on his Name], and

10.13　Because everyone who happens to call on [*Jesus*],* the Name of [the Logos], the supreme authority, shall be delivered [from the second death];"

> *****Primordial Adam** is the Name of the Ancient One, the Supreme Deity. **The Lord Jesus Christ** is the single Name of the Whole Second (Righteous) Adam (all his collective parts).*

10.14　[But you say]. "How, then, shall they call on [Jesus who is in the world] above, who they do not trust?

Indeed, how shall they trust [Jesus] when they never heard of [him]?

Indeed, how shall they hear about him when there are no preachers [to tell them about him]?

10.15　Indeed, how shall [the evangelists] announce the good news of the Age of Righteousness, [during] which the Carnal Mind [of the fallen souls of the First Adam] is engraved with [the Mark of God], unless [the evangelists] preach the Gospel of Peace, which sets them apart [from the First Adam]?"

10.16　On the contrary, all of you do not [trust the Lord Jesus Christ because] you have not subordinated [your Carnal Mind] to the Gospel of Peace. Wherefore Isaiah says, "Jehovah Elohim [alone] trusts us;" [R]

[R] Is 53:1

10.17　Therefore, [it is possible for you to be] convinced [that God woke up Abel, the Christ of the previous age, within Jesus of Nazareth, which delivered Jesus from the second death, that *Jesus* is the Name of the Logos, and that Jesus can do the same thing for you that God did for him] by you hearing the Word of God, [and] by you hearing [about the resurrection of Abel, the Christ of the previous age, in particular];

10.21a   Indeed, the Logos says to Israel, "I have extended my hands towards all you unbelieving children of the Day,[R]

[R] 1 Thes 5:5

10.18a   [But] you did not hear[R] the Logos, even though the spiritual message [of the Gospel of Peace] issued forth from the material bodies of all [the apostles, and] their narrative [was heard as far away as] the Roman Empire;

[R] Matt 13:13

10.18b   On the contrary, [Israel]

10.21b   Contradicted

10.19a   The Logos; Neither did Israel recognize [its actions][R];

[R]Jn 14:11

On the contrary, [even] Moses, [who performed miracles by the Logos while he was still attached to] the First [Adam, did] not [recognize] the Logos [within himself;[R]

[R] Jude 9

10.19b   So] I [AM] enraged [the daughter of Zion[R-1] by divorcing her,[R-2] and] incited [Israel] to [the point of] rivalry,[R-3] [by choosing[R-4] a spiritually] unintelligent people [who were] not a nation.[R-5]

[R-1]Lam 2:13
[R-2]Jer 3:8
[R-3] Deut 32:21
[R-4] 1 Pet2:9
[R-5]Acts17:26

10.20   Indeed, [Jehovah] declared boldly [through] Isaiah [saying] "The Logos was not discovered by [those who] worshiped me, [so] I revealed myself [to a people who did] not ask about me." *

> *Abram asked who the intelligence behind nature was, and Jewish scholars have been asking God questions ever since, but not many Christians ask questions. The proof is that not many Christians write about doctrine.*

Chapter 11

[627.4.C & 907.C]
God Did Not Reject Israel

11.01   [What should] I say, then? Has God cast away his people? God forbid! I, also, am an Israelite, of the seed of Abraham, of the Tribe of Benjamin.

11.02   God has not cast away his people, which he knew before * [they incarnated as the Nation of Israel].

> *Jehovah knew the souls that incarnated as National Israel from their inception. Many of these same souls are reincarnated in the Ashkenazi Jews today.*

God's Mind Is Spiritual

Look at Elijah [for example]. What does the Scripture say about how he communicated with God [to complain] against Israel, saying:

11.03   "Master, they have destroyed your altars and killed [all of] your prophets, except for me, and they are plotting to take my life [also];" *and

> * Elijah was talking about the personalities of the human beings who were the prophets of Israel. He was

Alternate Translation Of The New Testament/ Romans

thinking with his carnal mind. (See, also, Notes to Verses 4, 6 and 7b)

11.04 What was God's response? *

"I have reserved seven thousand males for myself who have not submitted to the [pagan god], Baal;"

> ** Jehovah was talking about the **Israelite souls that were born along with** the personalities of the prophets of Israel. **Seven thousand** is a round number that suggests the totality of Israelite souls.* (See, also, Notes to Verses 3, 6 and 7b)

Only Spiritual Israelites Are Elected

11.05 Accordingly, there is certainly, at this time, a remnant who are elected [by Christ], the Divine Nature, [to teach the Truth about God's Plan of Salvation for the nations], and

11.06 [When Christ], the Divine Nature, [teaches the Truth about God's Plan of Salvation for the nations], work can no longer [be considered to be] *labor* because, if it were not so, [that teaching the Truth about God's Plan for Salvation is not *labor*, then the one you call Christ], the Divine Nature, cannot be [Christ], the Divine Nature, because the work of [Christ], the Divine Nature, is not *labor*.^R *

^R Gen 3:19
Heb 4:11

> *Paul is saying that when Christ preaches through a personality, it cannot be called work because the personality need only be present for Christ to speak through him. Otherwise, the preacher has to labor to prepare a message. (See, also, Notes to Verses 3, 4 and 7b)

Carnal Israelites Were Blinded

11.07a   So, then, [all the personalities of] Israel did not obtain what they were searching for

11.08a   [Because] they refused to believe[R-1] [that Jesus of Nazareth was God's Son], and, [consequently], their inaccurate[R-2] perception [of him],

> [R-1] Duet 30:17
> [R-2] Isa 29:10
> Acts 28:26-27

11.09a   [According to what] David

11.08b   Wrote,

11.09b   Brought forth their own doctrine of [who Messiah is and how he shall appear and change the world], which [misunderstanding also] changed their character, and became a trap that

11.08c   [Continues] to bind [them], to this very day,

11.09c   [To the Law of Sin and Death, which] is holding them [R-1] captive in the unconscious part of the mind, UNTIL

> [The Jews believe that Jesus is the Son of God, and accept] the ransom [R-2] [that] he paid [for them], and

> [R-1] Ps 69:22-23
> [R-2] Rev 6:8
> [R-2] Rom 3:24,
> Eph 1:7

11.10   [The Serpent that ascended to the top of] the spine in the unconscious part of the mind to obscure their vision, so that they cannot see [clearly] in the unconscious part of the mind, returns [to the bottom of the spine and stays there] always;

11.07b   But [Jesus of Nazareth, the one that Christ] elected, obtained* [immortality],[R-1] and the rest were blinded [R-2] [by the god of this world],

> [R-1] Lk 4:25-27
> [R-2] 2 Cor 4:4

* Jesus of Nazareth is the only Israelite that obtained immortality, because it is impossible to understand God's plan of salvation apart from Christ. In this present dispensation, only those personalities that Christ is grafted to can expect to obtain immortality. (See, also, Notes to Verses 3, 4 and 6)

God Did Not Plan For Israel To Fail

11.11   Am I saying, then, [that National Israel] failed to overcome [their pride because God wanted them] to fall down [from their spiritually high place]?

No! Not at all! But, rather, that they sinned when [they allowed the First Adam], their other [prideful] self, [to influence them] to side-step [preaching] salvation to the Gentiles, [because they feared that they] would compete [with] them [to be God's chosen people].

Israel Failed Because of Sin

11.12a   Now, if [the First Adam], their other self, influenced them to side-step [preaching salvation to the Gentiles about]

(1)   The abundance of the world [of the one who rose from the dead], and

(2)   The deterioration of the abundance [of the existing world of] the Gentiles,

. . . how much more

11.12b   Will [the First Adam], their other self, [influence them][R-1] to side-step preaching to the Gentiles about] their completion?[R-2]

[R-1] Rom 7:5
[R-2] Col 2:10

National Israel Is Stronger Than the Nations

11.13a   Nevertheless, I am telling you [that National Israel does not have to be concerned about the spiritual strength of] the Gentiles, [because Israel's spiritual strength] is much greater; and

Paul Sent to Strengthen the Nations

That is why **I AM Adonay*** [has made me] his ambassador to the Gentiles, to render my services to them [as a preacher of the message of **Goodness by the Destruction of the Sin Nature**],

> ** I Am is the Name of God linked to the highest of ten degrees of power, and **Adonay** is the Name of God linked to **the lowest of the ten degrees**. I Am carries the DNA of Ancient Adam, the Son of God, and the Name **Adonay** is the Name that God takes when he resides in a man. The unity (**I AM Adonay**) is I AM (Ancient Adam) speaking through a man (in this case, Paul).*

11.14a   So that, somehow, by the flesh [of Christ Jesus, the spiritual male organ of the Lord Jesus Christ within me], coming near to them,

11.13b   [**I AM Adonay** might] increase [into them], and

11.14b   Stir up the spirit of the Gentiles, so that I might save some of them,

11.15   Because, if [Jehovah's] rejection of the Jews resulted in the reconciliation [of the Gentiles to God through Christ who is already in] the correct moral order, what shall the admission of [the Jews into the Kingdom of God] be,* but the resurrection of the [primordial kings** that] died?

> **Christ and, in particular, the Mind of Christ, is the door to the Kingdom of God (Jn 10:9).*

**Zech 3:8

8 Hear now, O Joshua the high priest, thou, and thy fellows that sit before thee: for **they are men wondered a**t: for, behold, I will bring forth **my servant the BRANCH**. KJV

The Branch is Messiah, the spiritual Son of David, the Son of God, and the men wondered at are the spiritually male human beings that he will reveal himself through. They are spiritually male because they are incarnations of these kings who were the first revelations of God in the flesh. They are all saviours through Jesus, the Great One who saves God's people from their sins (Ob 21).

National Israel Sanctified

11.16   Moreover, if [the Word of God], the root of the Holy [One* that] made [Adam], the first [man],$^{R-1}$ sanctified the whole mass of [earthen] humanity by sacrificing [Jesus,** the Second Adam,$^{R-2}$ then the Word of God, the same root of] the Holy [One that formed the First Adam and sacrificed the Second Adam], also [sanctified National Israel], the branches^{R-3} of [the Tree of Life] that broke off, [because National Israel are a part of earthen humanity who are all

sanctified by the resurrected Jesus Christ];

* The Holy One is Ancient Adam, the Tree of Life. The Word of God (Jn 1:1-2) is his root that attaches the Primordial Kings to him, who are his branches in the worlds that are his lower part. The Word of God and the kings are, collectively, called **ELOHIM**. Ancient Adam is **Elohim**, with its lower extremity (Elohim) ensconced in the earthen creature that they created in Genesis 1.

** The Word of God gave Jesus to humanity as a source of eternal life. He is the ransom paid in exchange for the bodies of fallen humanity, beginning with the Israel of God (the Christians and the Learned Jews), who are awakening to the reality of their fallen condition and asking Jesus to remove their sin nature.

^{R-1} 1 Cor 15:48
^{R-2} 1 Cor 15:48
^{R-3} Zech 3:8

Two Olive Trees

11.17   Also, if [National Israel were the branches of] a cultivated olive tree, and some of their branches were broken off, and [some of the branches of the Church],* a wild olive tree** [were grafted in amongst the remaining branches of National Israel, and, eventually, both the branches of National Israel, the cultivated olive tree,*** and the branches of the Church, the wild olive tree], became co-partakers of [the Word of God], the root [of the olive tree], and [of Jesus], the oiliness of the olive tree that came into existence [in this age],

The Church of the Lord Jesus Christ (Matt 16:18).

** Wild olive tree is a translation of Strong's #65, a word derived from Strong's #1636 which means, olive tree, and Strong's #66. Mr. Strong says that #66 in his Lexicon can be translated, fierce, and that word is, indeed, translated raging, in Jude 13.

The wild olive tree *is the Church that has the potential to grow up to the height that Adam attained to in National Israel, and higher, but the Church still has the violent, angry nature of the fallen First Adam. Therefore, the Scripture says that the branches of this wild olive tree were grafted to a root (the Word of God) whose nature* was contrary to it. James elaborates further, calling Christians **a double minded man** (Js 1:8).

Adam was **a cultivated olive tree** in National Israel, where he was fully regenerated to the point that Israel were a supernatural people. National Israel received an additional, righteous nature at the foot of Mt. Sinai that was separate and distinct from their fallen nature. There was no mixture in Righteous Adam. If Israel had only continued to follow after him, they would still be in the same place today. But they returned to their first nature.

*** **The cultivated olive tree** is **the Tree of Life**, which is a spiritual entity that consists of two parts: 1) The Root, and 2) The Branches. The Root is Ancient Adam, and the Branches are the Primordial Kings incarnated in his many-membered Son, mysteriously called, **these**, in the **Zohar**. The two, together, the Father and the Son, are called, **ELOHIM**, (a plural word), the Creator of Genesis 1.

11.18   In that event, [it would not be appropriate for] the branches [of National Israel, the cultivated olive tree] that were broken off, to exalt themselves above [the Church, the branches of the wild olive tree that were grafted in],

But, if [National Israel should be inclined] to exalt themselves [over the Church, they should remember that the branches of the Tree of Life] do not support [the Word of God], the root [of the Tree of Life], but, [on the contrary,

The Word of God], the root [of Ancient Adam, the Holy One, who formed the worlds], is the source of [all conscious existence for both the Jewish and the Christian branches of his Tree].

Alternate Translation Of The New Testament/ Romans

Israel

To Be Restored

11.19   So, [National Israel], the branches [of the Tree of Life, the cultivated olive tree] that were broken off, shall appear again, because **I AM** shall [rescue them from their earthen graves,[R-1] and] graft them back in;

[R-1] Matt 23:27

Deny Their Sin Nature

11.20   But, honestly, [National Israel, the branches of the Tree of Life] were broken off [because]

(1)   They did not believe [how important it is to be convinced of the Truth about their sin nature, and]

(2)   They did not highly esteem the Mind [of God that revealed that Truth to them];

Christians

Believe They Have A Sin Nature

But, you, [the Church], are standing [because] you exercise the high Mind [of God], the moral imperative [that] convinces you of the Truth [about your sin nature, and predisposes you to be in awe of [God], and to revere him;

Can Be Cast Down Also

11.21   So, if God was not lenient with [National Israel], the branches [of the Tree of Life that] he cast down, neither will he be lenient with [the Christians who think that they are in right-standing with him for any reason other than faith in Jesus Christ].

11.22   Therefore, [if Christians are to avoid being cast down like National Israel was cast down], they should understand why God is kind [towards some people], and severe [towards others]:

The Severity and Kindness of God

[God is] severe towards

[The people who] depart from [the high mind of God, and are not in awe of him, and do not revere him, and are not convinced of how important it is to believe the truth about their sin nature], but

God is kind towards [the people who exercise the high mind of God, the moral imperative that convinces them to face the Truth about their sin nature, and predisposes them to be in awe of God, and to revere him . . .

If they continue [to abide] in his morally excellent Mind;

[But, if they do not continue to abide in his morally excellent Mind], they will be cut off also;

The Mystery of Israel's Fall & Resurrection

Unbelief

11.23   So, [National Israel, the branches that were cut off from the Tree of Life], that continue in disbelief [to this day], will be grafted in also,

Disrespect For The Mind of God

Unless they continue to [disesteem the high Mind of God that reveals the Truth about their sin nature], because

God is able to graft them in again,

Grafted To The Root

Alternate Translation Of The New Testament/ Romans

11.24   Because, [when the cuttings] that come from [Jesus, the Branch^{R-1} of] the cultivated tree, are grafted to those* branches [of National Israel that were] cast down^{R-2} [by the Law, those branches [which are], themselves, the nature of [God], are grafted back into the root of] the cultivated olive tree, but [the *cuttings that] are grafted to [the non-Israelites are] grafted to an uncultivated olive tree, [whose* root and nature] are contrary to the nature of God** and

> * *The word,* **these**, *is a specific reference to the esoteric principle of the* **primordial kings**.

> ** *The Nation of Israel was born at Mt. Sinai when the primordial kings incarnated in the Hebrew children as they stood at the foot of Mt. Sinai.*

R-1 Zech 3:8
R-2 Rev 4:10

The Mystery of Israel's Failure

11.25   That is [the reason] why I do not want you to be in denial [about] this mystery, brethren, [that]

The hearts of the [female] side of [National] Israel, [who are still under the Law], were [spiritually] blinded because [they were not convinced of the moral excellence of the Mind of God, but, rather, chose to believe] the wisdom of their own [carnal mind;^R

^R Rom 7:25, 8:7

National Israel To Be Satisfied

Nevertheless, National Israel] shall be satisfied in the end time [also, when the man, Christ Jesus],^R enters into their multitude,

^R 1 Tim 2:5

National Israel's Sins Removed

11.27   Because, [at that time], when I take away their sin [nature, in accordance with] the Covenant[R] [that I made with their Fathers, Abraham, Isaac and Jacob], they shall come near to [me by] themselves, and

[R] Acts 3:25, 7:8

All Israel To Be Saved

11.26   This is how all Israel shall be saved, according to the way it is written [in prophecy]:

> A Deliverer shall come out of Zion, [and] He shall turn Jacob away from preferring the wisdom of his own [carnal] mind, which disrespects the Mind of God[R] [because] it reveals the truth about their sin nature.

[R] 1 Cor 2:16

National Israel, Enemy of The Gospel

11.28   [But, for now, National Israel, the branches of the Tree of Life that] were cast down [by the Law, are] enemies of the Gospel, because [the Church does not have the spiritual strength to convince them of the Truth [about their sin nature;

But] the [National Israelites who] prefer [God's merciful kindness above the Law], are joined to the Father through [his] beloved[R] [Son, the Lord Jesus Christ now].

[R] Matt 3:17, 12:5

Chapter 12

[1203.1.C]
12.01   I invite you, therefore, brethren, by [the authority of the Spirit of] Mercy [which comes from] God, that you present

your [personal souls, which are your spiritual] bodies, [to the Lord Jesus Christ, our altar, as] a burnt offering, [so that you might] agree with [the correct understanding of New Testament Doctrine, which is] your rational service to God, and be holy, and live.

Chapter 13

[OLM - 09 22 99]

13.01   There is [a spiritual] authority other than God, so let [Satan], the [spiritual] authority [that rules over] the animal nature, be subjected to the superior authority of God, because God is the [only] power [that] can arrange [us] in the correct moral order.

13.02   Therefore, whosoever resists [the personality that Christ Jesus lives in, also] resists [Christ Jesus], the authority of God's moral arrangement, and [Satan] seizes those who resist [Christ Jesus] their [true] self.

13.03   Satan's princes are afraid of [Christ Jesus'] authority, because [they do] evil [even though] they are terrified [of Christ Jesus'] good works. Therefore, [if] you are disposed towards Satan, do good, and [Adam, Jehovah's] thought form, shall possess [you].

13.04   The minister of God is given to you to do you good, but if you have evil thoughts in your mind towards him [even if they are unconscious or subconscious], you will experience fear, because the minister whose carnal mind is covered by Christ Jesus takes revenge upon [Satan], the one [who executes] the sowing and reaping judgment.

13.05   Wherefore, it is necessary that you submit yourself to [the minister in Christ Jesus], not only because he is come to punish [Satan and Leviathan within you], but [so that Christ

Alternate Translation Of The New Testament/ Romans

Jesus], your [renewed] conscience, [should dominate your carnal mind].

13.06 And for these same reasons, [that Satan and Leviathan in you should be destroyed and the life of the manchild preserved], the ministers [who] belong to God persevere in the exposure of sin continually, [and] are [therefore] heavily taxed in their emotions and in their physical body.

13.07 [Therefore], let the one who is judged deliver up his whole [carnal mind to the minister in Christ Jesus whose emotions and physical body] he is taxing; [indeed, let him deliver up Satan and Leviathan], the fearful ones who [make] him afraid of [the righteousness of God], and highly esteem the honorable [Christ Jesus, and the personality who carries Him, so that he might receive] eternal life [from Christ Jesus, the only one] who can give eternal life.

13.08 Let no man gather up the energy of another man [by relating to him with their carnal mind], but, rather, let us love one another [by relating to each other through Christ Jesus], because the one who communicates through Christ Jesus, satisfies the law, [and is a perfect man[R]].

[R] Jas 3:2

13.09a Therefore, do not set your mind [on carnal desires, or implement] any other solution [to your problems], because when your [human spirit] is gathered together with [Christ Jesus], you shall communicate in His nature, [and when you communicate in Christ Jesus' nature] you shall not commit adultery with Leviathan, and you shall not murder [Christ Jesus],

13.10 [Because] Christ Jesus does not harm His neighbor, [and], therefore, Christ Jesus satisfies the law [of sin and death].

13.09b You shall not do any of these things [any more, but] you shall communicate with your neighbor in the same manner [that] you communicate [with Christ Jesus within] yourself, [and Satan and Leviathan] will not steal [your energy anymore].

Alternate Translation Of The New Testament/ Romans

13.11a   But be aware that

13.13a   The fiery serpent, [the Primordial Serpent's] male sperm, is stretched out [towards Leviathan with] unbridled lust, and Leviathan, [who] is maliciously indignant [because Christ Jesus intends to marry the fiery serpent, his wife], is [very] jealous, and Satan, [who overcame Adam with] illusion, is quarrelsome [and] ready for a fight,

13.11b   [Because it is] the set time for Adam's timeline [to appear],

13.12a   [And] Christ Jesus is approaching, [and] the Primordial Serpent's timeline is coming to an end.

13.11c   So awake out of [your spiritual lethargy], for we are closer to deliverance [from this world] than when we first believed [that Christ could save us].

13.12b   Let us, therefore, separate from the activities of the carnal mind, and let us be baptized into the Christ Jesus, [our righteous] armor,

13.13b   [So that] we can live [out of] Christ Jesus' noble lifestyle,

13.14   [And] be baptized into the Lord Jesus Christ, [because the men who are married to the Lord Jesus Christ], do not concern themselves with the forbidden activities of [the spiritual insects in] their etheric body.

Chapter 14

[Mind, Hell & Death, Sheila R. Vitale, (Living Epistles Ministries, NY 2016)]

14.09   And this is the reason that Christ (Abel), who was lying dead [under Cain (the Carnal Mind)] revived, that He should be the supreme authority over both the [people] living [out of their Christ mind] and the [people existing through their] dead [carnal mind].

[691.2.C]
14.17   The Kingdom of God is not [experienced by eating] food [or] drinking [a beverage; it is a] mentality, a moral state of being called *righteousness*, which is experienced as the emotional calm, [or joy, that comes from the Spirit of Holiness, rather than irritation from the spirit of Satan, and it] emerges out of peace with God, which is the result of submission to [Jesus Christ], and which eventually materializes outwardly, in society, as life, personal liberty, and the freedom of the individual to pursue happiness.

[Message # Unknown]
14.17   The righteousness, peace and joy of the Kingdom of God is in the Holy Spirit, not in the spiritual philosophy[116] [of this world].

---

[116] Translation of **meat and drink.**

THE BOOK OF
1st CORINTHIANS

Chapter 1

[688.9.C]
1.21   Since the world knew of the wisdom of God from a source other than God, it pleased God to save those that [already] believed from disaster, by proclaiming [the truth publicly].

Chapter 3

[650.21.C]
3.10-15   I am a master builder who is building the foundation [of my immortal body upon the root of Jesus Christ], the grace of God, and others who are building [the foundation of their immortal body], should build [upon the root of Jesus Christ also], and

Everyone who builds upon Satan and Leviathan, the other foundation that is laid, should be careful,

Because, it shall be revealed whether we have built our foundation upon the [root of] Jesus Christ, which can be likened to gold, silver and precious stones, or [upon Satan and Leviathan, whose foundation can be likened to] wood, hay and stubble,

When [Christ Jesus, the Lake of] Fire, tests [our personality] with the fiery trials [that we must pass through to enter into the world to come, which is the seventh] Day [of Creation, the spiritual Day that never ends], which [tests] will reveal [which root] everyone's [personality is built upon], and

Every [personality] that survives the fiery trials [will receive the reward [of eternal life in Christ Jesus], and

Every [nefesh that does not survive] the fiery [trials], shall lose [his personality, as well as eternal life],

But the [Neshamah of Jesus Christ] shall be saved.

[688.8.C]
3.17   Anyone who corrupts the temple of the holy God, which you yourselves are, corrupts himself, . . And no one can experience being the temple [of God] until the seven plagues that [come from] the seven [Rings of the Lord Jesus Christ and Christ Jesus, the two witnesses], complete them.

Chapter 4

[OLM - 02 09 00]
4.05   So do not judge anything until the timeline of Christ Jesus arises within you, [because Christ Jesus] sheds light upon [Satan and the fiery serpent], the hidden darkness [of your carnal mind, and] distinguishes between the counsel of the left and the right side of the heart, so that everyone can be an accurate representative image of Jehovah's nature.

Chapter 5

[1003.1]
5.07   Therefore, now that Christ, our Passover [sacrifice] is breathing for us, thoroughly separate [yourselves] from the sin

[nature] of the Old [Man], because that is how you become sinless, [and] might [even] acquire a new material body.

[627.3.C]
5.08   Therefore, let us observe the feast [of Passover by] clearly [declaring] the truth [about our] sin[ful motives and behavior], rather than by [a physical feast, which form of observance is now] antiquated, [because] it does not deal with the corrupt [thoughts] and manipulations [of the Carnal Mind].

Chapter 7

[133.3]
7.37   Nevertheless if a man is standing immovably in Christ, not needing to unnaturally restrain his adamic sexuality, but having supernatural power to live out of Christ and has therefore decided to remain a physical virgin, he does a good thing.

7.38   So getting married is a single morally good act, but denying oneself marriage is a single morally good act of greater advantage.

7.39   A woman is knitted to her husband by spiritual principle for as long as he lives, but if her husband dies, she is not a slave to be apprehended by Christ, but as a free citizen, can choose whether or not to be married to the Lord.

7.40   In my judgment, spiritual women are supremely blessed if they dwell under the authority of the Lord. Although this is not the Father speaking through me, I, nevertheless, am speaking out of the Christ that is within me.

Chapter 8

[1246.2b.C]
8.01   Now, concerning [knowledge and its relationship to] sacrifices made to idols [in the heart], we know that we have all knowledge [through Christ, and that] knowledge [without Christ] inflates [the ego], but the love [of God, which is attachment to God], builds [up the person to be a house for God],

8.02   And if anyone thinks that he knows anything, [the truth is that] he does not know anything, yet, [about] what he needs to know [to acquire all knowledge through Christ];

8.03   Indeed, if anyone is bound to God, that same [person] is known [to God, and] receives [knowledge from] him, in the unconscious part of the mind;

8.04a   Now, concerning listening [to doctrine] that offers [the Seraph, the Image of Truth in the unconscious part of the mind, as] a sacrifice to the idol [in your heart],

8.05   Assuming [that] there are gods [that we can] relate to, whether in heaven or earth, there [would have] to be many angels and many gods, [because of the [many] idols in the hearts of all the brethren],

804b   But, we know [that there is] no God except [Jehovah], the One [True God, and] that idols [in the heart] have no form in the world;

8.06   But to us, [there is only] one, the [Eternal] God, the Father, the origin of everything [that exists, and] we in him, in the unconscious part of the mind; and] one Lord Jesus Christ,*

Alternate Translation of The New Testament/ 1 Corinthians

through whom the [Eternal God made] everything [that exists], and we [exist] through him, in the unconscious part of the mind,

> * The Lord Jesus Christ is the complete
> Adam (the First and the Second Adam),
> the creation of God.

8.07 But this knowledge is not in everyone, because, at this time, it is common for some to listen to doctrines of devils, and a partial [understanding of doctrine] soils [the Seraph, the Image of Truth that is] the witness ^R [to God] in the unconscious part of the mind,

^R 1 Jn 5:9

8.08 But whether we listen to [doctrine], or [do] not [listen to doctrine], we neither abound nor fall behind [in our attempts to draw closer to God, because [keeping] the Commandments of God] ,^R not doctrine, bring us closer to God,

^R 1 Jn 2:3; 5:2-3

8.09 But, be careful [to guard against the possibility] that, somehow, this privilege that you have [to be able to listen to doctrines of devils and] not soil [the Seraph, the Image of Truth in the unconscious part of the mind], should become a stumbling block [to your brethren who have a] weak [understanding of the doctrine of God, which] soils [the Seraph, the Image of Truth, the witness of God in the unconscious part of the mind],

8.10 Because, if anyone sees you, who have knowledge [in Christ], listening to doctrines [of devils from] a person who has an idol in their heart, how shall they, who have only a weak understanding of the doctrine [of God, which soils the Seraph, the Image of Truth, the witness of God in the unconscious part of the mind], bring into existence [the spiritual house] they are

Alternate Translation of The New Testament/   1 Corinthians

constructing [within themselves for God, if] they listen to doctrines of devils?

8.11   Shall [the efforts of] your brother, who Christ died for, [to make himself into] a house [for God], ^R come to nothing [because he saw] you, [who have knowledge] through [Christ, listening to doctrines of devils, when] he has only a weak understanding of the doctrine of God, which soils the Seraph, the Image of Truth, the witness to God, in the unconscious part of the mind]?

^R 1 Cor 3:10

8.12   Indeed, when you sin against the brethren like that, by wounding [the Seraph, the Image of Truth] in the unconscious part of the mind, because they have only a weak understanding of the doctrine of God, which soils the Seraph, the Image of Truth, the witness of God in the unconscious part of the mind], you sin against Christ;

8.13   Wherefore, if [my listening to] doctrines [of devils] makes my brother stumble and fall, I will not listen to dead doctrine during this age, so as to not make my brother stumble and fall.

Chapter 10

[429.1]
10.01a Moreover, brethren, I want you to understand that our fathers' dwelt [on the physical plane, which] is lower than the mental plane,[117] yet

10.03 They all ate the same spiritual food that [Moses] ate,

10.04 And they were all nourished by the same spiritual drink that [Moses] drank, [which food and drink] are the spiritual Rocks[118] that discipled [Moses], the Rock who was The Christ [to the Hebrews in the wilderness],[119]

10.01b And they all passed through the astral plane,[120]

---

[117] The physical plane where humanity exists is the lowest plane of existence. The next plane up is the astral, or emotional plane, and the one after that is the mental plane.

[118] The Greek word translated **Rock** is plural the first time it appears, and singular the second time. Michael, the spiritual drink, and the resurrected Adam, the spiritual food, are the Rocks that discipled Moses.

[119] The untranslated article **the** appears before the word **Christ**, indicating a personal Christ. (Read entire footnote in Appendices)

[120] Satan dominates the emotional plane, and all who hope to ascend beyond her power, must pass through her sea of spiritual energy. (Read entire footnote in Appendices)

10.02   Because all of the[ir human spirits] were immersed in Moses' [spirit], which was in [both] the mental and the astral planes,[121]

10.05   But [Christ, who Moses raised up in] the many of the [Hebrews], was overthrown in the wilderness, because [our fathers] preferred the fiery serpent over God.

[500.1]
10.20   But the ones (not the things) but the ones who sacrifice to devils, indeed, the ones who sacrifice to their carnal mind.

Chapter 11

[879.1.C]

MALE & FEMALE ROLES
The Male Instructs the Female

11.01   [My beloved brethren at Corinth], you should follow me as I follow Christ.

11.02   I praise you for reminding me of all the traditional ordinances[R-1] that you were given to keep,[R-2]

[R-1] Col 2:14
[R-2] Lev 18:4

---

[121] The spiritual man is simultaneously conscious on the physical plane, and on all of the planes of existence that he has ascended to.

Moses was conscious on the mental plane, which is higher than the emotional plane, which means that Moses had ascended to a place of authority over Satan. (See, **Note #*119*.**)

Alternate Translation of The New Testament/ 1 Corinthians

Male & Female Souls

11.03   However, I prefer that you should know that the whole [Adam, the spiritual] male [above, is] the head of Christ, [the Second Adam; ^R and Christ, the Second Adam], is the head of [the female soul of the spiritual Woman]; and the head of Christ [Jesus the only Mediator between the Whole Adam, the spiritual] male, and the female [soul of the spiritual Woman], is God, and

^R 1 Cor 15:47

Male & Female Head Coverings

11.04   Every [spiritual] male who prays [to another god]^R or prophesies [by the spirit of another god] covers [Christ, his] head, and dishonors him, and

^R Ez 14:3

11.05   Every [spiritual] female who prays [to another god],^{R-1} or prophesies [by the spirit of another god],^{R-2} dishonors [Christ Jesus], the head of [Christ], the spiritual male [that God gave to be an authority over the female soul of the Woman], which puts [that female personality (soul)] in the same spiritual condition as [a spiritual woman] who is still enslaved^{R-3} by the powers of this world ^{R-4} [that influence her through her Carnal Mind],

^{R-1} Ez 14:3
^{R-2} 2 Cor 11:4
^{R-3} Gal 5:1
^{R-4} Eph 6:12

It Is Better To Submit

11.06   Because [*the judgment* upon] a spiritual female who will not submit to [the wisdom of] the spiritual male who is in submission to Christ, his head, is ***to lose the gift of the Holy Spirit***. Wherefore, it is better for the spiritual female to be in submission to a spiritual male, who is in submission to Christ, his head, than [it is for her] to be without the Holy Spirit;

Alternate Translation of The New Testament/ 1 Corinthians

11.07   Indeed, the spiritual male who is in submission to Christ, his head, should not be in submission to the spiritual female, because Christ, who is the image of God,[R-1] has the opinion of God, but the spiritual female can only *reflect*[R-2] the opinion of God by learning from [the wisdom of] the spiritual male that she submits to,

[R-1] 2 Cor 4:4
[R-2] Pro 12:4

(Literal Understanding of Verses 8 & 9)

Woman Out of Man

11.08   [Because the man was not taken out of the woman, but the woman was taken out the man,[R] and

[R] Gen 2:22

Woman Is the Companion

11.09   The man was not created to be a companion for the woman, but the woman was created to be a companion[R] for the man],

[R] Gen 2:18

(Spiritual Understanding of Verses 8 & 9)

Man Existed First

11.08   Because [Christ Jesus],[R-1] the spiritual male [who is] the creation [of God],[R-2] did not come into existence from [the Church,[R-3] which is] the spiritual female,[R-4] but [the Church, which is] the spiritual female, came into existence from [the seed[R-5] of Christ Jesus], the spiritual male [who is the head of the

Church];[R-6]

[R-1] 1 Cor 15:45
[R-2] Rev 3:14
[R-3] Matt 16:18
Eph 5:25
Heb 12:23
[R-4] Eph 5:29
Rev 21:2
Rev 22:17
[R-5] Acts 13:23
[R-6] Col 1:18

11.09   So, then, since [Christ Jesus], the spiritual male, was not made to be [a companion for] the spiritual female, but [the spiritual] female [was made to be the companion of Christ], the spiritual male,

Spiritual Marriage

11.10   Therefore, if a spiritual female is not under the authority of a spiritual male whose head is Christ, one of the evil angels[R-1] will marry her,[R-2] and she will be [neither a spiritual male nor a spiritual female in Christ, but the concubine of an evil god];[R-3]

[R-1] Acts 16:18
Rev 12:7
[R-2] Matt 12:44
[R-3] Dan 11:38

11.11   So, because of the difference between a spiritual male and a spiritual female [which I have previously explained], the Lord desires that the spiritual female should not separate from the spiritual male,[R]

[R] 1 Cor 7:10-11

The Whole Adam

11.12   Because the spiritual female is a part of Adam, even though the spiritual female receives the opinion of God through the spiritual male, [who is the son of Man];[R]

[R] Lk 3:38

Authority In the Church

The Carnal Mind vs The Christ Mind

11.13   [The Carnal Mind] is not in submission to [Christ], the [spiritual] male, and worships [another god,^{R} wherefore, brethren], judge for yourselves: Is it proper [to allow] a spiritual female [to express the opinion of the Carnal Mind when a spiritual male is present?]

^{R} 2 Cor 4:4

11.14   Has not the engrafted^{R-1} Christ^{R-2} taught you that it is a disgrace for a spiritual male to submit to the [emotional] opinions of [the brethren who have received the Holy Spirit, which is] the long hair of the spiritual female?

$^{R-1}$ Js 1:21
$^{R-2}$ Col 1:27

11.15   But, [on the other hand, the brethren who have the Mind of Christ should not despise^{R-1} the emotional opinions of the brethren who have received the Holy Spirit, because], the spiritual female has been given the [emotional] opinion of the long hair of [the Holy Spirit] as a covering, until a spiritual male is sent to teach them.$^{R-2}$

$^{R-1}$ 1 Thes 5:20
$^{R-2}$ 2 Tim 2:2

Doctrinal Disputes

11.18   First of all, I hear that when you gather together, there are divisions among those of you who have different opinions [about who has spiritual authority], and about [how you should relate to one other, because of] your different roles in the Church,^{R}

^{R} 1 Cor 12:16-17

11.17   Wherefore, it is my understanding that you are better off not gathering together because of [your disagreement over whether Christ or the Holy Spirit is the superior anointing], and for this I do not applaud you,

11.16   Because the people who quarrel over the issue [of whether the believers with the Holy Ghost should submit to the believers who teach out of Christ, or, if the believers who have Christ should submit to the believers who have the Holy Ghost], cannot share the friendship and positive relationships based upon [their] mutual [belief in (1) The resurrection of the Lord Jesus Christ, (2) The forgiveness of sin, (3) The promise of immortality in the flesh, and (4) other] shared interests that [Christ], the Lord, intends for the churches of God^R to have;

^{R} 2 Thes 1:4

Wisdom, The Male Anointing

11.19   Indeed, wisdom identifies the spiritual males among you, who are approved to make you strong by speaking the Truth,$^{R-1}$ which destroys heretical doctrines,$^{R-2}$

$^{R-1}$ Jn 8:32
$^{R-2}$ Rev 10:9

11.20   So, when you gather together you should not share the Word of God,

11.21   Because [the believers who have birthed Christ believe that the Holy Ghost brethren] are starving for the word of God [and want to teach them] doctrine, and [the believers who have received] the Holy Spirit and are lusting for emotional [experiences, think that the brethren who have birthed Christ, are backslidden because they do not manifest the motions of the Holy Spirit, and] everyone has decided what he believes before you come together.

11.22   Now, is it not true that you have your own local churches where you can [either] share doctrine or experience the Holy Spirit? Why must [those of you who are in Christ] disrespect the other members of the Church of God who do not believe [in studying esoteric doctrine] like you do, and [why do those of you who have the Holy Spirit] shame [the brethren who do not want to participate in the emotionalism] that you have [in your services]?

Immortality & The Carnal Mind

11.23 Now, I passed on to you what I received from [Christ], the Lord [within me]:[R-1] that the Spirit of Life seized[R-2] [Christ], the Lord within Jesus [of Nazareth], and delivered up the fallen soul [that he was born with to destruction],[R-3] according to the Scripture,[R-4] and

[R-1] Rom 8:10
Col 1:27
[R-2] Matt 24:40
[R-3] Rom 8:7
[R-4] 2 Pet 3:10. 12

Christ, A Higher Soul

11.24 [Christ within Jesus] said, "I am glad that my [spiritual] body[R] will be broken [into many soul sparks] which will be formed into [the higher souls], that reflect [the mind of] Christ within Mankind," and

[R] 1 Cor 15:44

An Immortal Body

11.25 [Jesus] said, "The New Testament is in [the spiritual] Blood of [Christ], My [spiritual] body,"[R-1] [so] whosoever absorbs[R-2] [the Spirit of Life, that is in the Blood of Christ Jesus,[R-3] will receive a soul spark that] is not identical with, but similar to Christ Jesus, [who has] My [intellectual moral insight, and you will also receive an immortal material body] made from [the substance of] that [holy soul],

[R-1] 1 Cor 15:44
[R-2] Jn 4:13-14
Jn 6:54
Heb 6:7
[R-3] Rom 8:2

The Appearance of Christ

11.26 Provided that [Christ Jesus], their [new soul that is similar to my immortal soul], consumes [the spiritual understanding of] the Scripture and absorbs[R-1] [the Spirit of Life, that is the Blood of Christ Jesus][R-2] often enough so that [Christ], the Lord, [the Second Adam], appears in their physical body, [which appearance] proclaims the death of [the First Adam[R-3] who he has replaced].

[R-1] Jn 4:23
Heb 6:7
[R-2] Rom 8:2
1 Cor 15:47
[R-3] Js 3:11-12

Spiritual Death

11.27 Wherefore, whosoever consumes [the spiritual understanding of] the Scripture[R-1] and drinks in [the Spirit of Life[R-2] which is in Christ, our] Lord, with a wrong motive,[R-3] shall be responsible for [aborting[R-4] Christ, the holy] soul [of their New Man], and [polluting the waters of] the Spirit of [Life[R-5] that are in Christ], the Lord [who is destined to be born[R-6] within them].

[R-1] Col 4:3
[R-2] Rev 11:11
[R-3] Heb 4:12
[R-4] Heb 4:12
[R-5] Rom 8:2
[R-6] Rev 12:5

Testing Yourself

11.28 Indeed, test yourself in this way: Has the Second Adam, [your new holy soul, been formed] out of [the spiritual understanding of] the Scripture that you have consumed?[R-1] And has your physical body absorbed [enough of the Spirit of Life, that is in Christ, that it no longer gets sick and cannot die]?[R-2]

[R-1] Jn 6:50
[R-2] Jn 6:54
Jn 17:3

Separation From The First Adam

11.29 Because, [whosoever] consumes [the spiritual understanding of the Scripture] and drinks[R-1] in [the Spirit of Life, that is in Christ, must eventually] pass judgment upon himself[R-2] [as to whether or not] he is consuming [the spiritual understanding of the Scripture] and drinking in [the Spirit of Life, that is in Christ Jesus], without thoroughly separating [the spiritual] body of [Christ, which is] the Lord [within himself], from [the First Adam within himself],

[R-1] Heb 6:7
[R-2] Matt 7:1

Recognizing Christ

11.31 Because, if we separated ourselves thoroughly from [the carnal nature of] the First Adam, we would be able to recognize [Christ, the Second, spiritual Adam, within ourselves and within others];

Sickness & Death

11.30 [But, not separating Christ, the Second, spiritual Adam within yourselves, from the First, earthen Adam, who is also within us], is the reason why so many among you are sickly, and many have died;

Discipline & Recognition

11.32 Indeed, [Christ], the Lord with[in us], disciplines[R-1] us so that we can recognize [him when he is still lying down][R-2] under [the First Adam, so that Satan, the enforcer of the Sowing

& Reaping Judgment],[R-3] will not [be able to carry out the death] sentence[R-4] [that all the inhabitants of this] world [are subject to];

[R-1] Heb 12:6
[R-2] Matt 4:38
[R-3] Gal 6:7
[R-4] Rev 2:11
Rev 20:6, 14
Rev 21:8

Stay In Your Own Spiritual Space

11.33   Wherefore, brethren, when you come together [to fellowship], each one of you should stay in the [spiritual] place where you are when you consume [Scripture, your spiritual food], and not try to influence others, but

Lust To Minister

11.34   If anyone is [so] famished[R-1] [for the esoteric understanding of the Word of God that they are lusting to minister to the brethren who believe that the Holy Spirit is all that there is], let him consume [the esoteric understanding of the Scripture] at home,[R-2] [and not abuse the brethren who believe that the Holy Spirit is all that there is], which would result in [Satan,[R-5] the enforcer of the Sowing & Reaping Judgment,[R-3] harming him, because] he would be guilty [of the sin of pride],[R-4]

[R-1] Gen 25:29
Amos 8:11
[R-2] 1 Cor 14:35
[R-3] Gal 6:7
[R-4] Pro 16:18
[R-5] Job 1:12
1 Tim 3:6

Chapter 13

[688.13.C]

13.01   Though I speak the languages of [both] men and angels, if the love of [Christ, the regenerated female Adam], is not formed in me, I will have become [like] the sound [of the trumpet that was blown before] the judgment [that brought down the wall of Jericho], or the battle cry [of the Gentiles, before] they crash [against Israel],

13.02   And, though I have the faith [of the awakened Abel, the Malchut of the regenerated female of] the whole [Adam, and] possess the Word of God by which I understand the mystery of the whole Adam, [and] can move [the spiritual power of] the whole [Adam], the mountain [of God, when the awakened Abel within me] is experiencing spiritual intimacy with the whole [Adam]; if I do not have [the full 10 Rings of Christ Jesus, the regenerated female Adam, which is] the love of God, I am Leviathan, [not Christ Jesus],

13.03   And though I deliver up the body of [Leviathan, the pride of the spiritual dimension of] my neck, to the power of [God, and] though I am broken into pieces [so that] the whole [Adam] can come into existence through me, [these things] are not useful [to regenerate Christ Jesus, within] me, [the one who opposes] Leviathan,

13.04   [Now, love is the attribute of Christ, the fruit of the Holy Spirit, and the love of Christ is expressed as]: The kindness of Christ [that] endures for a long time [before he brings down judgment;

The nature of] Christ [that] does not envy [evil, or those who have attained wealth through evil deeds; the nature of] Christ [that] does not brag to build up his own self-image,

Alternate Translation of The New Testament/ 1 Corinthians

13.05 [The love of Christ] does not justify immoral behavior to preserve his own [reputation], or think evil of anyone else [to cover his own sins], and is not easily [moved to scapegoat others to ease the internal] irritation [of Satan's pressure to sin];

13.06 [The love of Christ] is not happy when injustice [overcomes Truth], but is happy [to hear that] Truth [has overcome the lies that lead to injustice];

13.07 [The love of Christ] hopes that the whole [Adam shall be awakened], and believes that the whole [Adam, the one who] covers [Leviathan, and] silences [the thoughts of Satan], shall endure [in the earth of mankind],

13.08 [And that] Christ, [the fruit of the Holy Spirit], shall never fall down [from the God world] again; but if there are warnings, they shall fail; if there are tongues, they shall become inactive; if there is a partial knowledge of the mysteries, it shall become ineffective,

13.09 Because [Christ, has only] a partial knowledge of the mysteries, [wherefore], he prophesies [only] out of that partial knowledge,

13.10 But when [Christ Jesus, who] is perfected [by the Lord Jesus Christ], comes into existence, then [Christ, the fruit of the Holy Spirit who prophesies only in] part, becomes inactive,

13.11 [Now], when I was [Abel, the spiritual] infant, [my] infantile, willful mindset reasoned like a [spiritual] infant, and spoke random, unintellectual words: but when [Christ Jesus, the regenerated female Adam], the adult [spiritual] man [who is the husband of the personality and lord of the physical body], came into existence [within me], he rendered [Abel], the [spiritual] infant who had not yet learned how to speak, ineffective.

13.12 [At this time] we see [the reflection of the spiritual worlds] in a dark mirror, because [we are back to back with the Lord Jesus Christ, the male Adam], but [in the world to come,

Jesus], the personality [of Ancient Adam], and [the personalities of Christ Jesus, the regenerated female Adam, shall couple, and] then I, [who] now know [the spiritual mysteries] in part, shall have face to face, spiritual intimacy with [Jesus, the male Adam, who] has been having [back to back] spiritual intimacy with me [all this time].

13.13   So, now [that] these three, [faith, hope and the love of God], remain permanently [in the earth, Abel], your hope [of glorification, shall awaken and become] your faith, [the first of the 10 Rings of the regenerated female Adam, who is] the love of [Christ to you], but the most Important of these [three] is [the love of Christ, the regenerated female Adam].

Chapter 15

[873.2]
15.01   Moreover, brethren, I declare that you are standing [because of] the gospel that I preached to you, which you have also received, and

15.02   By which you were saved, [and might] also [save] anyone [else], if you hold fast [to what] I preached to you, unless you have believed the exterior of the word of God, [which is] vanity,

15.03   Because I delivered what I received at the beginning to you also, that [the] Christ [child in National Israel] died because of our sins, according to the Scriptures, and

15.04   After he was roused from sleep on the third day [of creation], according to the Scripture, and

15.05   After that he was seen by Peter and then the twelve [disciples], and

Alternate Translation of The New Testament/ 1 Corinthians

15.06   After that, he was seen in the spirit by five hundred brethren at one time; of whom the greater part remain to this present [day], but some have fallen asleep, and

15.07   After that he was seen by James, and then all of the apostles, and

15.08   Last of all, he was seen by me also, one [of the National Israelites, who] miscarried [the Christ child],

15.09   Even though I am the least of the apostles, who does not qualify to be called an apostle, because I pursued the Church of God,

15.10   But [the Shekinah], the Grace of God, [which is] **the temple [of the point that is the beginning of creation, and the head of the Whole Adam who is below]**, did not [leave] me empty, [without a spiritual child], but, [on the contrary], the Grace [of God filled me with] the superabundant [anointing] of the whole [Adam]: Indeed, I did not work hard,[R] because [the Shekinah], the Grace of God, was with[in] me;

[R] Rom 11:6

15.11   Therefore, in this manner, whether I, or they, preached, [the only thing that matters, is that] you believed;

15.12   Indeed, we have preached that [the] Christ [child that went to sleep in National Israel] woke up [in Jesus of Nazareth before] he died, [and that, if Christ is awake in someone who dies, that person will stand up again]; So, how is it that some of you [still] say that it is not [possible for someone] to stand up again after he dies?

15.13   Indeed, if it is not possible [for someone] to stand up again after he dies, [this is the proof that the] Christ [child that went to sleep in National Israel] did not wake up [in that person];

15.14   So, if [Jesus] Christ [did not stand up again after he died], then [the Christ child that went to sleep in National Israel]

did not wake up [in Jesus either], and [the message of eternal life that] we have proclaimed [to you] is worthless, and your belief [in eternal life] is worthless [also];

15.15a   Indeed, [if what you say is true, that Jesus did not stand up again after he died], we are found to be false witnesses of God, because we have testified that God woke up [the] Christ [child that was within Jesus before he died;

But, God could] not have awakened [the Christ child within Jesus before he died,

15.16a   Because, if [Jesus] did not stand up again after he died, [it means that the] Christ [child that went to sleep in National Israel], did not wake up [in Jesus,

15.15b   Because], if [God did wake up the Christ child in Jesus before he died, Jesus would have stood up again after he died];

So, [if Jesus did not stand up again after he died, it means that the Christ child] did not wake up [in Jesus], and

15.16b   If the Christ child did not wake up in Jesus], in that event, [the Christ child will not] wake up [in you either], and

15.17   If [the] Christ [child that went to sleep in National Israel] does not wake up [in you, then], your faith is worthless, [because] you are still in your sins; and

15.18   Then, [in that event, the brethren] who fell sleep [believing that the] Christ [child that went to sleep in National Israel woke up] in [them], are fully destroyed [and will never rise again];

15.19   [Wherefore], If our expectation [of eternal life] is [based upon our faith that [the] Christ [child that went to sleep in National Israel] wakes up in this life, alone, then [how] shall we bring the mercy of the whole Adam into existence?

15.20   Indeed, [the] Christ [child that] woke up [in Jesus] is now become the firstfruits of [the many counterparts of himself that] went to sleep [in National Israel, when the First Adam did not stand up again after] he died;

15.21a   Indeed, the [First] Adam [separated from God] and died [to his immortality]

15.22   Because [the flesh of] everyone [who is] exactly like [the First] Adam dies off, but, after that, everyone [who the] Christ [child that went to sleep in National Israel wakes up] in, lives again;

15.21b   So, [because the Christ child that went to sleep in National Israel woke up in Jesus, the First] Adam stood up again after he died;

15.23   Indeed, [the] Christ [child that woke up in Jesus is] the firstfruits [of the many-membered Christ child that went to sleep in National Israel]; But, after that, [the] Christ [child must] appear in each person individually;

15.24   Then, when the [the Lord Jesus Christ] attains his goal of rendering **all** the authority and all of the power of the chief rulers [of the First Adam within the saints] utterly useless, he shall surrender the kingdom that God, the Father, provided [for him],

15.25   Because he must rule [over Satan's] soldiers in [the unconscious part of] the carnal mind [of] all of [the saints], until [the First Adam comes] under [his authority], and

15.26a   [In order to accomplish that, the Lord Jesus Christ], the last [Adam],

15.27a   Shall Subordinate the carnal mind of all [of the saints that the Christ child woke up in], under [himself], and

15.26b   Shall separate [the human spirit that belongs to God] from [Satan's] soldiers [in the unconscious part of the carnal mind [of those saints], and render them idle and completely useless;

15.27b   But, when [the Scripture] says [that] he will subjugate **all** [the authority and **all** of the power of the chief rulers of the First Adam within the saints], it is evident that **all**, does not include [the power of God];

15.28   Indeed, inasmuch as the Son [of God] shall subordinate everyone [who is] in the [First Adam], as well as himself, to the Whole [Adam who] subjected him, everyone [who is in] the Whole [Adam] will also be in submission to God,

15.29   Because Elohim banded together with [the Christ child within Jesus, who was] submerged under [the First Adam who] died [in the previous age; So] if [the First Adam who] died [in the previous age is] completely dead, then the Christ child did not wake up [within Jesus] and he is [still] submerged [under the First Adam within us also];

15.30   [So, if it is true that Jesus did not stand up again after he died], then, [both] we and the Christ child [within us who is still sleeping], are in continuous danger [of being overtaken by the First Adam, the evil ruler of this word];

15.31   I swear that [am telling you the truth], that defending yourself against me [when I reveal sin in you], is killing the unity [that Christ], the gentle gazelle [within me], has with Christ Jesus, our Lord;

15.32   [So], if I have encountered [your beast nature like an Ephesian gladiator], what advantage [has it] for me if the [First] Adam does not [stand up again after] you die? Let Christ] wake up [in you, and] let us eat [the flesh of the Lord Jesus Christ], and drink down [his] spirit[ual blood], because soon after [we do that], we shall die to the animal nature of [the First Adam].

Alternate Translation of The New Testament/ 1 Corinthians

[963.4.C]
15.34   Awake to [Christ Jesus, whose character] is equal to God's [standard of morality, which] does not have a [carnal] knowledge of sin: I am speaking to some of you [who are still living out of the First Adam, your] female [mind].

[Message Unknown]
15.41   Elohim's breath of life [glory] is appearing in this world as the human spirits of mortal men [the stars], but the individual mortal man varies in his ability to distinguish between good [Adam/Jesus] and evil [Satan, mortal man's unconscious mind (the sun of this world) and Leviathan, mortal man's subconscious mind (the moon of this world)].

[OLM - 02 03 99]
15.44   It is sown a natural body, it is raised a spiritual body, There is a natural body and there is a spiritual body.

[Message # Unknown]
15.45-47 In the beginning, the First Adam was a living soul, and after that, [Adam] was a living Spirit, and at the end [of the creative process], Adam was a man-faced creature [who revealed] the divine^R [nature] in the realm of time;

^{R} 2 Pet 1:4

And so it is written, [Jehovah] formed Adam, a man-faced creature, from the dust of the earth, [to cover Ancient Adam] in the realm of time; and

The First Adam was [formed from a] material, made like the animals, but the Second Adam was the Lord from Heaven.

[907.C]
15.54a   So, when [the material body that is [decaying is clothed with [a spiritual garment that provides] unending existence, and the mortal [soul that is dying] is clothed with [a spiritual garment that] prevents death, then, that which is written in the wisdom [of God], shall come to pass,

That, [the time shall come, when life] shall triumphantly swallow up death, [which shall cease to exist].

15.55　Where is [Satan, the Queen of] Hades, who [empowers] death to triumph [over life by] goading [mortal men to sin]?

15.56　[Satan, the unconscious part of the carnal mind of the fallen First Adam, is] the goad [that tempts mortal man] to sin, [which results in] death, [because]

The Law [of Jehovah's Righteous Sowing & Reaping Judgment], empowers [Satan, the unconscious part of the carnal mind of the fallen First Adam, to punish] the sin[ner].

[Message # Unknown]
15.57　Wherefore, [we] thank God, who gives us the victory over [sin and, therefore, over] death, through our Lord Jesus Christ.

Chapter 16

[Message # Unknown]
16.22　Anyone who truly loves the Lord will bring divine judgment upon Satan, the unconscious part of his own carnal mind.

THE BOOK OF 2nd CORINTHIANS

Chapter 3

[944.4.C]

3.01 Do we need to begin to recommend ourselves [over and over] again, or do we need, as some others do, letters of recommendation from you? No!

3.03a The letter of Christ [that recommends] our ministry is not written with ink, but with the Spirit of the living God; neither

3.02a Is our letter [of recommendation] written

3.03b On stone tablets, [but on] the fleshly tablets of your hearts, [so that] it might be conspicuously apparent

3.02b To all [of] Adam['s parts, so that] they might read [your] heart, and know us,

3.04 Wherefore, we have this great trust in God [that we are able to minister to you] through Christ,

3.05 Because we, ourselves, are not sufficient to explain anything [that the Lord has taught] us by ourselves, but our ability [comes from] God,

3.06 Who for that purpose has enabled us to serve [the spiritual food of] the New Testament; not [the literal meaning of the Word], but the spiritual [meaning of the Word], because, the literal [meaning of the Word] destroys [the spiritual] life [that the Word is intended to impart to those who hear it],

Alternate Translation Of The New Testament/ 2 Corinthians

3.07   But if the opinion of Moses' [other] personality [that he received from Jehovah on the Mountain] by engraved stone [tablets that did not disannul] death, [but], so powerfully [convicted the Hebrew children of their sins], that [they] could not meet Moses' eyes,

3.08   How is it possible that the ministry of the Spirit shall not be powerful enough [to disannul death]?

3.09   Because if the ministry of condemnation [ministered by Moses was] powerful [enough to convict Israel of sin], the ministry of righteousness [in Jesus' Blood, which is] much more exceedingly powerful [than the ministry of condemnation, shall surely save us from death],

3.10   Because even though [the ministry of condemnation] was esteemed to be powerful, [it was] not powerful in the sense that the power [of the ministry of righteousness] surpassed [it],

3.11   Because, if [the same Spirit that] is [so] much more powerful than [the Law that it] rendered [the Law] idle [dwells in you, it is also] powerful [enough to enable you] to remain [in your bodies];

3.12   [So, since] we have this great expectation [of eternal life for you], we are speaking [to you] plainly, and

3.13   Not like Moses, [who] put a veil over the [Christ] side of his personality [so that] the children of Israel could not perceive [the information that he received from Jehovah] concerning the end [of the age, when the Law] would be rendered entirely idle and useless, and

3.14   Their mind was rendered insensitive to the Spirit, and is veiled to this day when the Old Testament is read, but they will not remain veiled in Christ, [who] renders [the Law] idle and completely useless;

3.15　　But, even to this day, whenever they renew their knowledge of [what] Moses [told them], the veil is [still] upon their heart,

3.16　　But, whenever any [one of them] shall turn back to the Lord, the veil shall be removed;

3.17　　Indeed, [when] the Spirit of the Lord is in [an Israelite that has turned back towards him], the Spirit of the Lord [is] indeed, unrestrained in that [man];

3.18　　Indeed, everyone [who has] the opinion of the Lord is one of Adam's] unveiled personalities, so [when] we look at our reflection in a [spiritual] mirror [to see ourselves] as the Spirit of the Lord [sees us], the opinion that we have of ourselves changes to his opinion.

Chapter 4

[650.1.C]
4.18　　We do not give credence to the visible things of this world which are seen, but to the invisible things which are not seen, because the visible aspects of this world which we see are temporary, but the invisible things which we cannot see are eternal,

Chapter 5

[1246.9.C]
5.01　　We know that if this mortal soul of our temporary [physical body] were to dissolve, we [would still] have another soul, not made from the mind [of the First Adam, but born] of God, [existing], perpetually, in the spiritual worlds,

Alternate Translation Of The New Testament/ 2 Corinthians

5.02　　But, because [our mortal soul is] groaning, we long for our house from heaven to clothe us,

5.03　　Otherwise, [after] being stripped of [our material body], we shall be found naked;

5.04　　And we who are in this temporary body are not groaning because we want to be unclothed from the burden of [our] mortal soul, but, [rather], that [our mortal soul] should be swallowed up ᴿ by the life [of the Lord Jesus Christ];

　　　　　　　　　　　　　　　　ᴿ 1 Cor 15:54

5.05　　Indeed, [Jesus, who] is doing this for God, has given us [his] Spiritᴿ [as] a sign of good faith, [that he will do the same thing for us that Jehovah did for him], and

　　　　　　　　　　　　　　　　ᴿ 2 Cor 1:22

5.06a　　We are all confident, therefore,

5.07a　　Walking by faith,

5.06b　　Knowing that, while Jehovah is at home with [us in] the body, we are apart from [Jesus,

5.07b　　Who] has not appeared [yet],

5.08　　And we are confident [that] it would please Jehovah [for Jesus to be] present, rather than for [him] to be apart from the body,

5.09　　Wherefore, we aspire to please [Jesus] in the unconscious part of the mind, whether [he is] apart [from us], or present [with us in the body],

5.10　　Because each individual must [walk in] the footsteps of Christᴿ [who] ascended before all of us, to receive in this body according to what he has done, whether good and profitable, or worthless and evil, and

　　　　　　　　　　　　　　　　ᴿ Rom 8:1, 4
　　　　　　　　　　　　　　　　　Gal 5:16, 25

5.11   [Jesus, the Son of] God, the kindness of Jehovah, therefore, perceiving how terrified Adam, the species, [is concerning this judgment], has made [this explanation] available to you, [and] I hope, indeed, that your own conscience has also witnessed to [what] we have revealed [to you],

5.12   Not to set ourselves above you [concerning] your previous [sins], but that you may have the opportunity to boast more than us, of the glorious presence [of the Spirit of God] in the heart[R] [center of your emotional soul],

[R] 2 Cor 3:3

5.13   Because whether we are out of our mind [concerning what we are telling you about] God, or whether we are sane, [we are] on your [side], and

5.14   Because [our souls] are attached to Christ and are held fast by [him], we can [make] this judgment, that [if] one [crossed] over for the sake of everyone [who] died a natural death, then everyone was dead,

5.15   And that if [Jesus, the Christ], died for the sake of everyone, then they which are alive [because] he died, should not live for themselves, but for the sake of the one that died and rose again;

5.16   Wherefore, we no longer know anyone by [who they are in] the flesh, [and], if we have known Christ after the flesh, we do not know him that way anymore,

5.17   Therefore, if anyone [is] in Christ, [he is a part of] the new creation; The original [Adam] has gone away. Look! [Christ Jesus] is the new, [original creation];

5.18   Indeed, everything [is] of God [who] has changed us [into] himself through Christ, and has given us the assignment of exchanging [the soul of the First Adam for Christ Jesus];

5.20   Now, then, God has invited us to be [his] representatives, to beg you for the sake of Christ, through Christ [within yourself, to let] God change you,

5.21   Because he has made [Christ, who] did not have any knowledge of immorality, [the ransom]^R for [our] immoral [soul], that we might be made righteous by the Son of] God in the unconscious part of the mind.

^{R} 1 Cor 6:20. 7:23
Rom :24
Eph 1:7

Chapter 7

[Message # Unknown]
7.08   I regret that [my] letter [describing the sin that I saw in you] grieved you, but, on the other hand, I do not regret it, because, for a season, that same letter caused you the anguish [that leads to repentance], and

7.09   I did not rejoice because you were in anguish, but [I rejoiced] because that anguish cast down [your pride], and that that anguish led to the repentance [which] God [desires to grant to you, to the end] that you should not suffer loss because of us, [because]

If the Lord does not grant you repentance after we expose your sins, you will reap the loss of the Sowing & Reaping Judgment, because

7.10   The Godly [ones, who] repent [and] labor to cast down [their pride, experience] the anguish [that leads to] salvation, but the worldly [ones, who] labor without repentance, die, [even though they experience] anguish.

Chapter 8

[Message # Unknown]

8.01 Now that it has been revealed to you, brethren, that the divine influence of God has been bestowed upon the churches of Macedonia,

8.02 In that, despite an overabundance of tests and pressures which cast them down into poverty, the mystery of the riches [which are found in] unity [with Christ Jesus], overflowed into calm delight,

8.03 Because [Satan] was cast down[R] by the [miracle-working] power [of Christ], and not by the power of [Satan, who is] their own will [power],

[R] Lk 10:18

8.04 [After] we urgently requested permission to communicate the gift of [Christ],[R-1] the assistance [that Jehovah promised Adam],[R-2] to the saints, by means of a great deal of advice,

[R-1] Eph 4:7
Col 1:27
[R-2] Gen 2:18

8.05 And, as we expected, they opposed their own carnal mind and gave her over to [Christ] the primary controller [of their soul], and to us, [the teachers provided for them] by the Will of God,

8.06 To the extent that you desired that Titus should finish the work that we began in you, so that you should receive [Christ], the same divine influence upon your heart [that we have received].

Chapter 12

[1203.1.C]
    12.02   I became acquainted with the man, Christ Jesus, about 14 years ago. (I do not know whether [I was] in the body or out of the body), God knows; I know only this, [that] I was caught up to the third heaven

    12.03   [Where] I became acquainted with this man (whether in the body or out of the body I do not know;

    God [knows])

    12.04   That I was caught up into paradise and heard utterances that are illegal for the man [Christ Jesus] to speak [in public, because] they cannot not be expressed in human language, and],

    12.05a   [Now], I have [the same] opinion [that] this [man has, but], yet, it is not my opinion, [it is his opinion that I have, and I have it only because

    12.01   [I understand that] it is to my advantage to not have my own opinion,

    12.05b   But, rather, to keep my own opinion] very weak,

Chapter 13

[Message # Unknown]
    13.05   Test yourself like Jesus Christ did, to see whether your own righteous selves [Christ] can discern the difference

between himself and Satan and Leviathan [your old man], unless you are unfit to be tested [Christ is not formed in you].

THE BOOK OF GALATIANS

Chapter 2

[1221.1.C]

2.11 But When Peter Came to Antioch, I, [Paul], withstood [him, face] to face, even though [the other Jews who followed James] were [the ones] to be blamed for [teaching that male circumcision was required for the Gentiles],

2.12 Because, [it was] the other [Jews who] came [from] James to share New Testament doctrine with the Gentiles [that taught that the Gentiles should be circumcised, but when [Paul] came [to Antioch], they withdrew [from fellowship with the Gentiles], and separated themselves from [them], because they were afraid [of Paul, the apostle to the Gentiles, who was teaching that] circumcision [is not required for Gentile converts], and

2.13 In the same manner, the other Jews [who followed James believed] the hypocrisy [that the Gentiles should be circumcised] with so much spiritual conviction, that Barnabus, [a Levite], was led astray by that hypocrisy;

2.14 But when I saw that [the other Jews who came from James] were not walking uprightly according to the truth of the gospel [concerning male circumcision], I said to Cephas, [the apostle sent to the circumcision],

"If you, a Jew, live like a Gentile in front of everyone and not as the Jews live, why do you force the Gentiles to conform to Jewish customs?"

Alternate Translation Of The New Testament/ Galatians

2.15   We [are] Jews and not of the Gentiles, [but are] sinful by nature [as well as they],

2.16   Knowing, indeed, that Adam is not innocent [of violating the Law because] he performs the carnal commandments of the Law; But [he is innocent of violating the Law] by the faith of Jesus Christ, [who satisfies the spiritual law of God in the unconscious part of the mind];

Even we, [who are] in Christ Jesus, [must have] faith that we might be [found] innocent [of violating the law] by the faith of Christ, and not by performing the carnal commandments of the Law, because no flesh shall be [found] innocent [of violating the Law] by performing the carnal commandments of the Law,

2.17   [Because], even we, [who] seek to be found innocent of violating the Law] by [having faith in the faith of] Christ, are [still] found [to be] sinners in the unconscious part of the mind,

2.18   Because, if I act out my [ungodly thoughts, Christ, my sacrifice for sin in the unconscious part of the mind] dissolves, [and I am found guilty of] violating [the Law],

2.19   And I am dead, because [I exhibited the thoughts that violated] the Law, [which made me a sinner who fell short of the righteousness of] the Law; [But] I, [nevertheless], live for God, [who] crucified [me] to Christ,

2.20   Indeed, I live, but [it is] no longer I; [It is] Christ, the faith of the Son of God, who gave up [his life as Jesus of Nazareth to be] joined to me, who now lives in my flesh,

2.21   [But, Christ does] not negate the undeserved favor of God [that forgives the sins of the First Adam], because, if [the

First Adam can attain to] the righteousness of the Law through [the Holy Spirit], then, [it is] not necessary for Christ to die.*

> * *The Holy Spirit convicts us of sin, a perquisite for us to receive Christ.*

Chapter 3

[26.1]
3.13   Jesus Christ is the price[R-1] that the Father paid to purchase us out of this visible, physical world where we are subject to a law that we cannot keep,[R-2] by fastening him to a dead, mortal mind and physical body[R-3] that subjects him to this cursed age,[R-3] just like the rest of humanity;

[R-1] 1Tim 2:6
[R-2] Gal 13:10
[R-3] Rom 4:15

Because it is written, everyone who is fastened to a dead, mortal mind and physical body, has been prayed into such a weak position by an ungodly spiritual power.

[991.3.C]
3.27   For Christ has put on as a garment, as many as have been baptized into Christ.

Chapter 4

[26.1]
4.04-05 But when the time was right, God sent forth His Son, also under the law, but who through the Spirit of Holiness overcame the curse of spiritual weakness, and after being restored to spiritual power Himself, purchased the living soul that died from Satan, the unconscious part of the carnal mind, and the

Alternate Translation Of The New Testament/ Galatians

price He paid was His own purified soul life which He joined to them.

    4.04   But when the time was right, God sent his Son into this visible, physical world under the same conditions as the rest of humanity, which were subjected to [spiritual] weakness by the Serpent; but

    Jesus, because he was born with the Spirit of Holiness ***in addition to*** a dead, mortal mind and physical body, overcame the curse of spiritual weakness which was in his flesh and,

    After Christ Jesus was restored to spiritual power within himself, he purchased the whole dead, [fallen soul] from Satan by

    Giving up his existence as a mortal man who

    Was converted into a spiritual form that could be

    Grafted to the rest of the members of mortal mankind,

    Who are too weak to overcome Satan,[R] even if the Spirit of Holiness were to be added to them also.

    [R] Gal 6:14

Chapter 5

[688.9.C]
    5.04   The regenerated Adam is ineffective for you who are justified by the Law, because the grace [of God] has changed its course, and

    5.05   We now wait for the hope of [the restoration of our lost] righteousness [which we had] through [our union with the

Alternate Translation Of The New Testament/ Galatians

Holy] Spirit [of the first saved man, the Lord Jesus Christ, who is full well able to awaken the dead Abel, our] faith, and

5.06　　It no longer matters whether you are [physically] circumcised, or not [physically] circumcised, because [we are now reconciled to God through] Christ Jesus, [the male offspring of God that is to be born within us]; what matters [now], is that the faith [of the dead Abel within you] is activated by the [agape] love of God.

Chapter 6

[ ]
　　6.17　　From now on, no one can get close enough to me [in a way that will cause me to sin, which would] cut my body off [from this world, because] I have the mark of Jesus [who] carries away [my sins].

Alternate Translation Of The New Testament/ Ephesians

THE BOOK OF EPHESIANS

Chapter 1

[918.1.C]

The Ransom Price

1.01   To the Saints at Ephesus, and to those who are truly in Christ Jesus, [from] Paul, determined to be an apostle of Christ Jesus by God, and

1.02   [By] the Lord Jesus Christ: May you have peace with God, our Father, [through the intercession of the Shekinah, whose] favor [has supplied] us [with]

1.03   The Lord Jesus Christ, who is worthy of praise, [because] he speaks well of us [who are condemned to death], to God, the Father, and [because God] has rewarded us [with] Christ, a spiritual [advocate]^R in heaven, and

^R 1 Jn 2:1

1.04   Has chosen us [from with]in himself before the [unholy] conception of the world, that we should be an holy and unblemished [shape^R standing] in front of himself, through] the love of God, [which is eternal attachment through the judgment of sins],

^R Jn 5:37

1.05   According to the decree [of God], who determined beforehand that we should be adopted^{R-1} as sons by Jesus Christ, who is delighted to satisfy [us]^{R-2}

^{R-1} Rom 8:15-17
^{R-2} Lk 12:32

Alternate Translation Of The New Testament/ Ephesians

1.06　　With [the Christ child],[R] the concretization [of the Shekinah], the favor of God, (who has highly honored us [by attaching Christ within us to Christ Jesus], the opinion of God, [which is] the love of God),

[R] 2 Cor 4:4

1.07　　Who has ransomed us and forgiven our sins through his blood, [which is delivered to us] by [the Shekinah], the abundant favor [of God],

1.08　　Who [has been given] to all of us [in the form of the Spirit of Truth,[R] which gives us] an excessive amount of spiritual wisdom and intellectual, moral insight,

[R] Jn 15:26

1.09　　So that he can publicly reveal the secret of his kind intentions [towards us, who are called]

1.10　　To deal with the details of completing the ages, by gathering the whole [Adam], both [the Second Adam[R-1] who is] in heaven, and [the First Adam[R-1] who is] in the earth, into one [body] of Christ,[R-2]

[R-1] 1 Cor 15:47
[R-2] Rom 12:5

1.11　　In whom we have been chosen previously, according to the plan of the whole [Adam, whose] active energy works [in this world] according to his own advice,[R] [to accomplish his own] purpose,

[R] Is 63:5

1.12　　[Wherefore], we, who have [Christ Jesus], the opinion of Christ, commend you [who] hope[R] in him before you receive him,

[R] Col 1:27

Alternate Translation Of The New Testament/ Ephesians

1.13 Who were also marked[R-1] with the Holy Spirit of Promise,[R-2] because you believed in Salvation[R-3] when you heard [about it through] the Word of the true Gospel,

[R-1] Ez 9:4
[R-2] Gal 3:14
[R-3] Lam 3:26
1 Thes 5:8

1.14 Which [Holy Spirit] is the security deposit paid in advance, [until we receive Christ, Jesus' male child],[R] the ransom that is our inheritance, paid in full, [in exchange] for [the material bodies that Jesus] acquires through [Christ], the concretization of [the Shekinah, and Christ Jesus], his opinion;

[R] Rev 12:5

1.15 Wherefore, after hearing of your reliance on the Lord Jesus Christ, and also of your Godly love for all the holy ones,

1.16 I thank [God] for you, and mention you in my prayers, continually, [asking]

1.17 That God, the Father, reveal the knowledge of himself [to you by] giving you the Spirit of Wisdom[R] and [Christ Jesus], the opinion of our Lord Jesus Christ,

[R] Is 11:2

1.19 Who is the active energy [of the Lord Jesus Christ] that works to materialize the power of his exceedingly great, [reproductive] force toward those of us who trust him with our spiritual well-being,

1.20 Which [active energy] woke up the Christ [child within Jesus before] he died[R-1] [on the cross, and] was [still] operating within [Jesus] when he set up [Christ Jesus, the Second Adam, who is the Lord] from heaven,[R-2] [as] the right [column of the two columns[R-3] of spiritual authority within the Church],

[R-1] 1 Cor 15:3-4
[R-2] 1 Cor 15:47
[R-3] 2 Chron 3:17

Alternate Translation Of The New Testament/ Ephesians

1.18 [So] that you should be made aware of the vision [of God's plan for you, and] know what to expect from his invitation [to be joined to him through Christ Jesus, and] understand what abundance there is in [having] his opinion, [and understand the mystery of the Christ child]^R, the inheritance of the holy ones, and

^{R} Eph 3:4 (ATB)

1.21 [Now], the [spiritual] government$^{R\text{-}1}$ of the whole [Adam] has authority [over] the miracle working power$^{R\text{-}2}$ of the First [Adam], and [over] every [personal] name [that the First Adam is] called by, not only in this world, but also in the world [that is] about to come into existence,$^{R\text{-}3}$ and

$^{R\text{-}1}$ Is 53:9:6
$^{R\text{-}2}$ Rev 13:14
$^{R\text{-}3}$ Matt 12:32

1.22 [That is why] the whole [Adam was able] to subordinate^R the carnal mind [of the First Adam within Jesus of Nazareth to Christ Jesus], his head, [after which the Lord Jesus Christ] gave himself to be [a ransom] for the whole Church, and

^{R} Rom 1:4

1.23 [Now], the whole [Adam is waiting patiently$^{R\text{-}1}$ for] all [the personal souls of the First Adam to offer up]$^{R\text{-}2}$ the bodies [of the First Adam, so that Christ Jesus, the Second Adam] can satisfy$^{R\text{-}3}$ [them].

$^{R\text{-}1}$ Mk 12:36
$^{R\text{-}2}$ Ps 106:18
Rom 12:1
Rev 19:20, 20:10
$^{R\text{-}3}$ Phil 4:19

Chapter 2

[919.3.C]

One New Man

2.01 [But right now] you are [spiritually] dead,^{R-1} [because] your character flaws have caused you to miss the true meaning of life, [which is a relationship with God],^{R-2} and

^{R-1} Rom 8:10
^{R-2} Jn 17:3

2.02 Because, at one time, according to the ages of this world, you lived your life under the authority of [Satan], the dense, murky spirit that, at this present time, energizes the male children [of God, who] refuse to believe [that they are] the First [Adam],^R and

^R 1 Cor 15:47

2.03 We, also, at some other time, who, like all of you [now], were children [who were] the product of the anger [of God], who desired what is forbidden [to those of] us [who are] in the flesh, [but, nevertheless], satisfied the [evil] inclination of our [carnal] mind [and the lusts of] our flesh;

2.04 But God, who has abundant compassion, and [because of] the great love that he loved us with,

2.05a Even [when] we were dead because of our character flaws, [sent the Shekinah], the favor of God,

2.06a To wake up^R

^R 1 Cor 15:4

2.05b Christ, [the opinion of God, and] join us to his life,

Alternate Translation Of The New Testament/ Ephesians

2.06b [So that when] Christ Jesus, [who is] in heaven, marries[R] [Christ within us],

[R] Rev 19:7

2.05c We shall be saved together [with him],

2.07 That he might show in the ages to come, the exceeding riches of Christ Jesus toward us, through the excellent moral character of [the Shekinah], the favor[R] [of God, who is appearing to us today as the Lord Jesus Christ], and

[R] 2 Tim 4:22

2.08 Because you are saved by [the Christ child, the concretization of the Shekinah], the favor [of God, who] convicts you of the Truth,[R]

[R] Jn 8:46

2.09 Not of works, lest any man should boast, and

2.10 Because we, [the apostles], are the product that [God] manufactured through Christ Jesus, to [do] the good deeds [of teaching and counselling you], that God prepared [for us to do] before [you were saved, so] that you should [learn how] to live [a Godly life];

2.11a Wherefore, you may remember that, previously, when [Christ] was [buried under] the non-Israelite nations, your carnal mind manufactured and preached ignorant and inaccurate spiritual doctrine,

2.12 Because, at that time, you were separated from [the Lord Jesus] Christ, and not participating in the community of Israel, [so] the contracts[R] of promise were foreign to you, [and] you were in the world without any [reason] to expect [anything] from God,

[R] 2 Sam 23:5

2.13 But now, in Christ Jesus, you, who were, previously, distant, are brought near [to God] by the blood of [the] Christ [child], and

Alternate Translation Of The New Testament/ Ephesians

2.11b   [Through] the Mind of Christ, you [now] have the potential to study and understand the secrets [of God, like the Jews do],

2.14   [Because Jesus of Nazareth] dissolved the hostility in his flesh,[R-1] [and] made both [the First Adam and the Second Adam, the two columns of spiritual authority[R-2] within the believer, into one middle column called **Christ Jesus**], the hedge[R-3] [that we enter into to make] our peace [with Jehovah], and

[R-1] Eph 1:22 (ATB)
[R-2] Eph 1:20 (ATB)
[R-3] Jn 1:18

2.15a   Broke up the precepts of the religious dogma [of the Pharisees], rendering them ineffective,

2.16a   That he might reconcile both [Adams] to God by [nailing Christ, Abraham's] single [seed][R] to [his] body,

[R] Gal 3:16

2.15b   To make of the two [Adams], one new Adam,

2.16b   Thereby killing the enmity in his flesh, outright,

2.15c   [Thus], making peace within [Christ Jesus],

2.17   [Who] came [into this world] to preach peace [with God][R] to you who were distant, [as well as to those who] were near [to God],

[R] 2 Cor 5:20

2.18   Because, through [Christ Jesus], we have access, by one Spirit,[R-1] to both the Father [and the Son];[R-2]

[R-1] Jn 10:30
[R-2] 1 Jn 2:23
Eph 3:16 (ATB)

2.19   Therefore, you are now no longer foreigners [who] live near the holy ones, but [are] citizens of the same town, and the relatives of God,

2.22 Through whom you are, also [included], through the [eternal] Spirit, in the construction [of] the dwelling place of God[R]

[R] 2 Sam 7:13
Eph 3:1 (ATB)

2.20 That the apostles and the prophets are rearing up upon the foundation[R-1] of Christ Jesus [and the lord Jesus Christ, who] is the [chief] cornerstone,[R-2]

[R-1] 1 Cor 3:11
[R-2] Matt 21:42
Lk 20:17
1 Pet 2:6-7

2.21 In whom the whole structure is closely joined together, [and] growing into an holy temple[R] in the Lord,

[R] 2 Cor 6:16
Col 2:11

Chapter 3

[920.1.C]

The Christ Child

3.02 And, as you have heard, I have been given [the job of] working out the details [by which the Shekinah], the divine influence[R] of God, [is including]

[R] Heb 10:29

3.01 The non-Israelite nations [in the construction of God's house],[R-1] and that is the reason why I, Paul, am bound[R-2] to Christ Jesus,

[R-1] 2 Sam 7:12-13
Eph 2:22 (ATB)
[R-2] Eph 6:20
Phil 1:14

Alternate Translation Of The New Testament/ Ephesians

3.04   So that you might, intellectually, understand and remember the mystery of [the] Christ [child,[R-1] the concretization of the Shekinah],[R-2]

[R-1] Eph 1:18 (ATB)
[R-2] Eph 2:8

3.03   The mystery [that] I [previously] wrote to you about in lesser detail,[R] [which] was revealed to me by [the Spirit of] Revelation,

[R] 1 Cor 15:51

3.05   [That] the Holy [One] did not make known to the sons of Adam in other ages, [in the same way that] the Spirit [of Revelation][R] is revealing it to the apostles and prophets at this time,

[R] Eph 1:17

3.06   That the Non-Israelite nations should partake of the promises [of the forgiveness of sin,[R-1] and eternal life],[R-2] as equal [members] of the same body of Christ as the Jews, [because of] the good news [that Jesus of Nazareth defeated hell and death],[R-3]

[R-1] Acts 5:31
[R-2] Mk 10:30
[R-3] Eph 4:8

3.07   Which [promises] I am called to dispense [to the non-Israelite nations] as the gift[R-1] of [the Christ child], the concretization of [the Shekinah], by the active energy[R-2] that works [in this world, which] was given to me by God;

[R-1] Rom 5:15
[R-2] Eph 1:11

3.08   [Indeed], this [privilege of] announcing to the non-Israelite nations the good news of the abundant [life, that is in the] Christ [child], the concretization [of the Shekinah], the tracing that the non-existent [One made in the radiant splendor before the worlds were created], was given to me, the least of all the holy [apostles and prophets],

3.09 [To explain] the details of the mystery that is hidden from [the Church in] this age, that the unity of the shining [point and the palace that it created for itself, that became] Elohim, [is the beginning by which] God formed the Whole [Adam] for the sake of[R] Jesus Christ, and

[R] Eph 4:32 (ATB)

3.10 That the Church should find out at this present time that [humanity are] the First [Adam[R-1] who died[R-2] when he separated from Elohim], and that [Satan, the unconscious part of the carnal] mind [of the First Adam, is] authorized by God to enforce[R-3] Jehovah's righteous Sowing & Reaping Judgment, [one of God's] many ways of [teaching us] wisdom [in this world],

[R-1] 1 Cor 15:45
[R-2] 1 Cor 15:22
[R-3] Job 2:6

3.11 [Which] he intends to do, in accordance with his plan for this age, through Christ Jesus, the controller of our [separated soul],

3.12 Through whom we have [received] the confidence to boldly [strive for] admission [to the kingdom of God], because [God has given us] the moral conviction of Christ Jesus;

3.13 Wherefore, I ask that you should not be discouraged [when Leviathan, the subconscious part of your carnal mind, which is] the opinion of [the First Adam], pressures me [to disobey Christ Jesus, the opinion of the Lord Jesus Christ],

3.14 [Because], on account of that [pressure], I submit [Leviathan, the subconscious part of] my own carnal mind, [which is the opinion of the First Adam within me, to Christ Jesus, the subconscious part of my] Christ mind, [who is in submission to] the Father of our Lord Jesus Christ,

3.15 The Name [that signifies] the lineage of the whole [Adam, who is] in heaven, [and] in the earth [of humanity],

Alternate Translation Of The New Testament/ Ephesians

3.16 [Which lineage] gives you the abundance of spiritual power [that] is in [Christ Jesus, the Second] Adam, the opinion [of the Lord Jesus Christ], to empower [Christ Jesus in you], your [new], inner [man,[R-1] to have access] by [one] Spirit,[R-2] [to the Father through Christ Jesus, his Son],[R-3]

[R-1] Eph 4:24
Col 3:10
[R-2] Eph 2:18 (ATB)
[R-3] Jn 5:25

3.17 [So] that the moral conviction of Christ [Jesus, who can stand you] upright, might dwell in your heart [and attach you], through love,[R] to the root [of the Tree of Life],

[R] Col 2:19

3.18 So that the saints might comprehend the unity [of the Shekinah and her palace, which are collectively called], *Elohim*, and the profundity of the width, length and height of the whole [Adam], and

3.19 To make known the wisdom that goes beyond [the letter of the Word, which is] the agape love of [the Lord Jesus] Christ, that you might be filled with the Whole [Adam], the fullness that God completes [us with];

3.20 Indeed, the Whole [Adam], the overflowing abundance from above, is able to do more in us according to the active power of his energy [that works] in this world, than we can ask or comprehend,

3.21 [So that] Christ Jesus, the opinion of the Whole [Adam, may be revealed] through the Church, from age to age, and throughout [all] the ages, so be it!

Chapter 4

[930.1.C]

The Christian Life

4.01   I, the prisoner of the Lord [Jesus Christ], invite you to walk [according to] the lifestyle that the Lord [Jesus Christ] has called [you to],

4.02   Patiently tolerating one another with all of the modesty and humility [that arises out of] the sacrificial love[R] [of the Lord Jesus Christ],

[R] 1 Cor 13:3-8

4.03   Making [every] effort to [implement] the uniting principle of peace[R-1] to guard the unity of the Spirit,[R-2]

[R-1] Heb 12:14
[R-2] Ps 133:1

4.04   [Because you and the brethren who are] invited to your calling, [are] one [spiritual] body[R-1] and one Spirit,[R-2] and you all have the same confidence, [that there is only]

[R-1] Rom 12:5
[R-2] Eph 2:18
Phil 1:27

4.05   One Lord,[R-1] one [true] moral conviction[R-2] and one baptism, and

[R-1] 1 Cor 8:6
[R-2] Jn 14:6

Alternate Translation Of The New Testament/ Ephesians

4.06　　One God[R-1] [who is] the Father[R-2] of the whole [Adam], and [God], who is above[R-3] the whole [Adam is also] in all[R-3] [the members] of the whole [Adam], through [him], and

[R-1] Deut 6:4
1 Cor 8:6
[R-2] 2 Cor 1:3
[R-3] 1 Cor 12:6
Eph 1:23

4.07　　Every one of us is given a degree of the divine influence in accordance with the gift[R] [that comes from the] Christ [child within us];

[R] Eph 3:7

4.08　　Consequently, [the Scripture] says, [the soul that was] imprisoned [within the material body of Jesus of Nazareth overcame] her jailer[R-1] and ascended[R-2] into heaven [with the Supernal Mother, after which the Second Adam returned to earth and] gave gifts[R-3] to [the First] Adam;

[R-1] 1 Cor 15:55
[R-2] Rom 10:6
[R-3] 1 Cor 12:4

4.09　　Indeed, [Jesus' soul] would not have ascended if Elohim had not first descended[R] into the inferior parts of the earth, and

[R] Lk 2:11

4.10　　He that descended is the same [Elohim] that also ascended up above all[R] the powers [of the created world], that he might [pour out of his Spirit upon all flesh], to fill up all [of the members of the Second Adam with his life], and

[R] Phil 2:9

4.11　　He affirmed some [of them to be] apostles, some [of them to be] prophets, some [of them to be] evangelists, [and some [of them to be] teaching pastors,

Alternate Translation Of The New Testament/ Ephesians

4.12 For the complete equipping of the saints for official service, and for [the establishment] of the [governmental]^R structure of the body of Christ,

^{R} Is 9:7
Rom 13:1-3

4.13 Until we all come to the moral conviction that [God] is a unity,$^{R-1}$ and the knowledge that the son of God is the perfect male,$^{R-2}$ [that we might attain to the same] degree of [spiritual] maturity [that Jesus attained to when] Christ [Jesus] fills us up,$^{R-3}$

$^{R-1}$ Mk 12:32
$^{R-2}$ Lk 13:32
$^{R-3}$ Eph 3:19

4.14 [So] that we should not be simpleminded or immature^{R-1} anymore, or waver [in our opinion concerning] the spiritual doctrine of [the First] Adam, [who] unscrupulously [and] methodically plots to deceive [us];$^{R-2}$

$^{R-1}$ Matt 11:16
Lk 7:32
$^{R-2}$ Col 2:8
Jude 4

4.15 Indeed [we should be] speaking the truth^{R-1} in the sacrificial love^{R-2} [of the Lord Jesus Christ], that we might increase into the whole [Adam], who is the head of Christ [Jesus],

$^{R-1}$ Col 3:9
$^{R-2}$ 1 Cor 13:3-8

4.16 Out of whom the whole body [of Christ] is correctly joined together, by the ligaments of the whole Adam, [which] force [the First Adam],$^{R-1}$ by the active power [of God] that operates in this world, to unite [under his authority], to the degree that every part of the body [of Christ] increases in the sacrificial love [of the Lord Jesus Christ, until the governmental] structure of [the Second Adam] is formed^{R-2} [in them];

$^{R-1}$ 1Cor 15:47
$^{R-2}$ Gal 419

4.17a I am telling you with certainty, and testify to you, that [when Christ Jesus dwells in you], you will no longer live the depraved lifestyle^R of the other non-Israelite nations who

Alternate Translation Of The New Testament/ Ephesians

follow after [Leviathan, the subconscious part of] the carnal mind [of the First Adam,

^R Col 3:7

4.18a   Who] has blinded^R their understanding, and

^R 2 Cor 4:4

4.19a   They have become apathetic towards the whole [Adam], and

4.18b   Are not participating in the life of God, because of [that same] ignorance which has [also] hardened their heart,^R and

^R Rom 2:29 (ATB)

4.19b   They have surrendered themselves to sexual excess and avarice, and occupy themselves with physical and moral impurity,^R

^R Col 3:5

4.20a   But you,

4.17b   Who occupy the middle [column]^R of the Lord [Jesus Christ]

^R Eph 2:14

4.20b   Have not learned this from Christ [Jesus];

4.21   Indeed, you who have been taught the truth [that] Jesus [taught us], have heard this from [Leviathan, the subconscious part of the carnal mind of the First Adam];

4.22   So renounce the behavior of the old Adam [who] longs for that which is forbidden,^{R-1} and the delusion [of unhappiness] will waste away;^{R-2}

^{R-1} Col 3:5
^{R-2} 1 Jn 2:17

4.23   Indeed, renovate your spirit [by developing] your intellect, and

Alternate Translation Of The New Testament/ Ephesians

4.24 Be the clothing of the new Adam, who is morally innocent [concerning] holiness and truth, when compared to [Jesus Christ, God's standard], and

4.25 By doing that you will stop lying, [so] let everyone speak the truth to his neighbor and let us [sacrificially love][R-1] one another, because we are the limbs[R-2] of [Christ Jesus];

[R-1] 1 Cor 13:3-8
[R-2] Eph 5:30

4.26 So do not become enraged or exasperated, [which is] the sin [of pride, because], your rage will cause the sun [of Christ Jesus, your moral soul][R] to set, and [he will] go down [under the authority of [Leviathan, the subconscious part of] the carnal mind [of the First Adam];

[R] Mal 4:2

4.27 Neither give the Devil[R] a place [in your thoughts];

[R] Rev 20:2

4.28 Let the thief stop stealing[R-1] but rather let him experience the fatigue that comes from the hard work[R-2] of laboring at an occupation, and let his hands do the good [deeds] of giving to the destitute; [R-3]

[R-1] Ex 20:15
[R-2] 1 Thes 4:11
[R-3] Mk 10:21

4.29 Let no worthless communication [come] out of your mouth, but let [only] good [words] be discharged [from your mouth], which build the structure [of the government of the Second Adam], so that [your words] on that occasion might deliver the divine influence to those who can hear you, and

4.30 Do not be sad,[R-1] [because] the Holy Spirit of God [is a spiritual] sign [that] saves you [from Satan, the enforcer of the Sowing & Reaping Judgment], until the day [that the Christ

Alternate Translation Of The New Testament/ Ephesians

child], the ransom[R-2] [that the Second Adam is paying to the First Adam, is born in you], and

[R-1] 2 Thes 2:13
[R-2] Eph 1:7-14
Col 1:14

4.31   Let all bitterness [that perpetuates the pain of past hurts, and passion [that destabilizes your] emotions, and mental anger [that tempts you to plan vengeful acts], and public expressions of grief [that manipulate others to take vengeance on your behalf], and vilifying words [that curse the one that you are angry at, as well as their progeny], all [of which arise out of] the immoral character [of the First Adam], be removed from you, and

4.32   Be kind to one another, and full of compassion, forgiving one another, even as God, for the sake of [Jesus] Christ,[R] has forgiven you.

[R] Eph 3:9 (ATB)

Chapter 5

[931.2.C]

The Christian Life (Con't)

5.01   Be like the beloved children of God, [who] are following the example [of the Lord Jesus Christ], and

5.02   Let your lifestyle [reflect] the sacrificial love [of the Lord Jesus] Christ, even as he sacrificed [the First Adam, his other self, out of obedience] to God, [after which sacrifice] the sweet smelling odour [of the Shekinah] attached [his seed to our human spirit, thereby] giving his [holy child] to us, [to be] the living concretization of [the Shekinah within us],

Alternate Translation Of The New Testament/ Ephesians

5.03 But harlotry, adultery and incest, and physical and mental impurity, or the love of money, [are] all [sins which] are not suitable to even mention among the holy ones [of God];

5.04 Neither [are] obscenities, nor deceptive, or licentious, or irreverent speech, fit or proper, but, rather, [you should be] giving thanks,

5.05 Because you [should] know this, that any[one who is] a male prostitute, or any person that is defiled, or anyone who is greedy enough to defraud someone to enrich himself, which is idolatry, has no inheritance in the Kingdom of Christ, and of God;

5.06 [So] let no one delude you with empty words, because these are the things that bring punishment upon the unbelieving, obstinate and rebellious children of God;

5.07 Therefore, do not participate [in these attitudes and behaviors],

5.08 Because, [even though] there were times when you were [living like the First Adam, out of] the shadiness[R] [of the animal nature of the corporeal body, you are now living out of] the Light [that is] in the Lord [Jesus Christ, so walk] as [if] you were the children of [the Whole Adam, the one who carries] the Light [of God],

[R] Verse 11

5.09 Because the good character of [the Christ child], the fruit of the whole Adam, the Light bearer, is the moral equivalent of the Spirit of Truth;

5.10 So test [this] Elohim [that is in me, to see if Christ Jesus], the Lord [in you],[R] will accept him, and

[R] Matt 22:44-45

5.11 Do not participate in the shady lifestyle[R] [of the animal nature of the corporeal body, because it is] incapable of producing a [spiritual] child, [the ransom price that will liberate

Alternate Translation Of The New Testament/ Ephesians

you from the First Adam, who is enslaving you], but, rather, prove them to be wrong,

^R Verse 8 → rendered as: **R** Verse 8

5.12   Because it is shameful to even speak of those things which are done in secret;

5.13   Indeed, the whole [Adam], the Light [bearer], reveals all of those things to be wrong, and [Satan, the enforcer of the Sowing & Reaping Judgment], proves [to the sinners in Israel] what the Light [bearer] makes apparent;

5.14   Wherefore, [the Lord Jesus Christ] says, [let the Christ child that] is sleeping [within you] wake up,[R-1] [and let the Second Adam] enlighten you [through him], and let [the First Adam who] died [in the previous age] stand up again;[R-2]

[R-1] 1Cor 15:4
[R-2] Col 2:15

5.15   [So], see [to it], then, that you do not follow an unwise lifestyle, but live according to the wisdom [of the Scripture],

5.16   Because it is time for [the Christ child], the ransom [for the king's] doe, [who] married [the Snake, to be paid];

5.17   [So], avoid being ignorant [and] choose the thing [that] the Lord [Jesus Christ would choose, which] joins [you to the Shekinah, so that] Elohim [can appear in you], and

5.18   Be not intoxicated with wine, [because whoever is in] such a condition, is not saved, but be filled with the Spirit, and

5.19   Sing hymns and spiritual songs [from your] heart, [which] stimulate [Christ Jesus, the opinion of] the Lord [Jesus Christ], your [other] self, to speak to you in psalms, and

5.20   Be grateful at all times in the Name of our Lord Jesus Christ, for the Whole [Adam], and for God, [his] Father,

Alternate Translation Of The New Testament/ Ephesians

5.21   Submitting yourselves to Christ [Jesus] in one another, in the fear of God;

5.22   Wives, submit yourselves to your own husbands as [you submit yourselves to], the Lord Jesus Christ,

5.23   Because the man is the head of the wife, even as [the] Christ [child] is the head of the Church and the savior of the [corporeal] body;

5.24   On the other hand, [however], the woman's own husband [is subordinate to] the Whole [Adam within the woman], as the Church is subordinate to [the] Christ [child];

5.25   [So], husbands, love your wives [with the sacrificial love of God], even as also [the Lord Jesus] Christ [so] loved the Church [that he gave the First Adam, his other self, as a burnt offering,^R which sacrifice resulted in the Shekinah] giving [Christ, his holy child to us, to be the living concretization of herself],

^R 2 Pet 3:10

5.26   That he might cleanse and purify [us through] the baptism of immersion in the water [of the Holy Spirit, and] by the Word [of God], and

5.27   That he might recommend to his Church that they should [cling to] the unchangeable mindset of Christ Jesus], his opinion, [rather than the opinion of Leviathan, the subconscious part of the carnal mind of the First Adam, so that] they should be [found] without any moral stain and wholly unblemished;

5.28   [The male whose inner man is the Second Adam], sacrificially loves his wife [by burning the First Adam within himself, but the male whose inner man is the First Adam], his other self, loves the separated soul of] his own corporeal body, [which is the First Adam. Wherefore], males [who desire to overcome the First Adam within themselves], ought to sacrificially love their wives,

262

Alternate Translation Of The New Testament/ Ephesians

5.30   [Because], we are the limbs of the flesh and bone corporeal body [of Christ], and

5.29   No one [whose inner man is the Second Adam], ever, at any time, hated his own flesh, [but follows the example of] the Lord [Jesus Christ, who] nurtured [Christ after] he woke up, until he was mature [enough to stand up again after his body died], and

5.31   This is the reason why [the Second] Adam, shall separate from [Jehovah], his father, and [the Shekinah], his mother, and be joined to [Christ within] the flesh of the woman, to unify the two Adams;

5.32   I am speaking about a great mystery, indeed, concerning Christ and the Church;

5.33   Nevertheless, every one of you [males], in particular, [should resist the ungodly attributes of the First Adam, and] sacrificially love your wife like [Christ] sacrificially loves [you, his other] self; and the wife should be afraid [to overthrow the authority of] the male, [because the end of such folly is destruction].

Chapter 6

[963.4.C]
6.01   Children, obeying your parents in the Lord[R] is equal to the moral standard of the character of God,
                                                [R] Rom 13:1

6.02a   [So, make] the First [Adam within you] revere [the Lord Jesus Christ], your father, [and the Shekinah], your mother,[R] because they have the authority to assure you of
                                                [R] Ex 20:12

Alternate Translation Of The New Testament/ Ephesians

6.03　　A long life in the earth, with good [experiences, through Christ,^R

^R Prov 10:22-23

6.02b　　God's] divine prescription [that cures death].^R

^R Ps 56:13
1 Jn 5:11

To The Fathers

6.04　　Fathers, do not [make it so difficult for] your children [to please you that] they become exasperated [trying], but teach them [about the First Adam^{R-1} and how] to discipline [Satan],^{R-2} the unconscious [part of their carnal mind, and, *then*], call attention to their faults.

^{R-1} 1 Cor 15:47
^{R-2} Eph 3:10

To Employees

6.05　　Employees, subordinate yourselves to the authorities who have legitimate rule over you, and be alarmed [at the possibility of] Christ [Jesus], the single column^R [of God's merciful corrective judgment] in your heart, [separating into the First Adam, the left hand of God, and the Second Adam, the right hand of God, because Satan, the unconscious part of the carnal mind of the First Adam, the left hand of God, enforces Jehovah's righteous Sowing & Reaping Judgment, without mercy];

^R Matt 6:22

SPIRITUAL MARRIAGE

Conjugal Responsibility OF The Saints

6.06　　[So, do] not agree with the soul [of the First] Adam [who] serves Christ [by] *appearing* to do the will of God,^R

^R Jn 8:34
Jas 1:15

Alternate Translation Of The New Testament/ Ephesians

6.07a [But perform the spiritual] conjugal duty^R [that is due to Christ Jesus], the Lord in the midst of you,

^R 1 Cor 7:5

6.08a Knowing that every person, whether they are enslaved [by the First Adam], or unrestrained [through a relationship with Christ Jesus], the Lord, [who] does that good thing [of engaging in spiritual sexual intercourse with Christ Jesus]

6.07b Cannot be enslaved by [the First] Adam,^R

^R Jn 8:34
Rom 3:9
Rom 7:14

Christ Jesus' Responsibility To Provide

6.08b [Because Christ Jesus, the Second Adam], provides [them with everything that they need],^R and

^R Phil 4:19

6.09 [Because Satan], the unconscious [part of the carnal] mind [of the First Adam], knows that you have the authority to stop [her] from menacing^{R-1} [you, and to warn Leviathan], the subconscious [part of the carnal] mind [of the First Adam], not to do it either, [and Satan] the unconscious [part of your carnal] mind, [also knows that] you have authority over [her^{R-2} because] you are joined to [the Lord Jesus Christ, who is] in heaven, and,

^{R-1} Jn 10:10
^{R-2} Rom 16:20
Mal 4:3

JESUS' LIFE FORCE

The Blood

6.10 Finally, my blood brothers,^R be enabled in [Christ Jesus], the Lord, and in the mighty working of his [life]force

^R Acts 17:26

Alternate Translation Of The New Testament/ Ephesians

Full Immersion

6.11   To immerse yourselves[R] in the full body armor of God, that you might be able to stand against the deceit of the First Adam,

[R] 1 Cor 12:13

THE EVIL INFLUENCE

6.12   Because, [in order for the Second Adam] to exist [within you, you must] wrestle[R] with Satan, [the unconscious part of the carnal mind of the First Adam, the evil] authority [that emerged from] the soul of the First [Adam, after he seized the reproductive part of the creation, and formed] the flesh [vessels] that the shades, the spiritual depravity [that dwells in the world] above the sky, [are appearing in, in] this age;

[R] Col 2:15
Rev 20:2

THE MAN OF SIN

6.13a   Wherefore, resist the evil influence [of Satan, the unconscious part of the carnal mind of the First Adam[R-1] who] opposes . . .

CHRIST, THE DAYLIGHT

. . . [Christ] standing up [in you, and you will see the First Adam in] the day[light],[R-2] and when [the Christ child] is taken up,[R-3] the whole [body of Christ]

[R-1] 2 Thess 2:4
[R-2] 1 Cor 15:4
1 Cor 4:5
2 Cor 4:2
[R-3] Rev 12:5

TRUTH, THE SINLESS ENERGY

6.14   Will stand up [also]: Therefore, surround the generative parts [of your soul with the Spirit of] Truth, and [let

Alternate Translation Of The New Testament/ Ephesians

Christ in the midst of you be fully] immersed[R-1] [in the sinless energy of the Lord Jesus Christ, that the rings of power in] your chest [might be filled with that sinless energy that makes your character][R-2] equal to the character of God,[R-3] and

[R-1] 1 Cor 12:13
[R-2] 2 Cor 3:3
[R-3] 1 Cor 2:9
Rom 3.21a-3.22a (ATB)

6.13b   [Then] do

6.16   What is more important than anything that you have already done:

CHRIST JESUS, OUR MORALITY

Take up [the moral conviction of Christ Jesus,[R-1] which] extinguishes the evil influence [of the First Adam who] ignites [ungodly passions within you, and] shields you from all [of Satan's] arrows,[R-2] and

[R-1] Eph 4:31
Col 3:5
[R-2] Prov 26:18

ONE NEW MAN

6.15   Prepare the First Adam [to understand] the good news[R-1] about peace [with God[R-2] by first] binding him under [the authority of Christ Jesus, the Second Adam within you], and

[R-1] Eph 3:10
[R-2] Lk 2:14
2 Cor 5:20

THE HUMAN SPIRIT RESCUED

6.17 [After that], take up the Word of God, [which is the substance of Ancient Adam[R-1] who can] save[R-2] [the fallen human spirit that became Satan], the Sword of the Spirit,[R-3] and

[R-1] Dan 7:9
Acts 17:28
[R-2] Acts 4:12
[R-3] Ps 17:13

PRAYER FOR THE SAINTS

6.18 Pray always with prayerful petitions [for] everyone [who is] not in the Spirit [of Christ, the unconscious part of the Christ mind of the Second Adam], and, in all persistence, petition [God on behalf of] all the holy ones who are asleep,[R-1] [that], at the proper time, [Christ], the subconscious part of the [Christ mind of the Second Adam, should wake up[R-2] in them also], and

[R-1] 1 Thes 5:6-10
[R-2] 1 Cor 15:34
1 Cor 15:34 (ATB)

PRAYER FOR PAUL

6.19a That I may be given the opportunity to speak, and that, [when given that opportunity, that the Lord Jesus Christ] might open my mouth [and enable me to speak] boldly, and

6.20a That [the First Adam] might not interfere with [the discourse of the Lord Jesus Christ, when] he speaks from the unconscious part of my Christ mind

6.19b To make the mystery of the good news[R] understood,

[R] Lk 2:14

Alternate Translation Of The New Testament/ Ephesians

20b   For which [purpose the Lord Jesus Christ, our] elder [brother, has put the First Adam] in chains.^R

^R Ps 149:8
Vs 15 (ATB)
Matt 12:29

IN PAUL'S STEAD

6.21   [I have] [sent] Tychicus, a beloved brother and faithful minister in the Lord, to tell you how I am doing, so that you may know everything about me, and also

RECONCILED TO GOD

6.22   So that you might know [Tychicus], whom I have sent, so that [the Lord Jesus Christ, who is in] the unconscious part of our [mind], might call to [Christ, who is in] your heart, to come near [to God].

6.23   Peace to the blood brothers [of the Lord Jesus Christ] and [to Christ Jesus], the moral conviction in the midst of us, [from] God [the Father], who sacrificed* the Lord Jesus Christ [so that] he, [the Father], could be attached to [us].

> *The Father sacrificed, gave up, the use of Jesus Christ as a vessel that he could express himself through in the World of Action, because he preferred that Jesus' soul that overcame death should be shared with the rest of humanity. God abhors human sacrifice, and condemned Israel, his own people, over and over again because of this evil practice. Jesus is not a human or blood sacrifice that replaced animal sacrifices. It is Jesus' Spiritual Blood that lives in the hearts of many today in the form of Christ.*

6.24   May the divine influence [of the Shekinah and] the sacrificial love of our Lord Jesus Christ, [who are joined together] in an unending existence, be with [you] all.

THE BOOK OF PHILIPPIANS

Chapter 1

[242.1]
    1.21   When we die [to our Carnal Mind] we gain Christ.

Chapter 2

[1246.15.C]
    2.05   Let this mind^R be in you, which was also in Christ Jesus,

                                      ^{R} 1 Cor 2:16

    2.06a   Who did not plan, beforehand to seize [Jesus of Nazareth],

    2.07a   To disguise himself to look like [a man who] resembled Adam,^{R}

                                        ^{R} Gen 1:26

    2.06b   To come into existence as a [single] form of Elohim [that would] be equal to [the Name] Elohim^R [in heaven],

                                        ^{R} Gen 1:26

    2.08a   [But, rather], humbled himself,

    2.07b   And came into existence as a servant^R [of Jehovah],

                                        ^{R} Jn 8:35

2.08b   Submissive to the point of death, even the death of being [nailed to] a stake,^R and,

^R Matt 27:35

2.09   Consequently, Elohim has given him a Name [that is] higher [than the names of] all [the angels] ^{R-1} in the unconscious part of the mind, for the benefit of all [the souls that have the mark of his] Name,^{R-2}

^{R-1} Heb 1:6
^{R-2} Gal 6:17
Ez 9:4

2.10   [To the end] that every knee should bow at the Name of *Jesus*, [the angels in] heaven,^{R-1} [the angels attached to] the earth[en personalities^{R-2} of humanity, and the angels in prison] under^{R-3} the earth[en personalities],

^{R-1} Matt 22:30
^{R-2} Acts 12:15
^{R-3} 1 Pet 3:19

2.11   And that every tongue should confess that Jehovah [is] the Father^{R-1} of Jesus Christ, [who is] the opinion^{R-2} of Elohim,

^{R-1} Rom 15:6
^{R-2} Rom 3:23

Chapter 3

[1261.5.C]
3.01   Finally, brethren, I am not writing to you because you are lazy
   [in the work of] overthrowing [the First Adam in] the unconscious part of the mind,
   [I am writing to encourage you] to be happy in the Lord [while you are overthrowing him,

3.02 By being aware of [ungodly motives and thoughts that,
   Like] wild dogs that do not have a master, [roam freely in the unconscious part of the mind];
   Be aware of the injurious [doctrines of false] teachers;
   Be aware of [the Jews, who want to circumcise you only because] they are circumcised,
 3.03 Because we, who worship God in the Spirit,
   Boast in Christ Jesus, [rather than our own abilities], and
   Are not persuaded [by any strength we may have in] the flesh,
   Are [the ones who are truly] circumcised,
3.04 But, if anyone thinks that [they have reason] to trust in [their own] ability,
   I [have more reason than they do];
   Indeed, I have [good reason] to persuade [myself that
   All of my accomplishments come from my own] ability, [because]
3.05 [I am] of the stock of Israel, ^R

^R Rom 11:24

   Of the tribe of Benjamin,
   Circumcised on the eighth day,
   An Hebrew of Hebrews,
   Concerning the law, a Pharisee;
3.06 I was blameless concerning the righteousness of the Law, and
   [I was such] a fanatic that] I persecuted the Church [because they rejected the Law], ^R

^R Acts 7:58-8:1
1 Cor 15:9

3.07 But [I was willing] to lose the things that were important to me [because] I profited [from them],
   For [the character of] Christ;
3.08a Yes, indeed, I am willing to lose everything for the knowledge of Christ Jesus, my Lord,
   [Who is Adam from] above, for whom I have lost everything,
3.09 [Since] I found out [that] I am unrighteous,

[Because any righteousness that I may have comes from] the Law, but,
[On the other hand, that] I do have the righteousness that comes from God,
By faith, which is the faith of Christ,
3.08b But I consider [the things that I lost as worthless as] dog feces,
[In the hope that] I might acquire [the character of] Christ,
3.10 That I may know him, intimately, in the unconscious part of the mind, and
[Know] the power by which [the First] Adam [who died] stood up again, [R-1]
In the unconscious part of the mind, and
To share in his sufferings in the unconscious part of the mind,
[That] I might experience a similar death [to that of Jesus of Nazareth], [R-1]

[R-1] 1 Cor 15:4
[R-2] 1 Cor 15:20

3.11 [That], somehow, I might experience the dead [Adam] standing up [in me again also],
3.12 Not as though I had already received [the dead Adam standing up in me],
Or were already completely mature,
[But] I pursue [the resurrection of the dead Adam within me], [R]

[R] 1 Cor 15:20-22

So that I might seize Christ Jesus, [who] is [himself], pursuing me [for the same purpose,
[That he might stand up in me also];
3.13 Brethren, I do not consider myself to have [already] seized [Christ Jesus],
Or to be unified [with him],
But looking back [at how far I have come], I concede [that it is better], indeed, [that]
My personality should [continue to pursue the character of Christ, rather than] turn back, and

3.14   [That is why I have accepted] God's invitation to pursue the prize, [which is] Christ Jesus,
      [Who is Adam from] above;
3.15   Therefore, let as many of us as would [like] to be completely mature have this[same] mindset;
      But if any have a different mindset, God shall reveal this [truth] to you also,
3.16-17 [Because anyone who desires to be completely mature must] follow the rule,
      Which [is] to be mentally disposed [towards
      Christ] coming into existence [in] the unconscious part of the mind,
       And since] you have us for an example, brethren, take notice of how I walk, and
      Let us walk together [into the Age of Christ Jesus],
      Except that [we have] already attained to the Holy Spirit, [in] the unconscious part of the mind,
3.18   Because, as I have told you often, sobbing,
      Many [of the brethren that] the Holy Spirit walks around in, are enemies of the cross of Christ,
3.19   [Because they continue to hold] the female opinion in the unconscious part of the mind,
      [Despite the presence of Christ, who raises their soul] above
      The earth[en, animal soul that is unable] to rein in [the lusts of]
      The god [of] the womb [of creation, which] souls will be
      Destroyed by Elohim at the end [of the age];
3.20   But, we are citizens of heaven, and look for
      Our Saviour, the Lord Jesus Christ, [who] is from Elohim,
3.21   Who shall change this body that is humiliating for [Christ Jesus to dwell in],
      From one state to another, until it is] like the body [formed from]
      The energy [that] comes down from the opinion of [Christ Jesus]
      In the unconscious part of the mind,

By which [energy Christ Jesus] is able to put [all the souls that form his body]
In the correct moral order.

THE BOOK OF COLOSSIANS

Chapter 1

[917.1.C]

The Christ Child

Greetings and Salutations

    1.02a   To the Saints and the faithful brethren in Christ at Colosse:

    1.01   [From] Paul, an apostle of Christ Jesus by the will of God, and Timothy, our brother,

    1.02b   Salvation, favor and peace with God, the Father of our Lord Jesus Christ, to you.

    1.03   We give thanks to God, the Father of our Lord Jesus Christ, [and are] praying for you always,

The Church at Colossae

    1.04   Since we heard of your faith in Christ Jesus, and

Alternate Translation Of The New Testament/ Colossians

1.05 That you are expecting what is laid up[R-1] for you in heaven, [based upon what] you heard in the Message of the Gospel of Truth,[R-2]

[R-1] 2 Tim 4:8
[R-2] Jn 15:26
Jn 16:13
1 Jn 4:6

1.06 Which is come to you, and is bringing forth fruit [in you],[R-1] and is increasing [in you],[R-2] as well as [increasing] in all the world since the day [that] you [first] heard [it], and became acquainted with the favor of God [that one receives when he acquires a knowledge of] the Truth,[R-3]

[R-1] Jn 15:5, 8
[R-2] 2 Cor 10:15
[R-3] 1 Tim 2:4

1.07 [Which message] you also learned of Epaphras, our dear fellow servant, who is a faithful servant of [the] Christ [child][R] for you, and

[R] Acts 4:30

1.08 [Epaphras] also declared your sacrificial love for us [who are] in the Spirit, and

1.04b The sacrificial love that you have for all of the holy ones, and

Prayer For The Colossians

1.09 This is also the reason why we have not ceased from praying for you since the day that we heard of your desire to be filled with the knowledge of his Will, and the [spiritual] wisdom[R] and spiritual understanding [that come from] the Whole Adam,

[R] Verse 1:28

1.10 That your lifestyle might be worthy[R] of [Christ Jesus], the Lord, [dwelling in you, and that you might be] in compliance with everything [that God requires for] you to be fruitful, and to increase in the knowledge of God with every good deed [that you do], and

R Eph 4:1

1.11   To be strengthened by the [spiritual] government[R-1] of the Whole [Adam], according to the miracle working power [that arises out of] his opinion, [which results in] the endurance[R-2] and fortitude of the Whole [Adam appearing in you;

[R-1] Is 9:6
[R-2] Rev 13:10
Rev 14:12

Paul's Credentials

1.12   Wherefore], we express our gratitude to the Father, who has qualified us to participate in the opportunities [that are available to] the holy ones [who are] illuminated,

1.13   Who has rescued us from the authority of [the First Adam,[R-1] the principality[R-2] that rules over] the corporeal body, [by whom] we are transferred into the Kingdom of [Jesus Christ],[R-3] his beloved Son,[R-4]

[R-1] 1 Cor 15:47
[R-2] Verse 2:15
[R-3] Rev 1:9
[R-4] Lk 3:22

The Christ Child

1.14   [Through the effusion of] the blood[R-1] [of the Christ child],[R-2] the ransom[R-3] [that] pardons our sins,

[R-1] Heb 9:22
[R-2] Rev 12:5
[R-3] 1 Tim 2:15

1.15   Who is the firstborn[R-1] of the whole creature, the image[R-2] of the invisible God, and [the part of]

[R-1] Rev 1:5
[R-2] 2 Cor 4:4

1.16a   The Whole [Adam that is in the earth, who consists of

   (1) The First Adam

1.18   Who] died [in the previous age, and

   (2) The Christ child] who is the beginning,^R-1 and the head of the body,^R-2 the Church of the Firstborn of [the Supernal Mother];

^R-1 Rev 22:13
^R-2 1 Cor 11:21-30

Ancient Adam

1.17a   [But, the Ancient One]^R came before the Whole [Adam,

^R Dan 7:9, 13, 22

1.16b   Who exists] in heaven and in the earth, invisible and visible;

   Everything was created through Ancient [Adam, and] was created for him, and [came into existence] after him, including, thrones, or rulers, or elites, and

1.17b   The Whole [Adam] is sustained by [Ancient Adam, so Ancient Adam] has a rank [that is] higher than [the rank of] the Whole [Adam], and

1.19   [Ancient Adam] approves of the Whole [Adam] residing [within humanity], permanently,^R

^R Mk 10:30

1.20   Through [the Christ child, who] reconciles the Whole [Adam], whether [it is] this [First] Adam in the earth, or this [Second] Adam in heaven, to himself, making peace [between the two Adams],^R by setting [the First Adam] upright by [the effusion] of his blood, and

^R Eph 2:15

Alternate Translation Of The New Testament/ Colossians

Reconciliation

1.21a   You, [who] were sometimes estranged [from God] because of [Satan], the adversary[R-1] in [the unconscious part of] the [carnal] mind[R-2] of

[R-1] 1 Zech 3:2
Pet 5:8
[R-2] Rom 8:7

1.22   Your flesh body, have indeed, been reconciled [to God]

1.21b   Through the death[R-1] [of the First Adam, the one who influenced you to do] evil deeds, [so that the Second Adam[R-2] can] present your [soul to God], holy, unblemished and free of any legal charge,[R-3] as far as [God] is concerned,

[R-1] 1 Cor 15:47
[R-2] Rom 6:3
[R-3] Zech 3:1-2
Rom 8:33

1.23   **IF** you continue [to stand] erect and immovable in your conviction [of the Truth of] the Gospel that you have heard ([which] was preached to the whole creation under heaven, of which I, Paul, am made a servant), and not be moved away from anticipating [the realization of these promises in your lives; and

Exposure of Sin

1.24   This is the reason why I am happy] to supply you with what you lack [to be spiritually] well-off, [despite] the [mental and spiritual] pressure and physical hardships that I have suffered [from] exposing [your sin nature for your own benefit;

But I have, nevertheless, ministered to you] for the sake of [Christ's] body,[R] which is the Church,

[R] 1 Cor 11:29-30

1.25a   Of which I am made a servant for the purpose of administering that which was given to me, to fill you up

Alternate Translation Of The New Testament/ Colossians

The Mystery of God

1.26a   [With] the mystery of

1.25b   The Word of God[R]

[R] Rev 19:13

1.26b   That has been kept a secret from the generations of the ages,[R] which now, indeed, is made apparent to his holy ones

[R] Lk 10:24

God's Opinion

1.27   By [the indwelling] Christ [child], through whom God is willing to make known his valuable opinion, which is hidden from the Gentiles;

[So you have] reason to expect the opinion [of God to appear] in you [also],

1.28a   To remind [the members of] the Whole Adam [how to relate to] everyone [as Jesus would relate to them], and [to enable them] to teach[R-1] the spiritual wisdom[R-2] of the Whole Adam, whom we preach, and

[R-1] Verse 3:16b
[R-2] Verse 1:9

Paul's Goal

1.29   [This], also, [is the reason why] I labor, striving by the active energy [of Christ Jesus within me], which is the miracle working power [of God],

1.28b   So that we may present everyone [to God], complete[R] in Christ Jesus.

[R] Col 2:10

Chapter 2

[917.2.C]

The New Life

<u>The Great Assembly</u>

2.01 Wherefore, it is my desire for you and for them at Laodicea, and for as many as have not seen my face in the flesh, to know [about] the Great Assembly that I am possessed of, [even the Father and the Son],**R**

R 1 Jn 2:23

2.02a That all [of you] might be invited [to have] your hearts united together with [the Lord Jesus Christ],**R** the Son of God,

R 1 Cor 6:17
Verse 2.19

2.03 In whom are all the hidden secrets of wealth,**R-1** [which come from] a knowledge [of Ancient Adam,**R-2** the one who made us], and [his] spiritual wisdom, [which is the Word of God],**R-3** and

R-1 Ps 112:3
R-2 Verse 3:10
2 Pet 1:3
R-3 Verse 3:16
Heb 11:13
Rev 19:13

2.02b [Which should make] you entirely confident that [you will experience] an abundance of the sacrificial love [of the assembled Father and the Son,

IF] you recognize [that Christ Jesus, within me, is] the Father**R** of [the] Christ [child within you], and [that you need me], this [other] Father, [to help you] to understand the mystery of God;

R Js 1:18

An Orderly Lifestyle

2.04a   I am saying this

2.05   Because, even though I am absent in the flesh, I am, nevertheless, with you, rejoicing in the Spirit, to see your orderly [lifestyle],**R** and [the mental and emotional] stability that your faith in [the] Christ [child has produced in you];

R 1 Cor 14:40

2.06   Therefore, now that you have received Christ Jesus, the Lord,**R** and

R Verse 2:2

2.07a   Have built

2.06b   A life

2.07b   That is established upon [your] faith in [the Christ child] within you, [who], as you have been taught, [is] the root [of Christ Jesus], and [the reason that you] are overflowing with thanksgiving,

Deception and Seduction

2.04b   No one should [be able] to *deceive* you with persuasive language;

2.08   [But], watch out that no one *seduces* you through the philosophy of this world, [which] negates the philosophy of Christ, or [through] unfounded delusions[R-1] [about] the future [that they learned from] the traditions of [the First] Adam,[R-2]

[who was] cast down[R-3] [into] the orderly arrangement [of this] world [because of sin],

[R-1] 2 Thes 2:11
[R-2] Verse 21-22
[R-3] Gen 2:21
2 Pet 2:4
Jude 6
Rev 12:4

2.09 Because, [even though] the Whole [Adam], the permanent resident [of] the corporeal body which [exists] to contain divinity,

2.10 Fully equips[R-1] [Israel to resist the seductive philosophy of this world, the First Adam],[R-2] the principality who is the head of all [of the soldiers of Satan in the unconscious part of the mind], and the power [that enforces Jehovah's righteous Sowing & Reaping Judgment in this world,[R-3]

[R-1] Verse 3:10
[R-2] 1 Cor 15:45
[R-3] Job 1:12

Spiritual Circumcision

2.11 Was able] to sever [the unity between the] Christ [child within the men of National Israel and the Supernal Mother,[R-1] and the men of National Israel died,[R-2] even though] they were circumcised with the genuine circumcision [of the heart,[R-3] because the Supernal Mother] separated from [the Christ child, who was internalized within] their flesh bodies, and

[R-1] Rev 16:13-14 (ATB)
[R-2] Ps 82:6-7
[R-3] Deut 10:16
Rom 2:29

The Christ Child Aroused

2.12 He was buried[R-1] [under the carnal mind of the men of National Israel;

But the same Christ child that was buried under the carnal mind of the men of National Israel in the previous age], woke up [again within Jesus of Nazareth when John] baptized[R-2] [him, before he was crucified], and

[R-1] 1 Cor 15:4
[R-2] Matt 3:16
Mk 1:10
Lk 3:22

Jesus Resurrected

[Jesus], through faith in God and the energy of God that is active [in this world],

2.15a   Publicly[R-1] exhibited [his spiritual] victory[R-2] [over Satan's authority] within himself, by standing up again],

[R-1] 1 Cor 15:54
Jn 21:14
[R-2] 1 Cor 15:54-55

2.14a   [Thereby] obliterating [the judgment that] the hand [of Adam, the wall[R-1] that protects Israel, wrote] against us because we violated the Law, which] is contrary to [our nature,[R-2]

[R-1] Dan 5:25
Ez 40:5
[R-2] Rom 11:17

Sanctification

2.15b   Thus], wholly separating[R-1] us from [the First Adam], the principality[R-2] [who is the head of all of the soldiers of Satan in the unconscious part of the mind, and] the power [that enforces Jehovah's righteous Sowing & Reaping Judgment],[R-3] and

[R-1] Heb 2:11
[R-2] Verse 1:13
[R-3] Ex 21:24
Gal 6:7

Alternate Translation Of The New Testament/ Colossians

2.13a He has made you alive again^R

^R Rom 8:11
1Cor 15:22

2.14b By nailing [Christ, the seed^{R-1} of] himself, [to the cross^{R-2} of] your corporeal body,

^{R-1} Gal 3:16
^{R-2} Gal 2:20

2.13b Thus, joining himself to [the First Adam within you], who were [spiritually] dead^R because you transgressed [the Law, thereby] bringing the Whole [Adam, the one who] forgives you [when] you violate the Law, [into existence within you;

^R Eph 2:1, 5

But, [the First Adam still controls you, because he is] the flesh [of the foreskin^R that covers] the uncircumcised Christ child;]

^R Jer 4:4
Hab 2:16

Religion

2.16 Wherefore, [until the Christ child stands up in power within you], you should not let anyone condemn you concerning the food [that you eat or [the beverages that] you drink, or the degree to which you participate in religious festivals, or [observe] new moons, or the Sabbath,

2.17 [Because the Lord Jesus] Christ is about to appear [in this world, and cut away your corporeal] body, the shadiness that covers [him];

Opposition To Change

2.18 [So] do not let anyone who cannot recognize [that] the [Supernal] Mother is, indeed, [directing] you to do [the spiritual things that] delight [Christ Jesus], the Lord,^{R-1} judge your [behavior to be] incorrect

^{R-1} Ps 18:19

[Because] they are still] ceremonially worshipping angels, and their flesh mind[R-1] [which is the enemy of Christ],[R-2] has puffed [them] up,[R-3] [telling them that] they can intrude upon [your lives] without [a legitimate] reason;[R-4]

[R-1] Eph 2:3
[R-2] 1 Cor 8:1
[R-3] Rom 8:7
[R-4] 1 Cor 4:5

2.19   [Because the Christ child], the head [of their corporeal bodies],[R-1] has not] seized [them yet, so] the [spiritual] principal that unites[R-2] with [the Christ child to form] the Whole [Adam, the one] who fully supplies [R-3] the body [of Christ[R-4] with everything that it needs] to grow up [into Christ Jesus, the one who] knits them together[R-5] [in love, is not within them],

[R-1] Eph 5:23
[R-2] Verse 2:2
[R-3] Ph 4:19
[R-4] Col 1:8
[R-5] Eph 4:16

2.20   Wherefore, if you are dead[R-1] [as far as the First Adam is] concerned, [but] alive[R-2] through [the] Christ [child], the founding[R-3] principal of this [new] world [order called "the Kingdom of God," that is coming into existence within you], why would you subject yourselves to the ceremonial rules of the [present] world [order, such as]

[R-1] Eph 2:1, 5
[R-2] Verse 2:13
Deut 4:4
1 Cor 6:17
[R-3] 1 Cor 3:11

2.21   Do not touch [anyone who has a skin disease, or][R-1] do not eat [with Gentiles, or][R-2] do not relate to [morally unclean persons],[R-3]

[R-1] Matt 26:6
[R-2] Matt 9:11
[R-3] Jn 20:16-17

Alternate Translation Of The New Testament/ Colossians

2.22a Which commandments, [as well as those concerning]

2.23a The piety [that is associated with] modesty, no longer have any value,^{R-1} because they [only] deprive the [corporeal] body [of] satisfying the lusts of the flesh,^{R-2} and

^{R-1} 2 Cor 3:6
^{R-2} Verse 2:18

2.22b [Will] all [be] destroyed,^{R-1} [like the rest of] the doctrine of [the First] Adam^{R-2} [will be destroyed], after [their purpose] is used up;^{R-3}

^{R-1} Eph 2:15
Verse 2:8
^{R-2} Eph 4:14 (ATB)
^{R-3} Heb 8:13

2.23b Nevertheless, [whoever observes] these unnecessary [commandments], is said to possess the lower wisdom;

Chapter 3

[917.3.C]

The Christian Life

<u>The Mind of Christ Jesus</u>

3.01a [So], if [the] Christ [child] woke up [in you]

3.03a Since you died to [your carnal mind],^R

^R Rom 6:4

3.01b You should look [forward] to marrying [the Lord Jesus] Christ, who is married to the merciful side of God,^R [which is] above,

^R Mk 14:62

3.03b [So that] the life of [the] Christ [child, which is] hidden in God,

3.04 Might enlighten you, until the opinion of [the Lord Jesus] Christ, who is our life,[R-1] appears in [you][R-2] also,

[R-1] Jn 14:6
[R-2] 1 Jn 3:2

3.02 [Because] the high mind of [Christ Jesus, is] not [concerned with what is happening] on the earth;

The Character of The First Adam

3.05 Therefore, do not let your corporeal body, or your soul, engage in any physical, mental or emotional activities that [the First Adam indulges in], that [the] Christ [child who is] upon the earth, would not engage in], such as,

Behavioral Sin

Fornication, which is harlotry, adultery and incest,

Uncleanness, which is, specifically, sexual intercourse during a woman's menstrual cycle, and, in general, the illegal use of blood, including the drinking of blood for witchcraft rituals, and other hygienically unclean and immoral acts, including oral sex, anal intercourse, and bestiality, which is sex with animals,

Inordinate affection, which is uncontrolled passion, including lust manifesting as a compulsion that can never be satisfied, such as obsessive sexual behavior, all-consuming jealousy, lust to dominate, control and possess what does not belong to you, and addictions to alcohol, drugs, or food, which is gluttony, and gambling, in particular,

Concupiscence, which is lust, that is, longing especially for that which is forbidden,

Evil, which is injurious behavior or thoughts, and

Alternate Translation Of The New Testament/ Colossians

Covetousness, which is avarice, the excessive or insatiable desire for wealth, and greed, which is idolatry,

3.06   For which things God's passion[R-1] is coming upon his disobedient children,[R-2]

[R-1] Rev 14:19
[R-2] Eph 5:5

3.07 Whose lifestyle you also followed in the past; and

Mental and Emotional Sin

3.08   It is now also time to renounce [ungodly responses to these sins, as well, such as]:

Anger, which is passion of the mind,

Wrath, which is passion of the emotions,

Malice, which is malignity, that is, evil intentions,

Blasphemy, which is vilification, that is, evil speaking, especially against God, and

Filthy communication, which is base conversation, also base reasoning, which is the reasoning of the carnal mind; and

The New Man

3.09a   [You should also] stop lying[R-1] to one another [now that] you have stripped off the former Adam,[R-2] together with his [evil] actions,[R-3] and

[R-1] 1 Jn 2:22
1 Jn 4:20
[R-2] Eph 4:22
[R-3] Gen 3:6, 10, 12

3.10   Merged with the new [Adam,^R-1 who] is renovated^R-2 in the likeness^R-3 [of God], through a knowledge of the one who made him,^R-4

^R-1 Eph 4:24
^R-2 1 Cor 15:47
^R-3 Gen 5:1
^R-4 Phil 3:10

3.11a   [Because], there is no difference between the Greek and the Jew, or the circumcised and the uncircumcised [man], or the non-Israelite and the savage, or the bondservant and the freeman,

3.11b   When [the] Christ [child] is [attached to] the Whole [Adam, and] the Whole [Adam is attached to the Shekinah, the Supernal Mother];

The Love of God

3.12   Wherefore, you, who are the elect^R of God, should clothe yourselves with the sacrificial love of the Holy [One], which manifests as:

^R Rom 11:7, 28

Bowels of mercy, which is pity, that is, sympathy that comes from the inner man, ^R

^R Eph 3:16

Kindness, which is tolerance and excellence of character and behavior,

Humbleness of mind, which is humility attained by the humiliation of the carnal mind,

Meekness, which is humility, and

Long-suffering, which is fortitude, that is, endurance; and

3.13   You should put up with one another's faults, [and forgive the grudges] that you have against each other, as [the]

Alternate Translation Of The New Testament/ Colossians

Christ [child] forgave you,[R] and you should also forgive yourselves;

[R] Verse 1:14

3.14 But above all these things, [you should] love [the Lord Jesus Christ], the one who binds [R-1] [the Christ child within] you [to himself] to complete[R-2] you, and

[R-1] Matt 16:19
Matt 18:18
Verse 2:2, 19
[R-2] Col 2:10

3.15 Let the peace of God,[R-1] by which you are called to be one body,[R-2] govern in your hearts, and be thankful, and

[R-1] Lk 2:14
[R-2] 1 Cor 12:13

3.16a Sing spiritual songs from your hearts,, and hymns and psalms to Christ [Jesus], the Lord, and teach[R-1] [about the Shekinah], the favor of God, and warn[R-2] one another gently [about Satan, the enforcer of the Sowing & Reaping Judgment, the severity of God],[R-3] and let the [spiritual] wisdom[R-4] of [Ancient Adam, the Word of God dwell in all of you abundantly, and

[R-1] Verse 1:28ª
[R-2] Heb 3:13
[R-3] Rom 11:21-22
[R-4] Verse 2:3
Job 1:6-12

3.17 Whatsoever you do in word or deed, do everything in the Name of the Lord Jesus, giving thanks to God and the Father by him.

Personal Relationships

3.18 Wives, subordinate yourselves to one husband, as is proper in the Lord;

Alternate Translation Of The New Testament/ Colossians

3.19　　Spiritual males and husbands, in particular, love the spiritual females, and your wives, in particular, with the sacrificial love of God, and do not resent them;

3.20　　Children, obey your parents in all things,[R] because this pleases [Christ Jesus], the Lord;

[R] Ex 20:12
Eph 6:2-3

3.21　　Fathers, do not provoke your children,[R] or they will be discouraged [about their ability to please you];

[R] Eph 6:4

3.22　　Servants, obey those who have authority over your flesh [body][R-1] in all things, not just for the sake of appearance,[R-2] to make yourselves look good to other men,

[R-1] Eph 6:5
[R-2] Eph 6:6

3.24　　[But] knowing that you will receive the reward of your inheritance,[R] [which is the] Christ [child, the one who

[R] Eph 6:8

3.23　　Equips][R-1] you to do whatever you do out of your [Christ] mind, as if you were doing it for [Christ Jesus],[R-2] the Lord, and [not out of the emotions of the First] Adam,

[R-1] Verse 2:10
[R-2] Eph 6:7

Punishment For Willful Sin

3.25　　[Because], whoever is unjust shall receive [a just recompense[R] for] what he has done, and there is no respect of persons [with God]; and

[R] Eph 6:8
Gal 6:7

Chapter 4

[917.3.C]

Business Relationships

4.01   Those of you that have authority over others, be righteous [in your dealings with] your servants, and [pay them an amount] equal [to their labor], knowing that you also have a master in heaven, and

Pray For Yourselves

4.02   Continue in prayer, watching out[R] for yourselves [that you do right by your servants, while] giving thanks [for all that you have], and

[R] Eph 6:18

4.06   [Let the Shekinah, the Supernal Mother], the favor of God and [the spiritual reality of] the anointing oil,[R] preserve your motives, so that you always know how you ought to speak to every person [according to their ability to understand you], and,

[R] Acts 10:38

Pray For Paul

4.03   At the same time, pray that God will open a door for us to speak intelligently[R-1] about the mystery of Christ,[R-2] for which [cause] I am bound,[R-3] and

[R-1] Eph 6:19
[R-2] Eph 5:32
[R-3] Eph 6:20
Phil 1:13

4.04   That I speak in a way that clearly sets forth what I am supposed to say, and

4.05   That I relate to others with wisdom, [because this is] the season[R-1] for those who are strangers[R-2] [in Israel to be] rescued.[R-3]

[R-1] 1 Cor 10:11
[R-2] Lev 19:34
[R-3] 2 Cor 6:2

THE BOOK OF
1st THESSALONIANS

Chapter 1

[419.1]
    1.04   Knowing, brethren that you are joined to Jehovah, because you preferred God [over Leviathan].

Chapter 4

[78.1]
    4.13   But I want you to understand, brethren, about the sinful state of being of mortal man, so that your inability to change does not distress you like it does other natural men who are not anticipating the spiritual change that will transform their mortal mind into a righteous mind.

    4.15   Because the Word of the Lord that we have for you, is that we whose spirits have been grafted to the Spirit of the Lord Jesus Christ, and whose personalities have survived the purging from sin that occurs when He is grafted in, shall not enter into perfection ahead of the members of mortal man which are still abiding in death because of Leviathan, their mortal mind.

    4.16   Because the Lord himself shall come down from the Spiritual world where God is and, by his spiritual authority, preach the Gospel of the Kingdom through the mouths of mortal men: and the son of Man who was slain so that mortal mankind could receive his life, shall be resurrected out from the hell of this visible, physical world, as one man.

4.17 Then those of us which have received the engrafted Spirit of Jesus Christ, and survived the crucifixion, destruction, and slaughter, of Leviathan, their carnal mind (abiding life), shall take authority over (seize) the invisible powers and principalities (clouds) in the spiritual world (air) beneath the firmament, and meet the Lord, Jesus, in the spiritual world above the firmament, and from then on we shall be with the Lord, Jesus, all the time.

[480.6]
4.14 Because if we trust [the Word of God that says that] Jesus ascended and separated from his [physical] body, God will lead [us out of] the astral plane, in the same way [that He led Jesus out].

Chapter 5

[480.6]
5.06 Therefore, let us not [experience] the astral plane as others do, but let our consciousness be in the Mind of Christ, [who prevents Satan from] bubbling up,

5.07 [Because] when Satan, the astral plane, bubbles up, Satan, influences [the spiritual women who are active in] the astral plane,

5.08 But we who are of [the Spirit of Christ, who is] the Day, abstain from [Satan's] spirit [by] putting on [Christ Jesus], the faith [that] is committed to cover our heart, and cover [our carnal mind, and give us] hope that we shall be saved,

5.09-10   But Satan's violent passion has prostrated **CHRIST** Jesus], the timeline of god, who separated from his flesh for us so that our life should be preserved through union with Christ Jesus, our controller, whether our consciousness is in the mental plane of Christ **JESUS**, or in [Satan's] astral plane.

THE BOOK OF 2nd THESSALONIANS

Chapter 1

[1133.3.C]

1.01a   [From] Paul, and Silvanus, and Timotheus, to the church of the Thessalonians [that]

1.02a   The Holy Spirit of

1.01b   God our Father and the Lord Jesus Christ[R] [dwell] in,

[R] Chap 2:17b

1.02b   Peace to you from God our Father and the Lord Jesus Christ.

1.03   We thank God that we are bound to him always for your [sake], brethren, since it is necessary for the moral conviction [of God] to increase exceedingly] beyond the [human] ability of all of you to love each other with the love of God, [for] the unity* [of Christ to come into existence amongst you], and

> *There is a superfluity of words in Verse 1 concerning the brethren. All of the words **all, each** other, every **[one]** and **one** are not only unnecessary, the sentence would not make sense if they were all translated properly. So the King James translators excluded the implied word **one** when they translated the Greek word that means **every one**: The charity of every [one] **one**, all, each other. The word **one** would appear twice, if all of

> the words were translated according to their full meaning.
>
> My understanding of the verse is that the word **one**, Strong's 1520, is the wrong Greek word for that verse, somehow having been exchanged for Strong's 1175, translated **unity** two times in the Second Testament, and its First Testament counterpart, Strong's 1571, translated **unity** once. (Ps 133:1, 1 Cor 1:13, Eph 4:1-7, 13).

1.04   [For] our opinion [to be] in the unconscious part of the mind* of the churches of God, [and for it to be above [the carnal mind] so that the moral conviction [of God] should endure in you through all the persecutions and pressures that [you will have] to withstand,**

> * Some years ago the Lord revealed to us that Strong's 846, the Greek word that means, through the idea of a baffling wind] (backward); the reflexive pronoun self, can be translated, the other self in the unconscious part of the mind, or, simply, the unconscious part of the mind.
>
> ** The tribulation is a personal, spiritual experience that develops the character of Christ in the individual believer. All the trouble occurring in the world is the Sowing & Reaping Judgment.

1.05   [For you] to deserve the same judgment of God [that comes from] the kingdom of God above, [which] indicates that Abel [within you should be resurrected[R] like he was in Jesus of Nazareth, who] also experienced the painful process of having the nature of God] impressed [upon his soul],

[R] 1 Cor 15:4

1.06   If, perhaps, God should pay back [the First Adam within you] in the same way [that he paid back the First Adam in Jesus of Nazareth], by pressing [him] together [R-1] with [the

Second Adam, which] drives [the First Adam] into a narrow space **R-2** [underneath himself], and

R-1 Lk 6:38
Eph 2:15
R-2 NU 22:26
Matt 7:14

1.07   [Then] you, [who the First Adam is] being pressed down in, shall be loosed, [along] with us, [from the control of Satan and the Devil, when the Lord Jesus, [who is] in heaven, is revealed in the midst of [Christ Jesus], his angel**R** [in the earthen bodies of the priests of Judah,* and by] the miracle-working power [in] the unconscious part of [their] mind,

> *Christ Jesus is the high priest of Jehovah's Second Covenant with Israel (Heb 3:1), but he is not from the tribe of Levi. He is from the tribe of Judah, so the tribal designation of the priesthood must change as well (Heb 7:14). The apostles were the first priests of the Second Covenant, but they all died like Aaron and his sons (Heb 7:11). The priests of Judah, the image of the Lord Jesus Christ in the earth, will not die because Jesus will be born **with them** (Lk 1:35), like Elijah was **born again with** Mary (Mk 9:12-13, 1 Pet 1:23).*

R Gen 48:16

1.08   [Who are] not [coming] to execute justice [on them] that do not know God,**R-1** [or on them] that listen to the gospel, [but the Spirit of Life**R-2** that is in] the Lord Jesus Christ, [Jehovah's high priest], shall flash [through both groups like] lightning,

R-1 Lk 9:56
R-2 Rom 8:2, 11
1 Cor 15:45

1.09   [To make the First Adam within them] pay the penalty* for destroying perpetuity**R** [by preventing Abel], the personality of the Lord, from holding the opinion [of God] in the unconscious part of the mind, continuously,^R and

> *There is an untranslated word in Verse 9 (Strong's 1349) which "originally meant manner, tendency. Gradually it became the designation for the right of established custom or usage. The basic meaning of the word **involves the assertion by human society of a certain standard expected by its people which, if not kept, can bring forth ensuing judgment.** Thus it can be said that díkč is **expected behavior or conformity, not according to one's own standard, but according to an imposed standard with prescribed punishment for nonconformi**ty. It refers to **legitimate custom."** We have translated it, **penalty**, in Verse 9. (Complete Word Study Dictionary: New Testament © 1992 by AMG International, Inc. Revised Edition, 1993.)*

^R Heb 13:14

1.10   [Everyone that did not believe our evidence] in the day that [we were] among you, will be struck with astonishment^R when [the Lord Jesus Christ] comes in the saints [that] believed our evidence, because [the saints that] believed our evidence [will be able to hold] the opinion of [God] in the unconscious part of the mind, continuously,* and

> *Christ Jesus, the Second Adam, by his opinion and perceptions, will stand, continually, above the First Adam, in the unconscious part of the mind. The personality that experiences this state of being will have ascended to **the immortality of longevity**, the state of sinlessness that exists in the next age.*

^R Mk 5:42

1.11   This is the reason why Elohim prays for you also, that you should be worthy of the invitation of our God, and [that] all [of you should] be filled up with the virtue and the power [that comes from] always [holding] the morality of God [in the unconscious part of the mind, which brings] the activities that satisfy ᴿ [the soul into your lives], and

ᴿ Chap 2:17b

1.12 That the opinion of the Lord Jesus Christ, the Name of God, may be in you, and [that] you may be in him through [the Spirit of] Grace, [the Comforter who influences the emotions of the heart]ᴿ towards our Lord Jesus Christ.

ᴿ Jn 14:26
Chap 2:17b
Chap 3:18

Chapter 2

[1133.3.C]

2.01 Indeed, [we encourage you] to interrogate ᴿ [your other self] concerning the appearance of our Lord Jesus Christ and our gathering together with him in the unconscious part of the mind,

ᴿ Vs 6
1 Cor 5:4-7

2.02 [But], do not worry that you will waver [when it comes to choosing the opinion of God's] mind on the Day of Christ,* [which is] speedily approaching, [but, rather, remember what you have read in] our letters to you about the [Holy] Spirit and the Word [of God]:ᴿ

> *The two interlinear texts that we work with,* **Nestlé** *and* **Textus Receptus**, *have different opinions about the Greek word translated* **Christ**, *in this verse. Both Interlinears agree that the English translation should be,* **Christ**, *but they do not render this translation from the same Greek word.* **Nestlé** *says the Greek word is* **kurios**,

Strong's 2962, meaning, supreme authority; **The Textus Receptus** *says the Greek word is,* **Christos,** *Strong's 55 47, meaning,* **anointed,** *i.e., the* **Messiah,** *and epithet of* **Jesus. The Complete Word study Dictionary** *says that Strong's 5547 means* **everyone anointed with the holy oil, primarily to the high priesthood. Also a name applied to others acting as redeemers.**

^R Chap 1:12

2.03 Do not let anyone seduce you concerning the character of the First Adam, that he is the son [that] fell away from the truth [about the love of God] ^R and was morally ruined, because, unless he is exposed,

^R Vs 10, 12
Chap 3:4

2.04 [The people who] worship in the temple,^{R-1} [which is] the unconscious part of the mind, will make the reflection of God higher than the reputation of God, which will make him God;^{R-2}

^{R-1} 1 Cor 3:16
^{R-2} 1 Ki 12:20

2.05 Do you not remember that I told you about these things when I was still with you? And

2.06 Now you know [the truth about] your [other] self ^R in the unconscious part of the mind, which was withheld from you until the proper time to reveal

^R Vs 1

2.07 This mystery, [which is] withheld only until [the Lord Jesus] comes into existence in the midst [of the unconscious part of the mind] to elevate [the Woman who] violated the Law,^R and

^R Gen 3:6

2.08a   To adopt [Cain,^R at which time] the Spirit [of the Lord Jesus] shall appear conspicuously in the unconscious part of the mind to shut the mouth of

^R Rom 8:15, 23

2.09a   Satan

2.08b   By revealing

2.09b   [That she] appears [in the saints who possess] the energy of [the Holy Spirit, through] false prophecies, all [of which] are lies, ^R and

^R Rev 13:3

2.10   Deceit [that arise out of the First Adam who became] a moral ruin when he did not receive the truth about the love [of God],^R that he might be saved by Elohim in the unconscious part of the mind, and was fully destroyed,* and

> * The First Adam was fully destroyed concerning his relationship with God, which is righteousness and immortality, but he still exists. **Fully destroyed**, means both his male and female sides. He was cast out of heaven, the immortal dimension, and his soul that is attached to the earthen body died also. This is the reason why we all die. The First Adam, our higher soul, cannot keep our body alive because it lost its attachment to the heavenly (immortal) dimension, which is the love of God. **Attachment to heaven is the love of God. Separation from God's heavenly (immortal) dimension is death**. So it is possible to be dead and still exist, which state of existence and its environment, are called, **hell**.

^R Vs 3, 12
Chap 3:4

2.11a   This is the reason why God shall send the counterfeit Holy Spirit ᴿ

> ᴿ 2 Cor 11:13-15
> Acts 8:9, 17-23

2.12   To all of them [who] approve of the counterfeit [Holy Spirit, so that] they [who] do not [love] the truth, [which is] the moral conviction [of God],

2.11b   [Should] have the moral conviction of [the counterfeit Adam], the liar in the unconscious part of their mind [also];ᴿ

> ᴿ Rom 3:4

2.13   Indeed, we who are bound to God, give thanks always for the brethren who are joined to the Lord, [who has been] purifying your spirit through the moral conviction of the truth [that leads] to salvation, [that you have been receiving] from the beginning [of our ministry to you], and

2.14   This is the reason why Elohim has called you to obtain the opinion of our Lord, Jesus Christ, by our gospel

2.15   Before [you are tested by the counterfeit Holy Spirit, so that], perhaps, brethren, you will not be moved [by that seducing spirit] from the [legitimate] traditions ᴿ that you have been taught by the Word, or through our letters;

> ᴿ Chap 1:9

2.16a   Indeed, the Lord Jesus Christ and God, our Father, have given us perpetual intimacy [with them] in the unconscious part of the mind, [which is the true] love of God,ᴿ [so that we should] expect good things through

> ᴿ Vs 3, 10

2.17a   [The Lord Jesus Christ, the Father, and Christ Jesus, the Son],ᴿ the whole Word [of God, and]

> ᴿ Chap 1:1b

2.16b   [The Holy Spirit], the divine influence

2.17b [That] comforts [the emotions] of your heart,[R-1] [the only] foundation [R-2] and [acceptable influence to do] good activities; [R-3] And

[R-1] Chap 1:11, 12
Chap 3:4
[R-2] 1 Cor 3:11
[R-3] Chap 1:11
Chap 3:11,18

Chapter 3

[1133.3.C]

3.01 Finally, brethren, pray for us that the Word of the Lord should flow through us unhindered, so that his opinion [should be a sound foundation[R] of wisdom, knowledge and understanding] within you, and

[R] 1 Cor 3:11

3.02 That we may rescue you from the [First] Adam [who] became hurtful when he took [God's] place, [R] because everyone does not have the moral conviction [of God];*

> *Whoever has the moral conviction of God cannot be hurt by the First Adam because they will reject his thoughts. (Jn 14:30)*

[R] 1 Jn 2:18

3.03 Indeed, the Lord shall be your moral conviction; He shall be a foundation [of wisdom, knowledge and understanding that] will isolate you from the harmful [potential of the First Adam], and

3.04 We have confidence in the Lord concerning you, that you are doing, and will do the things that will join you [R] to [him through] us, and

[R] Chap 2: 3,10

Alternate Translation Of The New Testament/ 2 Thessalonians

3.05   That the Lord will direct [the emotions of] your hearts towards us [who love you with] the love of God [which attaches you to us], that [you should receive the strength] to endure [the trials and tribulations that precede the coming of] Christ in you;

3.06   Indeed, brethren, [all of] you who are joined to us in the Name of our Lord Jesus Christ should abstain from associating with every brother that is not walking after the transmission [of spiritual wisdom] that you received from us, but is living an immoral [lifestyle]*

> *It is clear from the beginning of Verse 7, that Paul is clearly talking about the hidden sins of the heart, evil motives, such as pride, envy and rebellion. This is the mystery of the esoteric doctrine of the Second Covenant: The cleansing of the unconscious part of the mind is possible, and through this cleansing, the return to immortality.*

3.07   In the unconscious part of the mind, because they should know how to follow [the way Jesus comported himself in the unconscious part of the mind], because we [did not deviate from following his example in the unconscious part of the mind] while we were among you, R

R Lk 1:51
Rom 1:21

3.08   Neither did we eat anyone's food without paying for it, but labored with our hands, [as well as in the Word, even though] it was painful and we were sad to be cut off from the anointing [while we were working] so that we would not set a bad example for any of you,

3.09   [Neither did we work] because we do not have the authority [to be paid for our spiritual labor of transmitting esoteric knowledge to you], but [we worked so] that we would be an example [that] you could follow,R

R Vs 9

3.10   Because when we were still with you and you were [spiritually] joined to us, [we taught you] that anyone who is not willing to work [to support themselves while receiving esoteric knowledge is not worthy] to eat [the holy doctrine], and

3.11   We hear that some who walk among you [who] are immoral [in the unconscious part of the mind] are going around [town, prophesying, but not by the influence of Jesus or the Holy Spirit], **R-2** and not even one of them is working [with his hands].**R-1**

R-1 Vs 9, 10
R-2 Chap 2:17b

3.12   Indeed, we have transmitted [our esoteric knowledge] to some of this sort who became joined [to us through that knowledge], and we exhort them by the Lord Jesus Christ, that they should work [with their hands] and desist from prophesying to others,**R** but prophesy to themselves;

R Chap 2:17b
Vs 11

3.13   But, brethren, do not be discouraged; **R-1** [Rather, wait on the Lord to influence you] to do good [deeds]; **R-2**

R-1 1 Thes 5:20
R-2 Acts 10:38

3.14   Identify any [of them that] does not repent and submit to our word [to stop prophesying], and do not [form a soul tie with him in] the unconscious part of the mind;

3.15   Yet, do not consider him an enemy but warn him gently

3.16   [That Satan does], indeed, [speak to us from] the unconscious part of the mind, [as well as Christ]; May the Lord of peace **R-1** be with you always, and give you peace through repentance. **R-2**

R-1 Gen 14:18
R-2 Lk 5:32
Acts 5:31

3.17   I, Paul, being supernaturally present in every letter that I write with my own hand, greet you;

3.18   [May the Holy Spirit] of our Lord Jesus Christ, the grace [that comforts our emotions and influences our heart towards good activities and deeds], be with you all. So be it. **R**

R Chap 1:12
Chap 2:17b

THE BOOK OF 1ST TIMOTHY

Chapter 2

[Message # Unknown]
    2.05   Elohim is united with the Mediator; And the Mediator is united [with] Elohim [and] Adam; And the Name of the Mediator is] The man, Christ Jesus

[906.3.C]
    2.06   Who [the Supernal Mother] gave as a ransom for the whole [creation, which] will be evident at the proper time.

[13.1]
    2.08   Let men pray everywhere to be caught up to the spiritual plane where they can lay hold of the ability to fulfill their duty towards God, thus fulfilling the commandment to love Him.

[347]
    2.14   The Serpent used witchcraft to trick the first Adam [the living soul] into using poor judgment, but the Woman was overtaken and seduced into the transgression.[122]

---

[122] The Greek word translated *not* is a negative particle which is used to describe man's worthlessness in relationship to God. **Negative particles** signify the *Serpent* or the *Devil* in parable form. (See, word study on Message #78, **The Harvest,** Part 9.) (Read entire footnote in Appendices)

Chapter 3

[1246.3.C]
3.16   Without objection, great is the mystery of devotion to God: Elohim, a righteous Spirit, became visible in the flesh, preached the opinion of God in the world, was recognized by the angels [in] the Gentiles, [and whoever] believed [him, was spiritually] elevated.

Chapter 4

[783.4.C]
4.01   Now the Spirit [of God] is distinctly laying out [for all to hear] that, in the final season [of this present age], some [believers] shall revolt against [God and] be persuaded to listen to demonic spiritual doctrines, the seductive

4.02   Lies of which shall desensitize their conscience, and deceive them [concerning

4.03a   Homosexual] marriage, which is forbidden, and [veganism, which teaches us to] abstain from meat and other foods that God made to be received with gratitude, [but]

4.03b   Those who are won over by the truth [of the Divine Doctrine], know [that]

4.04   The [soul, which is] the result of God's creative process, is good at its root, and not one part of the whole [soul] should be cast away if [the personality] receives [the Truth of the Divine Doctrine] with gratitude, because

4.05   [Cain, the animal nature], is sanctified by the word of God and prayer.

4.08   It is advantageous to discipline the physical body for the short season [that we are in the flesh], but the [mind] that arises out of a relationship with God, promises how possessing the life[style] of the [one preaching] benefits the whole [man] in this present life, as well as in the [higher states of consciousness [123] that we have to look forward to [in Christ Jesus].

4.08   It is advantageous to discipline the physical body for the short season [that we are living out of the carnal mind], but the [Christ mind] that arises out of a relationship with God, promises the life[style] that benefits the whole [man, not only] in this present life, [but also] in the [higher states of consciousness] that we look forward to [in Christ Jesus].

Chapter 5

[OLM – 06 07 00]
5.14   Let [the personalities of the Church of Jesus Christ] marry Christ Jesus, their New Man, and bear Christ, the [spiritual] child [that] disciples the household of God, so that the personalities [of the Church of Jesus Christ may learn] not to give [Satan], the adversary of [Christ Jesus, their husband], an opportunity to slander [Christ Jesus, their husband],

---

[123]   **12 Levels Of Consciousness**

1. Reconciliation; 2. Justification; 3. Sanctification; 4. Resurrected Christ in the individual marries the Lord Jesus who is above the firmament, and becomes a New Man [Christ Jesus]; . . . (Read entire footnote in Appendices)

Alternate Translation Of The New Testament/ 1 Timothy

5.15   Because [Leviathan] has already deflected some [personalities] away from [Christ Jesus, their husband, and turned them towards] Satan.

THE BOOK OF TITUS

Chapter 2

[Message # Unknown]
2.13   And one Saviour, Jesus Christ [the Revitalized Spirit], who has promised that the glory of the great God, Jehovah, should appear [in the individual human spirit to complete mortal man].

[719.1.C]
2.14   Who gave himself [to the earth] for us, and purchased us from the [Woman's] whole illegal family, and cleansed [us, so that we should be] an unusual people who are anxious to do good deeds on his behalf.

Chapter 3

[04/24/2024]
3.07   We can expect to inherit [perpetual life in the flesh when] we are justified by the Spirit of Grace.

Alternate Translation Of The New Testament/ Hebrews

THE BOOK OF HEBREWS

Chapter 1

[1202.12.C]

God Speaks

1.01   From time to time in the past, God spoke by different methods to [Abraham, Isaac and Jacob], the Fathers [of Israel], through the prophets,

1.02a   But, in these last days he has also spoken to us by his Son, who he subjected to *Elohim* [who] made ^R [the personal souls that]

^R Gen 1:1

The Personal Souls of Creation

1.03   Appeared in [the empty space where creation is taking place], ^{R-1} to enlighten ^{R-2} [them and] engrave ^{R-3} [them with] the opinion [of the Lord Jesus Christ, ^{R-4} the only] reality, ^{R-5} [who] upholds ^{R-6} all [of creation in the sea of the unconscious part of the mind, by the miracle-working] power [of the Holy Spirit, ^{R-7} and] the Word [of the Ancient Holy One, who became] the righteousness of [the Father ^{R-8} and] the High [Priest ^{R-9} who] marries ^{R-10} [the personal souls, and] washes away ^{R-11} [their] sins in the unconscious part of the mind, [which] makes [them]

^{R-1} Gen 1:2
^{R-2} Gen 1:3
^{R-3} Gen 1:16
^{R-4} 2 Pet 1:4

319

Alternate Translation Of The New Testament/ Hebrews

R-5 Heb 11:1
R-6 1 Cor 3:11
R-7 1 Cor 12:28
R-8 Acts 2:33
R-9 Heb 4:14
R-10 Rev 21:2
R-10 Eph 5:26
R-11 Rev 7:14

1.02b   Perpetual,

The Son of The Father Vs The Angels

1.05   And to which of the angels did [God] say at any time,

"You are my Son that I caused to be conceived **R** [in Mary's womb]?

R Lk 1:3

1.04   "[Who is] so much stronger than the angels, and so superior to them, [that] you inherited [the personal soul of Jesus of Nazareth, and became] a Name [that appears] in the unconscious part of the mind, [perpetually, from incarnation to incarnation];"

And again,

"I will be a Father to him and he shall be a Son to me,"

1.06a   But, when God introduced [Jesus Christ], the Firstborn [of the dead], **R** earthen [personal souls] to the angels, he said

R Rev 1:5

The Angels

1.07a   "Concerning the angels,

Alternate Translation Of The New Testament/ Hebrews

1.06b "Submit [the authority you have over] all [of the other dead personal souls] in the unconscious part of the mind [to my Son]," and he [also] said,

1.07b "[It is I, Jehovah], who formed the angels [R-1] in the unconscious part of the mind into the beneficent spirit[ual souls] [R-2] of the [Five-Fold] Ministry, [R-3] that, [through them, my Son [R-4] should] blaze [R-5] [like a shooting star] into the unconscious part of the mind [of the heirs of salvation];" [R-6]

[R-1] Gen 1:16
[R-2] 1 Cor 2:16
Eph 4:24
[R-3] Eph 4:11
[R-4] Vs 4
2 Jn 3
[R-5] Matt 2:2
Rev 22:16
[R-6] Rev 21:7

The Son

1.08a But to The Son he says,

1.09 "Because you have loved righteousness and hated lawlessness, God your God has [authorized you] to distribute [your spiritual blood [R-1] to the emotional female souls who are] your brethren, [R-2] [and] to smear it on [their minds, [R-3] so that they, too], can rejoice [over the birth of Jesus Christ, [R-4] their Lord, the Saviour of the World]," [R-5]

[R-1] 1 Pet 1:2
[R-2] Heb 2:11
[R-3] Ez 12:7
[R-4] Lk 2:11
[R-5] Jn 4:42

The Authority of God

1.08b [And the Son responded, saying]:

"Your throne, oh God, [is] perpetual, [and] the authority [you have given me to rule over] your kingdom, perpetually, is righteous;

The Names of God

1.10   "You [are the Ancient Holy One], [R-1] the beginning [of Creation, [R-2] the Second Adam], the Lord [from Heaven] [R-3] and [the Lord Jesus Christ], the foundation [R-4] of the earth[en personal souls], and the heavens are the work of [Elohim], your hands; [R-5]

[R-1] Dan 7:9,13,22
[R-2] Rev 22:13
[R-3] 1 Cor. 15:47
[R-4] 1 Cor 3:11
[R-5] Gen 1:1

"Garments" Are Souls

1.11a   "All [the angels] in the unconscious part of the mind change [their] garments [when] they grow old,

1.12a   "But I did not exchange [the soul of Jesus of Nazareth], the garment [that] I put on in the unconscious part of the mind, even though its [body] folded up [when it was crucified], because

1.11b   "[The soul of Jesus of Nazareth] remains consistently

1.12b   "The same in the unconscious part of the mind [for] years without end;

The Establishment of The Only Son of The Father

1.13   "Indeed, to which [personality] did you ever say,

" 'Sit at my right hand until I put [the angel who became your] opponent ᴿ under your authority'?

ᴿ 2 Pet 2:4

1.14 "Because it is not the function of all of [these] spirits [who became angels when they took on the flesh, to dominate the personalities] who are sent forth to inherit salvation, ᴿ

ᴿ 1 Pet 1:2

Chapter 2

[1202.12.C]
2.01 Therefore, if we are to avoid drifting [away from this great salvation, it is] superabundantly necessary [for us] to pay attention to [what we have heard],

2.02 Because, if what was said by [Moses and Aaron, the two] angels [that God sent to the Hebrew children in Egypt] ᴿ⁻¹ was accurate, and every wrongdoing and misunderstanding received a fair reward or punishment, ᴿ⁻²

ᴿ⁻¹ Ex 4:29
ᴿ⁻² Gal 6:7

2.03 How shall we escape [Jehovah's righteous Sowing & Reaping judgment] ᴿ if we neglect this great salvation that we began to receive [when] we first heard the Lord speak [about it, and later on] confirmed [to others],

ᴿ Gal 6:7

2.04 [How] God [is] witnessing [to these truths] with both supernatural [influences upon men], ᴿ⁻¹ prophecies, ᴿ⁻² various demonstrations of God's power over nature, ᴿ⁻³ and the gifts of the Holy Spirit, ᴿ⁻⁴ according to his own will,

ᴿ⁻¹ Jn 8:11
ᴿ⁻² Matt 24:4-51
ᴿ⁻³ Mk 4:39
ᴿ⁻⁴ 1 Cor 12:1-10

2.05   Because he is putting [the personal souls of humanity], not the angels, ^{R-1} in the right moral order in the world to come^{R-2} that we are telling you about.

^{R-1} Heb 1:6
^{R-2} Matt 10:30

Why Jesus?

2.06   But, some [who were] nearby protested earnestly saying,

"Who is [this] Adam, or the son of Adam, that he should be the one [who] resembles [Elohim]^R in the unconscious part of the mind?

^R Gen 1:26

Jesus Is Superior

2.07   "You have made the angels [who do] the work of your hands [in the earth] a little lower than [the only begotten of the Father], ^{R-1} the opinion and reputation [of God, but] placed them over [the ministers ^{R-2} who] decorate the unconscious part of the mind, and

^{R-1} Jn 1:14
^{R-2} Heb 1:7 (ATB)

2.08   "[You are saying that there is] nothing in the unconscious part of the mind [of Jesus that] he needs to bring into submission [at this] present [time], because

"[The only Son of the Father ^R purified] everything in the unconscious part of the human mind [of Jesus of Nazareth that could be purified], and

^R 2 John 3

"Subordinated [the angels in] the unconscious part of the mind [who were] not in submission [to him];

"But it does not appear [that] everything [in the unconscious part of our mind that can be purified has been purified, or that the angels in] the unconscious part of our mind [have been] subdued,"

Jesus, Higher Than The Angels

2.09   [And Paul responded, saying],

"Now that the divine influence [of the Holy Spirit and Jesus' Blood can be distributed to] anyone,[R-1] the angels [who have] a lower rank then Jesus [R-2] will look at the hardship that Jesus experienced [R-3] which led to the separation of his personal soul from his body, [R-4] and [understand that] he was crowned [R-5] with the opinion and dignity of God [R-6] [so that], in a little while, [*the personal soul* of] everyone that is among [those who receive Christ, the engrafted Word], [R-7] shall not die off, but shall separate from [the lusts of] the body [and continue to live through Christ; [R-8]

[R-1] Heb 12:24
[R-2] Heb 2:7 (ATB)
[R-3] Mk 15:32
[R-4] Jn 20:26
[R-5] Rev 14:14
[R-6] Rev 6:2
[R-7] Js 1:21
[R-8] Gal 2:20

2.10   "It is right [that the only Son of the Father, who made] everything[R-1] in the spiritual world [for himself], should complete [Jesus of Nazareth], [R-2] the Prince of Salvation,[R-3] [who is experiencing many] hardships in the unconscious part of the mind, [to convince] many sons [of Jehovah's] opinion, [in order to complete [R-4] them],

[R-1] Col 1:16
[R-2] Eph 4:13
[R-3] Rev 1:5
[R-4] Col 2:10

Sons of Jacob Through Jesus

2.11 "Because both [Jesus of Nazareth], the one that [the only Son of the Father] purified, ^{R-1} and those who [Jesus] purifies, ^{R-2} all come from [Jacob], ^{R-3} which is the reason why [Jesus] is not ashamed to call them his brothers, and

^{R-1} Rom 1:4
^{R-2} Rev 1:5
^{R-3} Jer 51:19

2.12 "To say [to Jehovah],

" ' I will announce your Name to my brothers; I will sing praises to you from the midst of [the children that form] the Church,' ^R and

^R Ps 149:1

2.13 "Again,

" ' I will put my trust in [Jehovah],' ^{R-1} and, again,

" 'Look! God gave me the children ^{R-2} in the unconscious part of the mind [to demonstrate] that [Jehovah's power is in the earth]' and

^{R-1} Pro 30:5
^{R-2} Is 8:18

Co-Heirs Through Christ

2.14 " Since the children certainly [have] a share ^{R-1} in [Jacob's] flesh and blood in the unconscious part of the mind, in the same manner, [Christ] ^{R-2} has a share of [the Father] in the unconscious part of the mind, that, [by the Father sending his only Son into the world to overcome] death, ^{R-3} he might render idle [R-4] the strength[R-5] that the Devil had [to cause Adam] to die, and

[R-1] Rom 8:17
[R-2] Gal 3:16
[R-3] 1 Cor 15:53
[R-4] 1 Cor 15:54
[R-5] 1 Cor 15:56

Guilty Under The Law

2.15   "Deliver them who are enslaved all of their lives [by lies, manipulation and submission to ungodly authorities, because] they are afraid of dying [R] [from disease, hunger, or] a life [without affection],

[R] Matt 10:28

Jesus' Blood Is The Atonement

2.16   "Because, honestly, [the only Son of the Father] did not [clothe himself with] angels, but he put on [Christ, the Son of the Father],[R] the seed of Abraham;

[R-1] Gal 3:16

2.17   "Wherefore, [Jesus] is obliged [in everything that he experiences] to be similar to his brethren, so that he might be a compassionate and trustworthy high priest [R-1] to God, to atone[R-2] for the sins of the people,

[R-1] Heb 4:14
[R-2] Rom 5:11

2.18   "Even [to the extent that] he experienced the pain of [being] tested [by the Devil's] suggestions [R-1] in the unconscious part of the mind, [so that] he is [now] able to assist[R-2] [those who] are [being] tested."

[R-1] Lk 4:3
[R-2] Gen 2:18

Chapter 3

[1003.1]
    3.01   Brethren, observe Christ Jesus,

The Apostle and High Priest [who] assents [to the New Covenant, tastes] the heavenly [bread that comes from God, and partners with] the Holy [Spirit to wield the powers of the world to come on] our [behalf,

The only Mediator that] invites you [to be] God's partner,

[991.3.C]
    3.11   So my Sowing & Reaping Judgment turned them back to the point of departure, [because] they could not enter in[to an immortal] body [while they were living according to the ways of this world],

    3.18   So Jehovah turned them back to the point of departure, [because] they could not enter into their [immortal] bodies until they believed [him],

Chapter 5

[530.1]
    5.05-06 So also Christ glorified not himself to be made a high priest; ...but he that said unto him, [unto Christ] Thou Art My Son, Today Have I Begotten Thee. That same God who said that also said to Christ in another place, Thou Art a Priest For Ever After The Order Of Melchisedec. The High Priesthood is the order of Melchisedec.

Chapter 6

[Message # Unknown]
6.02   [Which requires that] we be instructed concerning [the different kinds of] baptisms, the laying on of hands, the resurrection of the dead, and perpetual judgment,

6.03   But we can do this [only] if God turns us around.

6.01   Therefore, let us lay aside the principles of Satan, [the unconscious part of the carnal mind], and go on, rather, to the Doctrine of Christ, which [has the power to impart] the faith that is founded on God, the one who perfects [us] after we repent of dead works.

[Message # Unknown]
6.04   For those who were once weak, but who also experienced the illumination of the heavenly gift, and were made partakers of the Holy Ghost,

6.05   And experienced the good Word of God, and the powers of the world to come,

6.06   If they were to fall away again, would have to repent and experience the shame of having [their carnal mind] exposed and re-crucified to the Son of God [all over again],

6.07   Because the earth[en personality] that exposes itself to the rain [of the Holy Spirit] frequently, brings forth the appropriate [spiritual] food which causes [Christ], the one who plows [the personality, to expose and remove sins], to appear, [so that we] may receive blessings from God,

6.08   But [the personality] that gives birth to piercing demons, and an obstructionist [personality that] rejects and curses [God], is [married to Leviathan], whose end is to be burned [in the Lake of Fire].

[OLM - 06 14 00]

6.18 [Knowing that since] it is impossible for God to lie, we, the personalities [who] have fled [from Satan, Leviathan and Cain] in order to seize Christ Jesus [who] stands [in the high place, and] is the fulfillment of the calling to which we are appointed, have a mighty comfort,

6.19 That [Jesus Christ, the scout] who entered into [the spiritual city] within [the place between the eyebrows], the veil [of the high place], securely anchors our personality [in the spiritual dimension of the throat], which stabilizes [our volatile emotions].

Chapter 8

[23.1]

8.08-09 We are told that the way into the holiest place of all was not available to man when the first tabernacle was standing; only the high priest was allowed in, and

8.11, 13 Christ is the high priest of a multitude of blessings which come only through the true spiritual tabernacle, not the one made with hands, that is to say, not a natural building, but by the power of the eternal spirit, His human life produced no evil fruit, His soul had no evil spirits, no curses, no wrong thinking, He was preserved.

Chapter 9

[Message # Unknown]
9.09   Which was just a type of the real spiritual tabernacle which served for that time, in which were offered both gifts and sacrifices; But, these gifts and sacrifices could not redeem the priest's fallen nature.

[884.1]
9.11   But, the time came for Christ, [Jehovah's] high priest, the greater light [in the foundation of heaven], to come [into existence], not in a tent formed by the mind [of the first Adam], that is, not [in an earthen] habitation [like] this [one, but in] a more perfect [building],

9.12   And by the power of the eternal Spirit, his mortal life produced no evil fruit; and He was offered as a perfect sacrifice to God, and received the power to cleanse Israel from sin, and deliver them from the bondage of religious ritual into the spiritual place where they could serve the living God.

9.13   [Now], if the life of bulls and goats have the power to purify the [physical] flesh of all spiritual filthiness, how much more can the Mind of Christ Jesus...

... by the power of the Spirit of the ages, is not in any way separated from God, neither by demons, nor any other spiritual breach caused by sin, but is receiving all life, preservation and protection in the spiritual world of God through union with him . . .

9.14   Purify, clarify and restore your ability to understand spiritual truth and perform spiritual righteousness, so that you can serve the living God, spirit to Spirit, without needing to be justified through obedience to carnal rituals, because your mind is filled with spiritual filth.

[868.2]

9.15   And for this reason, [Christ] is the mediator of the New Testament, that he [might be] a ransom for the transgressions [that the first Adam committed] under the First Covenant, [and] that, by the death [of the first Adam], they which are called [to eternal life] might receive the promise of an inheritance [which will endure beyond this] age,

9.16   Because, where there is a testament, it is necessary that [the one who is standing up should] die, [so that] the one who is lying down [can stand up in his place],

[744.2.C]

9.18   And for this reason not even the first [contract] was inaugurated without separation.

[744.2.C]

9.24   Because engravings made by the mind [of the First Adam] have entered into the holy places [of the unconscious part of the mind of the people that] Christ has liberated, [which are] contrary to [the thoughts of the Second Adam, and] now [the Second Adam], the personality of God, is no longer appearing in [the foundation of] the heaven [that is] above us, and

9.25   Neither [does the First Adam] frequently appear down [here] as the high priest [who enters into the holy place [each] year with foreign blood;

9.26a   Wherefore, [the First Adam] must have suffered frequently since the foundation of the cosmos, [which is heaven, was taken] away,

9.27   But, Adam is permitted to die [to righteousness only] one time, and [in the event that it happens], after that, [he must experience the consequences set down by] the tribunal [for his crime, which is to be cast into the lake of fire],

Alternate Translation Of The New Testament/ Hebrews

9.26b But now, [the Second Adam] has appeared one time at the end of the age, to cancel the sin of this [First Adam], by suffering the loss of his [own corporeal body];

9.28 So, then, Christ presented [himself unblemished to God] one time on behalf of the many [souls of the First Adam, so that whoever] gazes at the Second [Adam, and] fully expects [him] to carry the sin[-filled soul] of each of them out [of their corporeal bodies] to physical and moral safety, will, himself [be found] without sin.

Chapter 10

[Message # Unknown]
10.05a Wherefore, when [Righteous Adam] came into the world, he said [to Israel], you prefer to make sacrifices and give offerings to God, and

10.06 God has had pleasure in your sacrifices and offerings [in the past],

10.05b But God has repaired and completed you, [and it is time for you] to be my body:

10.07 [So] come and see [that] the undifferentiated, engraved letters [that represent] God [in this lower world] are appointed to appear [in] the mortal men [where] the Kingdom [from] above [is found].

[1229.1.C]
10.09a And when

10.10a Jesus Christ offered up His body, once,

10.09b In accordance with the Will of [Jehovah]

Alternate Translation Of The New Testament/ Hebrews

10.10b To sanctify

10.09c [The members of His Church as] the Second [Witness to Jehovah's existence],

[Christ Jesus] said [to the people of Israel,

"[Jehovah] has removed [the Mosaic priesthood of Aaron and his sons], the First [Witness to His existence],

"And you are now to look [to me for atonement, so that]

10.10c "I may come [into existence] and be established [in the visible world].

[1007.1.C]
10.20 Elohim has given [us] a new, superior way to pass through the door to the most holy place; [grafting Christ Jesus], his living [blood relative, to the unconscious part of our mind, is better than] separating [our soul from our] flesh [which kills our material body];

10.22 So, let us approach [the most holy place] with truth [in our] heart, confident that Christ, [our] faith, [the Blood that the Lord Jesus] sprinkled in our hearts, has washed [away] the double-mindedness [caused by the thoughts of] the evil [one, and] cleansed the [spiritual] body [of our soul] with the pure water [of the Word],

[635]
10.26a The inward process [by which] the sin [nature] in the midst [of us] influences, seduces and deceives [us], cannot continue after we are apprehended by [the Lord Jesus], and acknowledge the truth,

10.28 [Because] anyone who sets aside the Law of Moses dies without mercy at [the mouth of] two or three witnesses;

10.26b [And] this is the reason why we [must] separate [from Cain], our sin nature, and sacrifice [Leviathan].

10.27a   Indeed,

10.29   How much greater punishment, [then], do you think [Leviathan, the one who] tramples down the Son, of God, and [Satan, the one who considers] the Blood of the Covenant an unholy thing, [and Cain, who] insults the Spirit of Grace by exercising Leviathan and Satan's authority to influence [Abel], the one who [looks] this [way] and that [way, to sin after] he was made holy by the authority of [Christ Jesus]?

10.31   [Wherefore, Cain] is afraid of the human avengers of [Abel's] blood that the living God is raising up

10.30   Because [Cain] knows that I [AM] awarded the just [legal decision to Abel], who [then] said, to me, Jehovah, I will repay [Cain] when Jehovah returns [and] prefers [Abel within] his people,

10.27b   [Wherefore], anyone [who] fears [God] should expect that [Jehovah's] divine justice is about to consume [Satan, Leviathan and Cain, Abel's] jealous opponent, in the Lake of Fire.

Chapter 11

[1008.1.C]
11.04   Abel offered a more excellent sacrifice than Cain [did] through Elohim, the anointing [in] the unconscious [part of Adam's mind], the gift that Jehovah [promised to Adam, to help his descendants transfer into the next age, and Abel continues] to speak [through] Elohim, the innocent witness [grafted to] the unconscious [part of the mind of Adam's descendants, even though Abel] is dead

11.05   Enoch cannot be found [in this world anymore, because Elohim sent him to the other, [righteous side of the Garden of Eden, where] he no longer experiences death], so that

[his] personality [could be grafted] to the unconscious [part of the mind of the many personal souls (personalities) of the fallen First Adam], in exchange for [mankind becoming the faithful and true][R] witness that pleases God,

[R] Rev 1:5, 3:14

11.07   The anointing warned Noah of things not yet apparent, [and Noah], moved by his reverence for Elohim, prepared a box that saved the household [of God in] the unconscious [part of his mind, and when] judgment [came] down upon the world, the anointing [that] inherited [him], justified [him],

11.11   Sarah, [who] had already matured to the age [when a woman becomes] sterile, miraculously ovulated [by the power of] the anointing [that Jehovah grafted to] the unconscious [part of her mind], and [her womb] also seized the seed, because she deemed the one who promised [her a son] trustworthy,

[Message # Unknown]
11.17   Abraham led Isaac to the conviction of the truth when he was tested, and presented [him with] the promise of [Christ], the [same] only begotten son that he, [Abraham], had received.

Chapter 12

[OLM - 12 16 98]
12.1   And for this reason, the aura of Christ Jesus is compassing about us, who have been curved [into a black hole] for such a long time, so let us put off all of these dark thought forms [who] stand around us on every side, thwarting [the righteous thoughts of Christ], endure Christ Jesus' corrective judgment], and spend our strength pursuing the assembling which has been revealed to us.

Alternate Translation Of The New Testament/ Hebrews

[818.1.C]
12.12 Wherefore, put your hands down [from their fighting position], and let your [Christ] mind, which the female Adam tore away (feeble) [from Jehovah], stand up, [because]

[OLM – 06 02 99]
12.13 Let the pattern of the spiritual atoms of your carnal mind be changed to the linear [straight] pattern of the Mind of Christ, so that the mind which is turned away from God should be healed.

Chapter 13

[231.1]
13.08 Remember, when considering the issue of your conduct, imitate the faith of your leaders who told you about the Word of God and Christ Jesus, who, although wrapped in flesh like [he was] in previous ages, is, nevertheless, [this time], a different age.

[1031.1.C]
13:11 The [Levitical] high priest brought the blood of the animals that were burned outside of the camp into the sanctuary for a sin offering, and

13:12 Jesus, likewise, in order to purify the people with his own spiritual blood, suffered the loss [of his animal body],

13:10 [But, the Levitical priests] who served [God] at [the altar of a physical] tabernacle, do not have the right to eat [the animal body of Jesus],

13:13a The one who bears the reproach of

13:14 Not having a body, [but] is looking forward to receiving [many bodies] that do not die,

Alternate Translation Of The New Testament/ Hebrews

13:13b [BECAUSE Christ, Jesus' blood] is issuing forth upon

[THE ALTAR of the unconscious part of the mind],

The battleground [where the priests from the tribe of Judah

Eat the living body of Jesus' personal soul (personality) that separated from his animal body, and

Drink the spiritual blood of the Supernal Mother (Elohim)].

[41.1]
13.15 Therefore, by the power of Jesus Christ [our altar which is within us], let us offer the sacrifice of putting Leviathan, our mortal mind, under foot continually, which will result in Christ Jesus in us being the [only] source of our thoughts and words, which words, because they are coming from Christ Jesus, will [always] give thanks to the Spirit of God.

THE BOOK OF JAMES

Chapter 1

[Message # Unknown]
    1.08   [and James 4:8] If you're experiencing contradictory thoughts and behavior which cause conflict in your emotions and your life, it's because you have two minds, one from the Serpent [Leviathan], and one from the Lord Jesus Christ [Christ Jesus], and it's this two-minded condition that causes your thoughts, feelings and behavior to be inconsistent.

    The solution to your problem is, to choose the thoughts and behavior of Christ Jesus, the one who imparts the power to live out of his mind by evacuating the ungodly spiritual sediment and trapped air known as demons and evil spirits, which influence you to live out of your other [evil] mind, no matter what you are feeling,

    1.18   [The Father] deliberately begat us [into the visible spiritual world], by the Lord Jesus Christ, who is the living expression of truth, so that we should be the first of his creature to sacrifice Leviathan unto himself.

[915.2.C]
    1.17a   Every gift [that comes from the Holy Spirit is] good, but everything that is given that descends from the Father of the shining lamps, above, completes [the Second Adam], who never changes his purpose or direction; nor do [the spiritual males of Israel], his shadow,

    1.18a   [Who] he begat of his own will with the Word of Truth,

1.17b [Ever] turn back [from keeping the Second Adam's commandments],

1.18b [So] that we should be the first fruit to ripen of a specie of creatures [that is born from] himself,

Chapter 4

[39.1]
4.01 Where does this state of open hostile warfare between two opposing forces, Christ and Satan, the unconscious part of the carnal mind, and an internal condition of insurrection between yourself and Satan, the unconscious part of the carnal mind, originate from?

4.02 You long to satisfy the cravings of your soul without giving up for one second, you will not stop for one second, you just want it, you even set your will against the Lord Himself when He says you cannot have it, and you still do not have, you set your will to obtain this thing, even in opposition to the Lord God, but you have not obtained it.

4.03 You finally give up and ask God, but you still do not receive peace because your sick soul man motivates you to ask for carnal things that will satisfy you temporarily, leaving you in the same spiritually needy condition, instead of asking for spiritual things that will impart eternal life to you.

4.04 You adulterous spirits and adulterous souls, do not you know that your failure to resist your union with the soul realm prevents you from entering into the kingdom of God. Everyone who does not align himself in warfare with Christ to overthrow his union with the soul realm, has declared himself openly to reject the kingdom of God.

Alternate Translation Of The New Testament/ James

4.05 Do you not know that the Scripture means what it says, when it tells you that your human spirit is trying to satisfy the lusts of your fallen soul by worshiping Satan, as God, and will do so without success until it destroys itself.

Chapter 5

[1230.6.C]

5.16 Confess your sins one to another and speak positive words out loud towards one another, because the prayer of [Christ], the righteous one, produces much strength to heal.

THE BOOK OF 1st PETER

Chapter 1

[980.3.C]

1.01   [I], Peter, an ambassador of Jesus Christ, to the elect resident foreigners [In Israel], and the converted Israelites in the Gentile nations of Pontus, Galatia, Cappadocia, Asia and Bithynia,

1.02   [Who were selected by] God the Father, [who] knew you before [you were born, to be] sprinkled with the blood of Jesus Christ, [have your heart] influenced by [the higher Mother, the Spirit] of the Divine [nature], and [have] increased peace [with God], through

(1) Submission [to Christ Jesus,[R] who] separates [you from the First Adam], and

[R] Cor 15:47

1.03   (2) Submission to God, the Father of our Lord Jesus Christ, [who], largely according to his mercy, has begotten the expectation of [eternal] life in us again,[R-1] through the resurrection of Jesus Christ from the dead,[R-2] and

[R-1] Jn 6:58, 14:19
[R-2] Rom 8:11, 10:9

1.05a   Through Christ, [our] faith,[R] [who], by the power of God, protects [us] until

[R] Vs 9a

1.04a   We inherit the unsoiled [soul] that does not corrupt or fade away, [R]

[R] Matt 6:19-20
Lk 12:33

1.05b   [Which is] the salvation [that] will be ready to be revealed at the proper time, and

1.06   [This is the reason] that you jump for joy for the season [that the Holy Spirit of Promise is upon you], but for now, if it is necessary, you are sad and in distress because of different kinds of negative experiences,[R]

[R] 1 Pet 4:12

1.07   So that the test of your faith, which is extremely more valuable than gold which perishes when it is tested in the fire, might be found to be a commendable [thing, because it develops] the honorable opinion[R] of Jesus Christ, [the quality by which] he appears [in us],

[R] Vs21

1.08   Whose opinion you love with the love of God, even though you have never seen him ([because] he is not appearing at this time), [but], you jump for joy and are filled with delight[R] that cannot be expressed in words [when you hear that]

[R] Lk 2:10 (ATB)
2 Cor 8:2 (ATB)

1.09a   He has provided [Christ], your faith,[R] to save your soul,

[R] Vs 21

1.10   Which salvation the prophets who prophesied by [the higher Mother], the Divine Influence upon the heart,[R] searched everywhere to find out [about], and

[R] Rom 11:6

1.11   They [also] sought [to know] what sort of person would explain, in plain [language], the predictions [that came forth] from within themselves, of the sufferings of Christ[R-1] and the glory that would follow, and in which time period the Spirit of Christ [would raise Messiah from the dead],^{R-2}

^{R-1} Is 53:5
^{R-2} Rom 8:11

1.09b [Which is] the ultimate result of [his sufferings], and

1.12 To whom it was disclosed that [the things that they predicted were] not [for] themselves, but [were] for us who minister [these things] which are now announced to you by [those of us who] preach the gospel to you by the Holy Spirit [of Truth which is] sent down from heaven,^R which things the angels desire to look into;

^R Jn 15:26

1.13 So, support the procreative power of your mind [by] being completely sober concerning your expectation of the revelation of Jesus Christ, the one who carries [the higher Mother], the Divine Influence upon the heart,

1.14 As submissive children, not conforming to your previous [lifestyle] in which you ignorantly craved that which is forbidden,^R

^R Eph 2:3

1.15 But, [rather], since he who has called you is holy, all of your behavior should be holy,

1.16 Inasmuch as it is written, "Because I am holy, you should be holy,"^R and

^R Lev 20:26

1.17 Since the Father, who you call upon [to save you], judges each man's work without respect of persons,^{R-1} foreign residents [living in Israel] should have the same fear of [God's] judgment^{R-2} [that natural-born Israelites have],

^{R-1} Cor 5:10
^{R-2} Eccl 12:13, Rev 14:7

1.18   [Because], as you know, you were not ransomed[R-1] from your profitless and idolatrous behaviors[R-2] with corruptible things such as silver and gold, as the traditions handed down from your fathers[R-3] say,

[R-1] 1 Tim 2:6
[R-2] Eph 2:3
[R-3] Gal 1:14

1.19   But [you were ransomed] with the valuable blood of Christ, [our Passover] Lamb,[R] which [is] unstained and without any character flaws,

[R] 1 Cor 5:7

1.20   Whose [coming] was accurately predicted before [Jesus], the foundation[R] of the world [was laid], but is, indeed, rendered apparent for you in these end times,

[R] 1 Cor 3:11

1.21   Who by [Christ],[R-1] do believe in God, that he raised [Jesus] up from the dead,[R-2] and gave [him to be] your faith,[R-1] that [having] his opinion,[R-3] [your] hope might be in God, and

[R-1] Vs 9a
[R-2] 2 Cor 4:14
[R-3] Vs 7

1.22   [Now that] your souls have been purified through obedience to the [Holy] Spirit of Truth, your clean heart has sincere brotherly affection for the brethren, [who] love each other intently with the love of God,

1.23   [Because you are] not being born [again][R-1] of perishable seed, but by the immortal Word of the Living God,[R-2] [so that] you can remain [in the earth of humanity until] the end of the age,

[R-1] Jn 3:7
[R-2] Js 1:8

1.24   Because all flesh is like grass, and your own opinion is like all the flowers of the grass: The flowers fall off and the grass withers,[R]

[R] Is 40:6-7

Alternate Translation Of The New Testament/ 1 Peter

1.25   But the Word of the Lord remains for the [entire] age;^R Indeed, [it] is this [eternal] Word by which the gospel is preached to you.

^R Is 40:8,
Matt 24:35

Chapter 2

[Message # Unknown]
2.12   I see that you have purified your mind through obedience to the truth, by the power of the Spirit, which has resulted in a sincere love for the brethren. Therefore, love one another with a spiritual love that touches each other through Christ Jesus, your new man.

Chapter 3

[Message # Unknown]
3.04   [Let your beauty be the] Adam [who is] concealed [in your] heart; [He is] humble and tranquil [to the point that] he cannot be disturbed by anything that happens outside of himself, and he cannot decay.

[590.1.C]
3.14   But if you [behave] contrary [to your fallen nature, Christ Jesus] will boil Satan, and impress, or engrave you with his Righteous [Nature], and you will be supremely blessed, but Leviathan the one who [Cain] is in awe of, will be alarmed [at the appearance] of [Christ Jesus], your other self;

3.17   Wherefore, it is good to choose [to do] the more noble thing, because it is the Will of God that you should be

Alternate Translation Of The New Testament/ 1 Peter

impressed, or engraved [with the Righteous Nature of the Lord Jesus Christ], rather than the injurious nature [of Satan],

[1259.4.C]

3.18 And also Christ, [the Angel within Jesus of Nazareth, whose character is] equal [in morality] to the character of God, suffered once for the sins of [the Angels whose character fell short of the character of God], that he might bring us, [the sheep souls of] the Angels [who are the incarnating kings, to Jehovah], by putting [our] sheep souls to death, but, on the other hand, making the Angels [who are the incarnating kings within us], alive,

3.19 By [which Angels that were made alive, Christ] also went to the Angels [that were] imprisoned [in other bodies, and] preached [to them],

3.20 Which disobeyed Jehovah at the time when He was waiting patiently in the days of Noah, for the Angels [to build the Tabernacle in] the eight [sheep] souls that were to be saved by [devolving into] the waters [of the primordial sea (Jehovah's spiritual amniotic fluid)], and coming into existence [again]after the flood, so that Jehovah could] enter into the ark [that Noah] was preparing for the most holy place, the first room of the Tabernacle],

3.21 [Through] which [devolution of soul] we also, in the same manner, are now saved through baptism (not [by] putting off the body, which is filthy, but by [receiving] a good conscience towards God) through [Christ], the angel [who dwells with us] because of the resurrection of Jesus Christ, [who directs the correct] answers towards [those who would accuse us, and]

3.22 Who, [having] gone to the righteous side of the Angels, is in heaven, the unconscious part of the mind, [all] Angels and authorities and powers, being made subject to him.

Alternate Translation Of The New Testament/ 1 Peter

Chapter 4

[590.1.C]
    4.01   Wherefore, now that Christ's animal nature has been impressed/engraved [with Jehovah's Righteous Nature, you should], in like manner, equip yourself with that same Mind, because when your animal nature is impressed engraved with [the Righteous Nature of Christ], you will be able to restrain [your carnal mind], and stop sinning,

    4.02   And it is the Will of God that [you stop indulging in] the lusts of fallen] Adam for the remainder of the time that your animal nature will spend in this existence.

[Message # Unknown]
    4.08   And above all things have fervent charity among yourselves: for **converting the sinner from the error of his way** shall cover the multitude of sins.

THE BOOK OF
2nd PETER

Chapter 1

[801.6.C]

1.03a [Jehovah] has given us everything that pertains to life and godliness

1.04c [So that] you, [too], might be partakers of the divine nature

1.03b Through a knowledge of [how Jesus], who has invited us to have his opinion and the highest standards of uprightness, beginning with our sexual standard and spreading out to every other aspect of our relationships with others

1.04a Escaped the corruption that is in the world through lust, [which is

1.04b The very reason why these] exceeding great and precious promises are given to us.

Chapter 2

[60.1]

2.04 Because, God did not grant leniency to the spiritual men that sinned, but thrust them out of the visible, spiritual world of God's Spirit, down into the visible, physical world which exists underneath the earth of mortal man, and put them into prison [the carnal mind] by joining the[ir spirit] to the darkness [Satan], the spirit which rules in mortal man, *for the purpose of preventing their personality] from marrying, until the judgment which will restore her virginity has been completed.*

[20.1]

2.13   The Divine Moral Order was already present in before Adam e broke God's Law and lost its protection, and

2.12   Now, these human animals who live their entire lives without thinking before they act, routinely obey the impulses of the Satanic realm within [the unconscious part of their carnal mind]. They do not bear live young, but increase without conscious thoughts because they are programmed to expand, and

2.14   The pain and torment associated with the righteousness of God being tread under the foot of the Satanic realm, the unconscious part of the carnal mind of each and every man born, from Adam to Moses, has ruled over mankind ever since, in violation of God's moral order, (even though our failure is much more understandable than Adam's because he had the spiritual strength to resist the Snake); Nevertheless, we, fallen Adam's descendants, are now born into this existence in the weakened spiritual condition that Adam received when he fell.

2.15   But God's favor prevents us from experiencing any loss similar to Adam's, [whose] momentary deviation stripped the protection of right standing with God from us all without giving any of us anything to say about it,

2.16-18   [Because even though] one man made us all sinners and brought many sins into this world, God's gift of salvation has the power to make many sinners righteous. For although one man's sin made many unrighteous, one Man's obedience to God has made many sinners righteous.

Alternate Translation Of The New Testament/ 2 Peter

Chapter 3

[1109.1.C]

3.01   Now, this is the second letter that I am writing to those who I love through a soul tie [with Christ Jesus], to remind your enlightened minds,

3.02   To remember the words that were spoken previously by the holy prophets. and the commandment of us, the apostles of the Lord and savior,

3.03   [That] we shall know that the last days have come upon us [when] the First [[Adam who is] within [us], taunts us [with] false teachers [who tell us that we can] follow the forbidden lifestyle that we long for,

3.04   Saying, "What happened to [Jehovah's] promise [that his Son] would appear in the unconscious part of the mind [of Abraham's descendants? Because] nothing has changed since [Abraham, Isaac and Jacob], the patriarchs, fell asleep. Everything is just like it was when [Elohim] created it in the beginning."

3.05   Because [these false teachers] are not of those who delight in this hidden [truth, that] the heavens [that came into existence through] the ancient of days, when] the earth [was mixed with the waters of the soul that became a sludge, and] stood up [as individual personalities and] the egos [that are contained with] in [them], and

3.06   That the world that Elohim formed [around those ego-personality clusters] was then overcome [by the power of the] soul, and completely destroyed;

3.07   And the ego-personality clusters [that exist in Christ Jesus] now, [were formed by that] same ancient of days, but are stored away and guarded against [the destructive opinion of the soul, until] the day of the trial of [the First] Adam, [who] was ruined [when] he disrespected [Jehovah by not obeying his instruction];

3.08   But you who I love through a soul tie [with Christ Jesus], are not ignorant of this hidden thing, that one day [in the World of Creation where] the Lord is, is experienced as one thousand years [in this world], and [that] one thousand years [in this world, is experienced] as one day [in the World of Creation], and

3.09   [That] God is long-suffering towards us because he is not willing that the Son of Man that has been born within us should be fully destroyed, but that the whole [Adam]* should come to repentance;

> *** The whole Adam** is The First Adam, the man of the earth, The Second Adam, the Lord from heaven (1 Cor 15:47), and the Son of Adam (Man) (Matt 16:28), who is born of the seed that Jehovah gave to Abraham (Heb 11:11) and Jehovah's breath (Gen 2:7) that he breathed into Adam at the beginning.

3.10   Indeed, the day of the Lord will come as a thief in which [the Holy Spirit], the whirlwind [from the two] heavens [of the World of Emanation and the World of Creation], shall come near to [Jehovah's breath, the primordial] elements in the unconscious part of the mind, [that became Satan and the Devil],[R-1] and set them on fire [until] they liquefy, [R-2] [and Cain, that wicked one], [R-3] is consumed, and the First Adam, who has] to work [for his food because of Jehovah's curse], [R-4]

[R-1] Rev 20:2
[R-2] Jer 6:29
[R-3] Mal 4:3
[R-4] Gen 3:17-19

Alternate Translation Of The New Testament/ 2 Peter

3.11   Shall see what the holy behavior [that comes from] godliness ought to be, [after] all these things are loosened, [if he plucks them out of his eye],^R

^R Matt 5:29

3.12   [Then you will be] looking for and eagerly awaiting the appearance of God, the day when [the Holy Spirit, the two] Heavens [of the World of Emanation and the World of creation], start the fire that loosens the primordial] elements [in the unconscious part of the mind, that became Satan and the Devil], and burns them with fire [until] they liquefy (melt), [and Cain, that wicked one, is consumed];

3.13   Indeed, we anticipate a new higher soul and a new earth[en personality], according to the promise ^R [that Jehovah made to Abraham, that] the justified one will dwell in the unconscious part of the mind [of his descendants],

^R Gen 22:17

3.14   Wherefore, [if] all of you that I love through a soul tie [with Christ Jesus] anticipate [receiving] these things, [you should] make every effort [to be] morally unblemished and blameless in the unconscious part of the mind, [where] peace [with God] is obtained, and

3.15   Consider that the long-suffering of our Lord is [for our] salvation, even as our brother Paul, who we love through a soul tie [with Christ Jesus], has written to you, according to the wisdom given to him,

3.16   In all [his other] epistles, in which he speaks about these things which are hard to understand, which the unlearned and [those whose opinions are] unstable,^R pervert, as they also do [with] other scriptures [as well], to the destruction of [Christ Jesus], their other self in the unconscious part of the mind;

^R 1 Ki 18:21
Eph 4:14
Js 1:8

3.17   Therefore, all of you who I love through a soul tie [with Christ Jesus; Since now that] you know about these things

Alternate Translation Of The New Testament/ 2 Peter

before they happen, be careful to avoid them so that you do not make the same mistake that [Cain],^R that wicked one made, who was led away from the stable path of [Christ Jesus], his other self,

^R 1 Jn 3:1
Jude 1:1

3.18   May the divine influence upon your heart and your knowledge of our Lord and Savior Jesus Christ increase, [and may] the [moral] opinion [of God be found in] the unconscious part of your mind, which permits you to pass from the Church] age to the [next] age [of Christ Jesus].

THE BOOK OF
1st JOHN

Chapter 2

[338.3]
    2.13   Little children,[124] you have been overcoming the wicked one[R-1] since you had [spiritual] intercourse with the Lord Jesus Christ,[R-2] so now I am forming you into 1) young members of the two-witness company, and 2) [young] fathers[125] who have a doctrinal understanding that the immature Mind of Christ [the

---

[124] The Greek word translated **little children**, in verse 13, **Strong's** #3813, means, **infant**. An infant's sex can be determined by looking at his body, but not by observing his behavior. Infantile behavior is sexually undifferentiated: It neither signifies discipleship, that is, exposure and correction of sin mind, nor warfare, either against Leviathan [conscious, mortal mind] in their own mind, such as young fathers engage in, or against Leviathan in other mortal minds, as well as their own, such as mature fathers engage in.

[125] **Fathers** are mortal men who have the spiritual authority to reproduce the nature of the Lord Jesus Christ in other mortal men (1 Cor. 9:2). (Read entire footnote in Appendices)

first Adam (the living soul)] was separated from Jehovah[126] in the beginning;[R-3] and

> [R-1] Matt 13:28
> Is 14:29 (AT)
> [R-2] Pro 29:30 (AT)
> Zech11:11-12 (AT)
> [R-3] Gen 2:23-25 (AT)
> Dan 8:6-7 (AT)
> Rom 5:6 (AT)

2.12,14 [You, my] Disciples,[127] you have been overcoming the wicked one since the Lord Jesus Christ engrafted himself to [Abel] your fallen soul, and [Christ] began to mature in you, and Christ Jesus began to forgive your sins, and now I am forming you into [strong young fathers] (See, *Note #124*), mature members of the two-witness company, who are experiencing the resurrection of the first Adam, the one who was separated from Jehovah in the beginning.[128]

[245]
2.15   The Word of God is not in the man who communes with Leviathan or Satan, so do not commune with them.

---

[126] That is, a doctrinal understanding of **what happened**.

[127] The Greek word translated **little children**, in verse 12, **Strong's** #5040, means, **disciple**. The most obvious sign that someone following Christ Jesus has entered into discipleship, that is, training to be like the master, is **correction** (Pro 13:24; 23:13-14; Heb 12:6-7.) (Read entire footnote in Appendices)

[128] Waging war against Leviathan in one's own mind, as well and in other men's minds results in the first Adam [the living soul] rising from the dead as one's own renewed Christ mind, which is in Jehovah's image (1 Cor 15:3-4). (Read entire footnote in Appendices)

Chapter 5

[607.4.C]

Spiritual Completion

5.01   [Whoever is] complete[R-1] believes that Jesus is the regenerated Christ[R-2] of God, and is attached to the regenerated [first Adam,[R-3] and is] also attached [to Christ in] whoever [Jesus has] regenerated[R-4] him,

[R-1] Col 2:10
[R-2] 1 Cor 15:4
[R-3] 1 Cor 15:45
[R-4] Matt 19:28

Attached To God

5.02   And this is how we disciples know that we are attached[R-1] to God: When we are attached to God, we keep his commandments,[R-2]

[R-1] Mal 1:2-3
[R-2] Ex 20:1-17

The Love Of God

5.03   Because God [demonstrated his] love for us [when he gave us his] commandments, and keeping his commandments is not a hardship [when his son is born[R] in us],

[R] Rev 12:5

Our Faith

5.04   Because, when God regenerates the whole [Adam], he subdues the [spiritual] world [within himself], and he succeeds [in subduing] this [spiritual world] through [the Lord Jesus Christ, the beginning and end of] our faith;^R

^R Heb 12:2

Overcoming The Fallen Nature

5.05   Whose [spiritual seminal fluid provides the seed that] subdues the world [of our fallen nature], unless we do not believe that Jesus is the Son of God,^R

^R Rom 11:20

Joseph & Abraham

5.06   [Because] Jesus Christ is the one who came into existence by the spirit[ually female seed of] the seminal fluid [of Joseph, the son of David],[R-1] and by [the male] spirit[ual] blood [seed of Abraham];[R-2] not only by [the spiritually female seed of] the seminal fluid of [Joseph, the son of David],[R-1] but by [the spiritually female seed of] the seminal fluid [of Joseph, the son of David][R-1] *AND* [the male spiritual] blood [seed of Abraham];[R-2] and the Spirit of Truth[R-3] is [one of]

[R-1] Lk 3:23
[R-2] Gal 3:16
[R-3] Jn 1:17

Three Witnesses In Heaven

5.07   The three witnesses in heaven that [Jesus is the Son of God]:[R-1] *the Father*,[R-2] *the Word [of God]*,[R-3] and *the Holy Spirit*,[R-4] and these three [comprise *Ancient Adam*,[R-5] who is] one, whole [spiritual man,[R-6] and]

[R-1] Heb 4:14
[R-2] Pro 9:1
[R-3] Rev 19:13
[R-4] Pro 24:3
[R-5] Dan 7:9
[R-6] Acts 17:28

Alternate Translation Of The New Testament/ 1 John

Three Witnesses In The Earth

5.08   There are three that bear witness in the earth [that Jesus is the Son of God, the human] spirit,[R-1] [the spiritually female seed of] the seminal fluid [of Joseph, the son of David],[R-2] and the [spiritual] blood [seed of Abraham],[R-3] and these three [comprise Christ Jesus,[R-4] who is] one [whole spiritual man].

[R-1] Rom 8:15
Gal 4:6
[R-2] Lk 3:23
[R-3] Gal 3:16
[R-4] 1 Tim 2:5

Jesus Greater Than Moses

5.09   [Now, if] we believe the evidence [that God gave to prove that Moses[R-1] was] a completed man,[R-2] [we should also believe] the evidence [that] God [gave to prove that Jesus is greater than Moses], and this is the evidence that God has presented with respect to his Son:

[R-1] Ex 7:14-18
[R-2] Col 2:10

Eternal Life Is In Jesus Christ

5.11   God has given us eternal life[R-1] and that life is in [Jesus Christ], his Son,[R-2] and this is the evidence: [that God has given us eternal life through Jesus Christ]:

[R-1] Jn 17:3
[R-2] Jn 6:54

Christ In You[R-1]

5.12   Whoever is possessed by [Christ Jesus],[R-1] the Son [of Jesus Christ], has [eternal] life,[R-2] and whoever is not possessed by [Christ Jesus, the Son of Jesus Christ], the Son of God, does not have eternal life; [and],

[R-1] Col 1:27
[R-2] Jn 10:28
Rom 6:23

361

True Witness, False Witness

5.10   Whoever believes [that Jesus Christ is] the Son of God, is possessed by [Christ Jesus], *the witness of God within himself*; but [the personality] that does not believe [that Jesus Christ is the Son of] God, is possessed by [Satan and Leviathan, their carnal mind], **the false witness**[R] [that God is] within himself, [because the carnal mind of fallen Adam] does not believe the evidence that God testified to [concerning] his Son,

[R] 1 Thess 2:11

The Nature Of God

5.13   I have written these things to you [who] believe [that it is possible to acquire Christ[R-1]], the nature,[R-2] of the Son of God, to help you to become intimate [with the Lord Jesus Christ],   the Son of God, [who is the way[R-3] we begin to attain] eternal life through [Christ[R-1]], the nature of [God,[R-2] and

[R-1] Gal 3:16
Col 1:27
[R-2] 2 Pet 1:4
[R-3] Jn 14:6

God Hears Our Prayers

5.14   When we have the nature[R-1] of God within us], we are bold enough [to believe] that [the Father] hears[R-2] us when we ask for anything that is according to his Will,[R-3] and

[R-1] 2 Pet 1:4
[R-2] Jn 9:31
[R-3] Lk 22:42

According To His Will

5.15   We know that if [the Father] hears everything that we ask for, we [also] know that we will receive everything that we desire [that is according to his Will for us];

Alternate Translation Of The New Testament/ 1 John

Remission of Sin For The Ignorant[R-1]

5.16a   [So], if anyone sees his brother sin a sin that does not call for capital punishment,[R-1] and he asks [the Father to pardon that man,[R-2] the Father] will give life[R-3] to [that man whose] sin does not call for capital punishment. [However], there is a sin that calls for capital punishment, and I am clearly telling you not to pray for [the man who is guilty] of it.

[R-1] Lk 12:48
[R-2] Jn 20:23
[R-3] Jn 10:10

Repentance For The Sons

5.16b   [Also], if any one perceives that his brother[R-1] [who] has been granted [eternal] life, [might be] sinning a sin that could result in the death [of the resurrected Christ within himself, and reveals it to him], and [the son of God] asks [to be forgiven] he will not die,[R-2] [but you should know that] instructing [the sinner who will not repent, and] praying for him, will not [stop Satan], his sin nature [who is the enforcer of Jehovah's righteous Sowing & Reaping Judgment, from bestowing] death upon him.[R-3]

[R-1] Matt 12:50
[R-2] Jn 20:23
[R-3] Heb 6:4-6

Christ Does Not Sin

5.18   We know that [Christ, the one who] is born of God,[R-1] does not sin, but, on the contrary, [Christ, the one who] God has begotten,[R-2] guards [Abel, his other self, against Cain, the daughter of Satan], the evil one,[R-3] [who desires] to engage in spiritual sexual intercourse of the mind with [him];

[R-1] Heb 5:5
[R-2] Heb 11:7
[R-3] Rev 18:9

The Power to Forgive Sins[R-1]

5.17   [Nevertheless], everything that is unjust and unfair is sin, [and all sin is punishable by death],[R-2] but sometimes sin does not result in death [when you repent and Christ Jesus forgives your sin].[R-3]

[R-1] Lk 5:24
[R-2] Rom 6:23
[R-3] Jn 20:23

Jesus, The Only Reality

5.19   [Now], we know that all [the denizens of] the world [of Forms, the Astral Plane], where the unclean spirits and demons][R-1] are lying [in bed with Satan], the evil one,[R-2] but we [also] know that the Son of God is come, and [that] he has given us the understanding that Jesus Christ, the Son of God, is the only one who is true,[R-3] and that we are a part of his reality,[R4] which is the eternal life of God,[R-5] [and]

[R-1] Matt 12:43
[R-2] Rev 18:9
[R-3] Jn 14:6
Rev 3:14
[R-4] Col 1:8
[R-5] 1 Tim 6:15

God Is Inside Of Us

5.20   We [also] know that [the reason that] the Son of God has come, and has given us understanding, [is] that we may know the Truth,[R-1] and the Truth is that [Christ Jesus], the Son of Jesus Christ, is in[side[R-2] of] us, and that this [Christ Jesus] is the [only] genuine [source of] the eternal life of God.[R-3]

[R-1] Jn 8:32
[R-2] Lk 17:21
[R-3] 1 Tim 6:15

Alternate Translation Of The New Testament/ 1 John

Idols In The Heart

5.21   [Wherefore, brethren], may [Christ Jesus] guard all of you [spiritual] children from [Satan and Leviathan, your carnal mind, which are] the idols [in your heart].**R**

R Ex 14:7

THE BOOK OF
JUDE

Chapter 1

[Common Salvation, Sheila R. Vitale (Christ-Centered Kabbalah, NY 2014)]

1.01   Jude, the servant of Jesus Christ and brother of James, to [the brethren] whose [human spirit] is separated [from their bestial nature] by God the Father, and [whose personality] is preserved [through union with] Jesus Christ, and are called [to return to the immortality of innocence]:

1.02   May the mercy, and the peace, and the love of God be multiplied unto you.

1.03   Beloved of God, it was morally necessary for me to write to you, to exhort you to seriously strive [to recover] the faith that was given to the Saints at one time, [wherefore], I have made every effort to write to you concerning the salvation that does not produce the atonement,

1.04   [Because], it is written, that [in the last days, the Kings] from the previous ages who had no fear of God and were condemned by him, shall refuse to honor our only master, the Lord Jesus Christ, and will secretly enter into [your subconscious] alongside Adam, [your righteous mind], with the intent of changing the accepted [use of your physical bodies], into vehicles [to be used] to satisfy [their] insatiable desire for [sexual] pleasure, and

1.05   I will, therefore, remind you of what you once knew, [that when Christ did not rise] in the people after the Lord saved them out of the land of Egypt, [their personalities and their

Alternate Translation Of The New Testament/ Jude

physical bodies] were destroyed, [because there was no place for the male seed to attach itself],

1.06   And [that] the Angels which did not guard themselves at their beginning, but left their own residences [to join with the earth], were imprisoned by the judgment [that] shackles them, [through] perpetual [reincarnations], to the dark under[side of mortal mankind, until the great day [of Jubilee, when everything will be restored to its rightful owner], and

1.07   [That these same fallen Kings who] were separated from [Jehovah], their source, [and who] also came under [Elohim's] justice, [which] burnt [them] in the [lake] of fire, are examples of [Jehovah's judgment upon] lust [for spiritual ascension], which corrupted the flesh of the other [species that] they were attached to with lascivious thoughts, and

1.08   Likewise, in the same manner, [these fallen Kings], indeed, also pollute your flesh; indeed, they slander [Christ], the opinion of God, and render secular authority that promotes liberty, null and void, [to bring to pass] their dream [of a one-world Utopian society that they will rule over];

1.09   Indeed, when Michael, the Archangel, verbally distinguished [between] the Devil, [Moses' emotions, and Christ], Moses' living, [spiritual] body, he dared not bring an official judgment of blasphemy against [the fallen Kings within Moses], but said [to them], the Lord charges you [with blasphemy]; and

1.10   As much as, indeed, the physical, irrational beasts [that] these [Kings influence] do not understand that they are speaking evil of Elohim, nevertheless, they know how to do the things that [cause Christ] to wither and shrivel up, [and enjoy doing them];

1.11   Woe unto them because they are following Cain's lifestyle, and making the same mistakes as Balaam, who hired

Alternate Translation Of The New Testament/ Jude

out his anointing for pay, and Korah, who disputed [Moses' right to rule over Israel];

1.12   These [Kings] are [like] reefs in the sea [that shipwreck the souls that are born from the] love of God, so hold your [ship] on a good course, fearlessly teaching true doctrine [and avoiding] the souls that have no spirit [in their sails; but] bear up alongside [Adam to take his energy, because] these [Kings] are uprooted [spiritual] trees, stripped of [their outer bodies and] unable to reproduce themselves, who died [when they left their primordial residences, and] died again [on the other side of the flood];

1.13   They are gloomy shadows that wander into the unconscious part of the female mind [with] their own [interpretation of the Scripture], and guard themselves from loss or injury in this age by incarnating as the wild, turbulent [emotions of Leviathan's male] Rings, [which are collectively called, *the pride of man*]; and

1.14a   Enoch, [the disciplinarian of the world before the Flood], prophesied of these saying, behold, the Lord [Jesus Christ] will enter into [the world to come] through the 7th [Ring] of the Sons of Wisdom

1.15a   To judge the whole

1.14b   Adam,

1.15b   To convince all of his souls of all [their] ungodly actions, and of all the wicked, carnal [words that their] wicked [selves] have spoken against their [righteous] selves, and

1.16   [The bodies that these fallen Kings are incarnate in] are discontented grumblers, whose mouths speak prideful [words] that flatter people for their own benefit, [whose main purpose in life is] to satisfy their own lusts;

Alternate Translation Of The New Testament/ Jude

1.17   Indeed, beloved, you should remember the predictions of the apostles of the Lord Jesus Christ,

1.18   How they told you that in the last day, there would be false teachers who would follow after their own ungodly lust [to teach, rather than the Spirit of Truth], and

1.19   That there would be those who would hold on to their bestial nature, and refuse to separate it from the Spirit [of Truth];

1.20   But you, beloved of God, are rearing up [Christ Jesus], the holy one, upon [the foundation of] your faith, [which you received by] praying in the Holy Spirit,

1.21   So, let the love of God guard you against loss or injury [in this age, rather than the raging emotions of the fallen Kings], by looking to the mercy of our Lord Jesus Christ, unto eternal life, and

1.22   Have compassion on some, by thoroughly separating [their bestial nature from the Spirit of Truth], and

1.23   Save others by pulling them out of the fire; indeed, be compassionate, but take care that you do not stain the flesh of your body [when you draw near to] that which is detestable,

1.24a   [Because of your] exuberant joy [over their reconciliation to God];

1.24b   Now, to him that is able to keep you from stumbling, and to stand up [Christ Jesus], the very presence of God's unblemished opinion in you,

1.25a   To God, our Saviour, through Jesus Christ, our Lord, whose wisdom alone [is greater than the wisdom of] Glory (Hod), Majesty (Malchut) and Dominion (Gevurah), [the left column,

1.25b   May his] authority [be over] all [worlds], both now, and to all ages. Amen.

END NOTE

^A The Lord is telling me that Jesus did not die. On the contrary, Christ, the spiritual man within the mortal man Jesus (born of a woman), was resurrected, or arose out of, the physical body that He dwelled in.

Now, because the personality (mortal soul) known as Jesus of Nazareth was completely fused (married) to Christ, the spiritual man within himself, the two, Christ and the personality, Jesus of Nazareth, escaped from (ascended out of) the physical body (prison house, grave) that they were woven together with.

Jesus' physical body was an aspect of the material manifestation of the spiritual state called *death* (this whole world system). Christ and the soul (mortal personality) known as Jesus of Nazareth, breathed out of Jesus' physical body before that physical body died, which spiritual exodus caused Jesus' physical body to dissolve. The flesh and bones of a personality that escapes from its physical body, and lives, dissolve.

An earthen carcass is left behind in this world **ONLY** when the physical body dies **BEFORE** the personality (mortal soul) of the man exits the body.

We know that the physical bodies of Elijah and Moses were never found, so it is difficult to determine whether the physical body dissolves at the exact instant that the spiritual man departs (which would mean that it was a miracle that Jesus' body held its shape long enough for Joseph of Arimathea to transport it to the cave where Jesus' grave clothes were found (so that the world could relate to his resurrection)], or, if the abandoned physical body dissolves over a period of time.

Alternate Translation Of The New Testament/ End Note

My response to those who would say, *I believe that Jesus died because He said, 'destroy this temple and I will raise it up in three days,'* is, as follows:

The whole point behind the *Alternate Translation Bible* is that when you look at the Scripture *in the raw* (Interlinear Text), you will discover that more than one translation can be rendered from each word, phrase, or idea,

The Interlinear text of John 2:19 reads:

Destroy temple this and in three days I will raise up it up in three days.

If we move the words around, we can say: *In three days I will raise up it and destroy this temple.*

The Greek word translated *destroy*, *Strong's* 3089, can also be translated *dissolve*, the Greek word translated *and*, *Strong's* 2532, can also be translated *then*, and the Greek word translated *it*, *Strong's* 846, can also be translated *myself*. Also, there is a Greek word that is not translated, *Strong's* 3588, which can also be translated *it*. The King James translators did not translate this word because they could not find any use for a second *it*, but since we are translating *Strong's* 846 *myself*, we will use the second *it* in our *Alternate Translation*.

Also, the tense of a verb is frequently the result of *translator's license*, because the Hebrew text (I am not sure about the Greek, but it appears to be true in the Greek also) is very ambiguous, since it is written without any vowels or punctuation.

In view of all of the above, we can now say,

On the third day I will raise myself up [out of] this temple, and it will dissolve.

Alternate Translation Of The New Testament/ End Note

WITNESS:

Luke 13:32, And he said unto them, Go ye, and tell that fox, Behold, I cast out devils, and I do cures today and tomorrow, and ***the third day I shall be perfected***. KJV

When we weave the two Scriptures together, we get an ***Interspersed Alternate Translation***, as follows:

And he said unto them, Go ye, and tell that fox, Behold, I cast out devils, and I do cures today and tomorrow, and [on] ***the third day*** I will ***be perfected***, and arise [out of] this temple, and [this temple] shall dissolve,

HALLELUJAH!!!

APPENDICES

Matthew

Footnote #1

Satan, the enforcer of the Sowing & Reaping Judgment, is a translation of ***Strong's*** #3985, translated ***tempted*** in Matt. 4:1,

Matt 4:1
> ⁴ THEN WAS JESUS LED UP OF THE SPIRIT INTO THE WILDERNESS TO BE TEMPTED OF THE DEVIL.

and ***tempter*** in Matt. 4:3.

Matt 4:3
> ³ AND WHEN THE TEMPTER CAME TO HIM, HE SAID, IF THOU BE THE SON OF GOD, COMMAND THAT THESE STONES BE MADE BREAD.

The phrase ***thou shall tempt*** in Matt. 4:7 is a translation of ***Strong's*** #1598, another Greek word.

Matt 4:7
> ⁷ JESUS SAID UNTO HIM, IT IS WRITTEN AGAIN, THOU SHALT NOT TEMPT THE LORD THY GOD.

Strong's #3985, can be translated ***to scrutinize*** or ***to discipline***, and ***Strong's*** #1598, means ***to test thoroughly***.

Jesus taught his disciples, who were still under the influence of Satan, the unconscious part of the carnal mind, that Jehovah's Law prohibits the carnal mind from testing the authenticity of Christ in another man.

Christ is the only one permitted to pass judgment on the authenticity of Christ in another man.

Alternate Translation Of The New Testament/ Appendix – Matthew

Satan disciplines mortal men who are in rebellion against Jehovah's Righteous Spiritual Law. This is **the Sowing & Reaping Judgment**,

Christ Jesus teaches and corrects the mortal men who willingly submit to his correction. This is **the White Throne Judgment**.

Footnote #2

Spiritual genetic material is an interpretation of the English word *stone*, which can signify the pit of a fruit, which contains the entire genetic blueprint of the whole tree.

The *white stone* promised to the overcomers in Rev. 2:17, signifies *the spiritual genetic heritage of the Light*. (*White*, *Strong's* #3022, means Light).

Rev 2:17

[17] HE THAT HATH AN EAR, LET HIM HEAR WHAT THE SPIRIT SAITH UNTO THE CHURCHES; TO HIM THAT OVERCOMETH WILL I GIVE TO EAT OF THE HIDDEN MANNA, AND WILL GIVE HIM A **WHITE STONE**, AND IN THE STONE A NEW NAME WRITTEN, WHICH NO MAN KNOWETH SAVING HE THAT RECEIVETH IT.

Rom 13:12

[12] THE NIGHT IS FAR SPENT, THE DAY IS AT HAND: LET US THEREFORE CAST OFF THE WORKS OF DARKNESS, AND LET US PUT ON THE **ARMOUR OF LIGHT**.

1 Thess 5:5

[5] YE ARE ALL THE **CHILDREN OF LIGHT**, AND THE CHILDREN OF THE DAY: WE ARE NOT OF THE NIGHT, NOR OF DARKNESS.

Footnote #3

Spiritual bread signifies a man who is so possessed by the Word of God, that his wisdom, teaching and counsel *feeds* Christ in other men.

Satan, the unconscious part of the carnal mind that Jesus received from Mary, suggested to Jesus that he bring the promise of spiritual ascension to pass in his own strength, rather than wait for the Spirit of Elijah to accomplish it for him.

Footnote #5

Righteous Adam is called ***Christ Jesus*** when he is regenerated in a man by Jesus' Holy Spirit ***Abel*** is the descendant of Righteous Adam, who went to sleep after the Woman committed adultery with the Snake.

Gen 2:21

[21] AND THE LORD GOD CAUSED A DEEP SLEEP TO FALL UPON ADAM, AND HE SLEPT: AND HE TOOK ONE OF HIS RIBS, AND CLOSED UP THE FLESH INSTEAD THEREOF;

Footnote #6

The ***whole Word of God*** includes the knowledge (1) that Satan is the unconscious part of the carnal mind that all mortal men are born with, (2) that Christ must be formed in the individual, (3) that the Holy Spirit is not Christ, and (4) that the Mind of Christ must overthrow the carnal mind, if the individual is to experience ***the end of their faith***, which is the salvation of their soul.

1 Pet 1:9

[9] RECEIVING THE END OF YOUR FAITH, EVEN THE SALVATION OF YOUR SOULS.

Footnote #8

The physical body is the temple of the Holy Spirit,

1 Cor 6:19

> [19] WHAT? KNOW YE NOT THAT YOUR BODY IS THE TEMPLE OF THE HOLY GHOST WHICH IS IN YOU, WHICH YE HAVE OF GOD, AND YE ARE NOT YOUR OWN?

. . . and the Body of Christ, which is the Mind of Christ, is the temple of God (Elohim).

Footnote #10

Jesus of Nazareth was still a mortal man when Satan, the unconscious part of the carnal mind that Jesus inherited from Mary, tested him. Jesus became *The Christ* after he brought that carnal mind into submission to the regenerated Adam (see, *Note #4*) within himself (Rom 1:4), and Righteous Adam was rejoined to Jehovah above though the mediatorship of the Spirit of Elijah.

Matt 11:14

> [14] AND IF YE WILL RECEIVE IT, THIS IS ELIAS, WHICH WAS FOR TO COME.

Footnote #11

The carnal mind that Jesus inherited from Mary told Jesus that he had the power to reconnect his earthen self to the God world above by means of an earthly power.

This is what the Jews believe, that an earthly power can restore the glory that Israel experienced in the previous age.

The truth, however, is that the only way back up to the God world is by a line that is let down from above to below, and Jesus is that line.

Alternate Translation Of The New Testament/ Appendix – Matthew

Zech 1:16

¹⁶ Therefore thus saith the Lord; I am returned to Jerusalem with mercies: my house shall be built in it, saith the Lord of hosts, and a line shall be stretched forth upon Jerusalem.

Footnote #Error! Bookmark not defined.

Christ was killed by the Serpent, the progenitor of the carnal mind, in the previous age.

Rom 5.8-5.9 – AT:

5.8 *But the love of God is uniting the members of the whole living soul into himself through the imparted Christ, we being sinners because the death of the imputed Christ in the past age, is overshadowing us."*

5.9 *Much more preferable than being justified at this present time, by the resurrected Christ life then, there's something even better than that our souls shall be saved from God's judgment, upon this fallen creation, because of him. (ATB)*

Footnote #19

The regenerated Adam within Jesus had spiritual sexual intercourse with the dead Abel, Adam's root system, within the disciples, and Abel rose from the dead within the disciples, with a new name, Christ.

1 Cor 15:3

³ For I delivered unto you first of all that which I also received, how that Christ died for our sins according to the scriptures;

Christ is the virile female seed that is capable of producing the male offspring of Righteous Adam.

Alternate Translation Of The New Testament/ Appendix – Matthew

Footnote #24

Leviathan, the Devil and Satan, are present-day expressions of the Ancient Serpent who appeared in the Garden. They are all spiritual females.

Rev 20:2

> ² AND HE LAID HOLD ON THE DRAGON, THAT OLD SERPENT, WHICH IS THE DEVIL, AND SATAN, AND BOUND HIM A THOUSAND YEARS,

Footnote #Error! Bookmark not defined.

Thayer says that the Greek word translated *Jerusalem*, *Strong's* #2414, means *double peace*, and we have already translated it that way. But, for this verse, the Lord had me investigate the roots that the Hebrew word translated *Jerusalem*, is derived from.

Much to my surprise, I found out that the Hebrew word translated *Jerusalem* is derived from two Hebrew words, *Strong's* #3384, *mother*, and *Strong's* #3389, *mother-thresher*, or *matricide, the murder of a mother*.

Spiritually speaking, the Earth is the mother of creation, and the Primordial Serpent, who is appearing as Satan and Leviathan today, is the spiritual earth.

Rev 20:2

> ² AND HE LAID HOLD ON THE DRAGON, THAT OLD SERPENT, WHICH IS THE DEVIL, AND SATAN, AND BOUND HIM A THOUSAND YEARS,

Jehovah generated the spiritual substance of the creation, but the Primordial Serpent murdered Adam to acquire it and form it in her own image.

The world, as we know it, therefore, is an illegal formation of the spiritual substance of Jehovah's creation, which the Lord Jesus Christ will rearrange in his own image in the age to come.

The followers of Christ, who are fearlessly facing the truth about humanity's fallen state of being in preparation for deliverance from this present world, which is hell, know that Satan is the mother, and Leviathan is the father, of mortal humanity.

Jesus came to restore us to our first estate (Jude 6), which is the nature (image) of God.

JUDE 1:6

⁶ AND THE ANGELS WHICH KEPT NOT THEIR FIRST ESTATE, BUT LEFT THEIR OWN HABITATION, HE HATH RESERVED IN EVERLASTING CHAINS UNDER DARKNESS UNTO THE JUDGMENT OF THE GREAT DAY.

Footnote #30

Satan speaks the truth in a manner designed to stir up the sin of pride within Peter,

Gen 3:5-6

⁵ FOR GOD DOTH KNOW THAT IN THE DAY YE EAT THEREOF, THEN YOUR EYES SHALL BE OPENED, AND YE SHALL BE AS GODS, KNOWING GOOD AND EVIL.

⁶ AND WHEN THE WOMAN SAW THAT THE TREE WAS GOOD FOR FOOD, AND THAT IT WAS PLEASANT TO THE EYES, AND A TREE TO BE DESIRED TO MAKE ONE WISE, SHE TOOK OF THE FRUIT THEREOF, AND DID EAT, AND GAVE ALSO UNTO HER HUSBAND WITH HER; AND HE DID EAT.

. . . which sin would result in Peter's fall from the spiritual dimension of the throat, the spiritual place of safety that Peter had ascended to through his relationship with Jesus, the Christ.

Mark

Footnote #36

The Greek word translated *tempt* can also be translated *to discipline* or *to scrutinize* (see, *Note #1*), and *scrutinize* can also mean *to weaken*.

In (Matt 4.01), Jesus *disciplines the Devil*, the personalities who are in agreement with Satan and Leviathan, their carnal mind...

> **Matt 4.01 – AT:** *Then Jesus, by the power of the Spirit that He had just received, led Himself, or His soul life, up into the realm of spiritual power, where He would be disciplined, or tested with respect to the Devil, who is His own fallen soul.* **(ATB)**

... but in Mk. 1:13, Jesus weakens Satan within the disciples who are intimate, or in agreement, with Righteous Adam, so that Jesus' disciples can discipline Satan, the unconscious part of their carnal mind.

> **Mk 1.13 – AT***: Indeed, [Adam] appeared in the left side of [Jesus'] heart to weaken Satan [within the personalities that Jesus was spiritually intimate with, so that Jesus' disciples] could discipline [Satan], take charge over [Cain], the fiery serpent [within themselves], and become angels that minister [to Jesus' friends]* **(ATB)**

Footnote #38

Conscious, subconscious and unconscious.

The carnal mind of mortal man:

Cain is the part that is *conscious*, or aware of the visible, *physical* world, and lusts for it;

Cain, the fiery serpent, is the *subconscious* part of the mind that is aware of Satan's spiritual planes of consciousness; and

Satan is the *unconscious* part of the mind that has all knowledge of the Ancient Serpent's creation.

The Christ mind, our inheritance:

The Spirit of Christ is the *unconscious* part of the mind that has all knowledge of Jehovah's eternal creation, as well as the Ancient Serpent's temporary creation;

Cain, the fiery serpent married to Righteous Adam is the *subconscious* part of the mind that is aware of the Kingdom of God, which is the God Mind; and

Abel married to Cain, the fiery serpent, who is married to Righteous Adam, is the part of the mind that is *conscious*, or aware of the visible, *spiritual* world, and desires it.

Footnote #39

The fiery serpents that marry Christ Jesus become *seraphim*.

Is 6:2-3

[2] ABOVE IT STOOD THE SERAPHIMS: EACH ONE HAD SIX WINGS; WITH TWAIN HE COVERED HIS FACE, AND WITH TWAIN HE COVERED HIS FEET, AND WITH TWAIN HE DID FLY.

[3] AND ONE CRIED UNTO ANOTHER, AND SAID, HOLY, HOLY, HOLY, IS THE LORD OF HOSTS: THE WHOLE EARTH IS FULL OF HIS GLORY.

Footnote #43

The Ring called *Majesty* (*Malchut*) (Ez 1:18) carries the female seed which, when joined to the male seed of Righteous Adam, produces the man child of Rev 12:5.

Ez 1:18

¹⁸ AS FOR THEIR RINGS, THEY WERE SO HIGH THAT THEY WERE DREADFUL; AND THEIR RINGS WERE FULL OF EYES ROUND ABOUT THEM FOUR.

Rev 12:5

⁵ AND SHE BROUGHT FORTH A MAN CHILD, WHO WAS TO RULE ALL NATIONS WITH A ROD OF IRON: AND HER CHILD WAS CAUGHT UP UNTO GOD, AND TO HIS THRONE.

Jesus' disciples were guarding their spiritual virginity.

Rev 14:4

⁴ THESE ARE THEY WHICH WERE NOT DEFILED WITH WOMEN; FOR THEY ARE VIRGINS. THESE ARE THEY WHICH FOLLOW THE LAMB WHITHERSOEVER HE GOETH. THESE WERE REDEEMED FROM AMONG MEN, BEING THE FIRSTFRUITS UNTO GOD AND TO THE LAMB.

Footnote #45

The English word ***millstone*** in the King James translation is rendered from two Greek words: (1) ***Strong's*** #3458, ***millstone***, and (2) ***Strong's*** #3684, ***belonging to an ass***.

Strong's #3684 appears only twice in the King James Translation, in Mk 9:42, and in Matt. 18:6,

Mk 9:42

⁴² AND WHOSOEVER SHALL OFFEND ONE OF THESE LITTLE ONES THAT BELIEVE IN ME, IT IS BETTER FOR HIM THAT A **MILLSTONE** WERE HANGED ABOUT HIS NECK, AND HE WERE CAST INTO THE SEA.

Matt 18:6

⁶ BUT WHOSO SHALL OFFEND ONE OF THESE LITTLE ONES WHICH BELIEVE IN ME, IT WERE BETTER FOR HIM THAT A **MILLSTONE** WERE HANGED ABOUT HIS NECK, AND THAT HE WERE DROWNED IN THE DEPTH OF THE SEA.

Alternate Translation Of The New Testament/ Appendix – Mark

... and is linked as an untranslated word to ***Strong's*** #3458, ***millstone***, both times.

The King James Translators swallowed up the word ***donkey*** because they could not fit it into their translation, but the Doctrine of Christ explains it.

The spiritual donkey is not a domesticated animal pulling a physical millstone, but Cain, the rebellious animal nature that is ***covered*** by the spiritual millstone, the symbol of the glorified man manifesting as the Spirit of Judgment.

Matt 21:44

44 AND WHOSOEVER SHALL FALL ON THIS STONE SHALL BE BROKEN: BUT ON WHOMSOEVER IT SHALL FALL, IT WILL GRIND HIM TO POWDER.

Luke

Footnote #47

Adam exists in two stages of maturity: (1) Resurrected in an individual, but not yet rejoined to the Godhead above, Adam is that man's male, spiritual mantle; (2) Joined to the whole Godhead above, Adam is King of the whole visible world in that man's heart.

Gen 1:26

[26] AND GOD SAID, LET US MAKE MAN IN OUR IMAGE, AFTER OUR LIKENESS: AND LET THEM HAVE DOMINION OVER THE FISH OF THE SEA, AND OVER THE FOWL OF THE AIR, AND OVER THE CATTLE, AND OVER ALL THE EARTH, AND OVER EVERY CREEPING THING THAT CREEPETH UPON THE EARTH.

Footnote #48

The carnal mind perceives the Scripture with natural understanding, but the spiritual, Christ Mind, discerns the Scripture spiritually.

1 Cor 2:14

[14] BUT THE NATURAL MAN RECEIVETH NOT THE THINGS OF THE SPIRIT OF GOD: FOR THEY ARE FOOLISHNESS UNTO HIM: NEITHER CAN HE KNOW THEM, BECAUSE THEY ARE SPIRITUALLY DISCERNED.

Babylon and Jerusalem, the city of God, exist in both the natural and in the Spiritual worlds.

Rev 21:10

[10] AND HE CARRIED ME AWAY IN THE SPIRIT TO A GREAT AND HIGH MOUNTAIN, AND SHEWED ME THAT GREAT

Alternate Translation Of The New Testament/ Appendix –
Luke

CITY, THE HOLY JERUSALEM, DESCENDING OUT OF HEAVEN FROM GOD,

Judah was the pregnant woman in Jesus' day, and the Church, and each member in particular, is the pregnant woman today.

Rev 12:1-2

¹ AND THERE APPEARED A GREAT WONDER IN HEAVEN; A WOMAN CLOTHED WITH THE SUN, AND THE MOON UNDER HER FEET, AND UPON HER HEAD A CROWN OF TWELVE STARS:

² AND SHE BEING WITH CHILD CRIED, TRAVAILING IN BIRTH, AND PAINED TO BE DELIVERED.

There is no male or female in Christ Jesus. Every human being, both physical males, and physical females, are spiritually female in relation to God, and can, therefore, bear the Christ child, Elohim's righteous mind.

1 Tim 2:15

¹⁵ NOTWITHSTANDING SHE SHALL BE SAVED IN CHILDBEARING, IF THEY CONTINUE IN FAITH AND CHARITY AND HOLINESS WITH SOBRIETY.

Rev 12:5

⁵ AND SHE BROUGHT FORTH A MAN CHILD, WHO WAS TO RULE ALL NATIONS WITH A ROD OF IRON: AND HER CHILD WAS CAUGHT UP UNTO GOD, AND TO HIS THRONE.

The spiritual understanding of the phrase, *So everyone went into his own [spiritual] city to engrave the pregnant woman . . .*, is that the people of Israel were summoned to Righteous Adam's spiritual city to be sealed, or marked, with Elohim's nature, their only defense against the Dragon [mark of the beast] devouring the Christ Mind that was to be grafted to them.

Rev 12:4

⁴ AND HIS TAIL DREW THE THIRD PART OF THE STARS OF HEAVEN, AND DID CAST THEM TO THE EARTH: AND

> THE DRAGON STOOD BEFORE THE WOMAN WHICH WAS READY TO BE DELIVERED, FOR TO DEVOUR HER CHILD AS SOON AS IT WAS BORN.

Conception of the Christ Mind was available to all of Israel by the Spirit of Elijah, the ***Saviour of Israel***, but Mary was the only one who was physically impregnated, and she bare Jesus, the ***SAVIOUR OF THE WORLD***.

1 Jn 4:9

> ⁹ IN THIS WAS MANIFESTED THE LOVE OF GOD TOWARD US, BECAUSE THAT GOD SENT HIS ONLY BEGOTTEN SON INTO THE WORLD, THAT WE MIGHT LIVE THROUGH HIM.

The Spirit of Elijah incarnated as the man, Jesus (see, Message #396, ***Jesus & John - Elijah & Elisha???***), who was glorified, and now Jesus is Saviour of Israel.

Acts 13:23

> ²³ OF THIS MAN'S SEED HATH GOD ACCORDING TO HIS PROMISE RAISED UNTO ISRAEL A SAVIOUR, JESUS:

AND Saviour of the whole World.

Jn 4:42

> ⁴² AND SAID UNTO THE WOMAN, NOW WE BELIEVE, NOT BECAUSE OF THY SAYING: FOR WE HAVE HEARD HIM OURSELVES, AND KNOW THAT THIS IS INDEED THE CHRIST, THE SAVIOUR OF THE WORLD.

Footnote #49

Christ Jesus, Elohim's time line, is swallowing up this present spiritual generation of fallen men.

Matt 17:17

> ¹⁷ THEN JESUS ANSWERED AND SAID, O FAITHLESS AND PERVERSE GENERATION, HOW LONG SHALL I BE WITH YOU? HOW LONG SHALL I SUFFER YOU? BRING HIM HITHER TO ME.

Alternate Translation Of The New Testament/ Appendix – Luke

Every individual who is pregnant with Christ, is pregnant with one member of Elohim's many-membered, renewed time line.

Footnote #51

The root of ***Strong's*** #4166, translated ***shepherds*** four times in Luke 2 (verses 8, 15, 18 and 20), is from a root which means *to assemble*. The spiritual significance of this word is ***incarnation****, **the gathering of spiritual beings into physical bodies***.

Lk 2:8

⁸ AND THERE WERE IN THE SAME COUNTRY **SHEPHERDS** ABIDING IN THE FIELD, KEEPING WATCH OVER THEIR FLOCK BY NIGHT.

Lk 2:15

¹⁵ AND IT CAME TO PASS, AS THE ANGELS WERE GONE AWAY FROM THEM INTO HEAVEN, THE **SHEPHERDS** SAID ONE TO ANOTHER, LET US NOW GO EVEN UNTO BETHLEHEM, AND SEE THIS THING WHICH IS COME TO PASS, WHICH THE LORD HATH MADE KNOWN UNTO US.

Lk 2:18

¹⁸ AND ALL THEY THAT HEARD IT WONDERED AT THOSE THINGS WHICH WERE TOLD THEM BY THE **SHEPHERDS**.

Lk 2:20

²⁰ AND THE **SHEPHERDS** RETURNED, GLORIFYING AND PRAISING GOD FOR ALL THE THINGS THAT THEY HAD HEARD AND SEEN, AS IT WAS TOLD UNTO THEM.

The mortal man that Christ is grafted to is an incarnated immortal, because the Immortal One is within him, and the emotional animal [personality] can ascend into immortality *IF* her carnal mind is overthrown. (See, also, *Note #49.*)

Alternate Translation Of The New Testament/ Appendix – Luke

> **Ez 1.28b – AT:** *And when I, [Ezekiel], saw [Elijah's] shape appear in Jehovah's [energy] cloud, my [fallen] personality was overthrown, (ATB)*

Accordingly, we have translated **shepherds**, **the assembled** in Luke 2, verse 8, and **incarnated immortals**, in verses 15, 18 and 20.

Footnote #52

Elohim condensed his spiritual Son into a human body.

Job 10:11

> [11] THOU HAST CLOTHED ME WITH SKIN AND FLESH, AND HAST FENCED ME WITH BONES AND SINEWS.

Footnote #53

The Greek word **prototokos**, **Strong's** #4416, is translated **firstborn** eight times in the Scripture, but the only time this word refers to the human child, Jesus, is in Luke 2:7.

Lk 2:7

> [7] AND SHE BROUGHT FORTH HER FIRSTBORN SON, AND WRAPPED HIM IN SWADDLING CLOTHES, AND LAID HIM IN A MANGER; BECAUSE THERE WAS NO ROOM FOR THEM IN THE INN.

Every other Scripture using this word refers to the spiritual man, Christ Jesus.

Footnote #55

The Greek word translated **manger**, is derived from the verb, **to eat**, and means, **a trough, or an open box in which feed for livestock is placed.** Christ Jesus is the bread from heaven which, when eaten, imparts immortal life.

Jn 6:51

> [51] I AM THE LIVING BREAD WHICH CAME DOWN FROM HEAVEN: IF ANY MAN EAT OF THIS BREAD, HE SHALL LIVE FOR EVER: AND THE BREAD THAT I WILL GIVE IS MY FLESH, WHICH I WILL GIVE FOR THE LIFE OF THE WORLD.

We have translated the word *firstborn* to mean **Christ, the spiritual child** who is the bread from heaven and, accordingly, we are translating *manger* to mean the place, or physical body, that the spiritual child was placed in.

Footnote #56

Fallen humanity.

Matt 12:29

> [29] OR ELSE HOW CAN ONE ENTER INTO A STRONG MAN'S HOUSE, AND SPOIL HIS GOODS, EXCEPT HE FIRST BIND THE STRONG MAN? AND THEN HE WILL SPOIL HIS HOUSE

Matt 12:44

> [44] THEN HE SAITH, I WILL RETURN INTO MY HOUSE FROM WHENCE I CAME OUT; AND WHEN HE IS COME, HE FINDETH IT EMPTY, SWEPT, AND GARNISHED.

Footnote #58

The engrafted Word, which is the Mind of Christ.

Jas 1:21

> [21] WHEREFORE LAY APART ALL FILTHINESS AND SUPERFLUITY OF NAUGHTINESS, AND RECEIVE WITH MEEKNESS THE ENGRAFTED WORD, WHICH IS ABLE TO SAVE YOUR SOULS.

Footnote #59

The world above and ***the world below*** are states of consciousness which correspond to the left and right sides of the heart. The world below is this present world, which is under Satan's dominion,

2 Cor 4:4

> [4] IN WHOM THE GOD OF THIS WORLD HATH BLINDED THE MINDS OF THEM WHICH BELIEVE NOT, LEST THE LIGHT OF THE GLORIOUS GOSPEL OF CHRIST, WHO IS THE IMAGE OF GOD, SHOULD SHINE UNTO THEM.

... but the one who dwells in the world above, has dominion over Satan.

Jn 1:38

> [38] THEN JESUS TURNED, AND SAW THEM FOLLOWING, AND SAITH UNTO THEM, WHAT SEEK YE? THEY SAID UNTO HIM, RABBI, (WHICH IS TO SAY, BEING INTERPRETED, MASTER,) WHERE DWELLEST THOU?

Footnote #60

The Lord Jesus is incarnating in the mortal men who prefer him over their carnal mind.

Christians who have Christ, the humble seed, grafted to them,

Jas 1:21

> [21] WHEREFORE LAY APART ALL FILTHINESS AND SUPERFLUITY OF NAUGHTINESS, AND RECEIVE WITH MEEKNESS THE ENGRAFTED WORD, WHICH IS ABLE TO SAVE YOUR SOULS.

... and who have made their fallen personalities bow down to Christ Jesus so that Christ Jesus can express his nature and purposes through them, are ***righteous incarnated immortals***.

Satan is also incarnating in the mortal men who prefer her. These men are ***evil incarnated immortals.***

Rev 12:7

⁷ AND THERE WAS WAR IN HEAVEN: MICHAEL AND HIS ANGELS FOUGHT AGAINST THE DRAGON; AND THE DRAGON FOUGHT AND HIS ANGELS,

Footnote #62

Conversion means that you start living out of your Christ Mind, and stop living out of your carnal mind.

Acts 17:6

⁶ AND WHEN THEY FOUND THEM NOT, THEY DREW JASON AND CERTAIN BRETHREN UNTO THE RULERS OF THE CITY, CRYING, THESE THAT HAVE TURNED THE WORLD UPSIDE DOWN ARE COME HITHER ALSO;

Footnote #63

Cain and Abel are the inseparable germ seed of creation, Jehovah's nature and the Primordial Serpent's nature inseparable for the life of the ages. The only question is, which nature will prevail over the whole man? The answer is, of course, the nature of Christ, but not without much spiritual wrestling.

The turtle demonstrates this spiritual principle. Cain is the hard shell that blocks Abel's spiritual development,

Ez 11:19

¹⁹ AND I WILL GIVE THEM ONE HEART, AND I WILL PUT A NEW SPIRIT WITHIN YOU; AND I WILL TAKE THE STONY HEART OUT OF THEIR FLESH, AND WILL GIVE THEM AN HEART OF FLESH:

. . . and Abel is the heart of flesh that responds to the call of the Lord Jesus.

Abel must overcome his spiritual straightjacket (shell) to mature into Christ Jesus, who covers the pair, and preserves (saves) the personality (soul) that they inhabit.

Alternate Translation Of The New Testament/ Appendix – Luke

Footnote #67

The Holy Spirit is the flower produced by Jesus, the Christ, the true vine, and Christ Jesus is his fruit. The Holy Spirit is seed, Christ Jesus is mind. The Holy Spirit is a free gift, Christ Jesus grows to maturity...

Eph 4:13

[13] TILL WE ALL COME IN THE UNITY OF THE FAITH, AND OF THE KNOWLEDGE OF THE SON OF GOD, UNTO A PERFECT MAN, UNTO THE MEASURE OF THE STATURE OF THE FULNESS OF CHRIST:

... as a result of much labor and care.

Lk 8:15

[15] BUT THAT ON THE GOOD GROUND ARE THEY, WHICH IN AN HONEST AND GOOD HEART, HAVING HEARD THE WORD, KEEP IT, AND BRING FORTH FRUIT WITH PATIENCE.

Footnote #69

Obtaining the riches of this mortal world in Leviathan's strength results in spiritual and physical death.

Lk 12:20

[20] BUT GOD SAID UNTO HIM, THOU FOOL, THIS NIGHT THY SOUL SHALL BE REQUIRED OF THEE: THEN WHOSE SHALL THOSE THINGS BE, WHICH THOU HAST PROVIDED?

Footnote #72

Abel and Cain are the male and female aspects of one dual being. They cannot be separated from one another.

When Abel, the male, is exercising authority over (on top of) Cain, the female, the whole mortal man comes under the authority of the Mind of Christ, but when Cain, the female, is exercising authority over (on top of) Abel, the whole man falls under the authority of Satan and Leviathan, the carnal mind of mortal man.

Abel is the subconscious part of the Christ mind in the individual personality, and Cain is the conscious part of the carnal mind of mortal man.

Cain is the veil that covers spiritual potential of the personality in Christ Jesus.

Abel is the potential spiritual male sexual organ of the personality, and Cain is the foreskin that covers Abel.

Spiritual circumcision severs Cain from Abel so that he can fulfill his spiritual potential through union with the grafted Christ.

Jas 1:21

> [21] WHEREFORE LAY APART ALL FILTHINESS AND SUPERFLUITY OF NAUGHTINESS, AND RECEIVE WITH MEEKNESS THE ENGRAFTED WORD, WHICH IS ABLE TO SAVE YOUR SOULS.

Footnote #74

The fiery serpent is called Abel and Cain as soon as Abel begins to reject the Dragon's thought patterns and manifest the thought patterns of the grafted Christ (Jas 1:21).

Jas 1:21

> [21] WHEREFORE LAY APART ALL FILTHINESS AND SUPERFLUITY OF NAUGHTINESS, AND RECEIVE WITH MEEKNESS THE ENGRAFTED WORD, WHICH IS ABLE TO SAVE YOUR SOULS.

Footnote #75

In Luke 13:31, the Pharisees tell Jesus that He should go away, leave town, because Herod wants to kill him.

> **Lk 13:31**
>
> ³¹ THE SAME DAY THERE CAME CERTAIN OF THE PHARISEES, SAYING UNTO HIM, GET THEE OUT, AND DEPART HENCE: FOR HEROD WILL KILL THEE.

But Jesus knew that the Pharisees were lying,

> **Lk 23:8-11**
>
> ⁸ AND WHEN HEROD SAW JESUS, HE WAS EXCEEDING GLAD: FOR HE WAS DESIROUS TO SEE HIM OF A LONG SEASON, BECAUSE HE HAD HEARD MANY THINGS OF HIM; AND HE HOPED TO HAVE SEEN SOME MIRACLE DONE BY HIM.
>
> ⁹ THEN HE QUESTIONED WITH HIM IN MANY WORDS; BUT HE ANSWERED HIM NOTHING.
>
> ¹⁰ AND THE CHIEF PRIESTS AND SCRIBES STOOD AND VEHEMENTLY ACCUSED HIM.
>
> ¹¹ AND HEROD WITH HIS MEN OF WAR SET HIM AT NOUGHT, AND MOCKED HIM, AND ARRAYED HIM IN A GORGEOUS ROBE, AND SENT HIM AGAIN TO PILATE.

... and that it was Satan, the unconscious part of their carnal mind, that was motivating them to drive Jesus away.

Footnote #77

Lazarus, ***Strong's*** #2967, is a translation of the Hebrew name Eleazar, ***Strong's*** #499, the one that God helps.

The name ***Lazarus*** in this parable teaches us that God's favor, or the lack of it, is demonstrated by God's helpful intervention in the everyday life of the faithful. Lazarus' spiritual change of position from a needy to a prosperous man, is the proof that God was with Lazarus and, conversely, the prosperous man's change of position from king and priest to a spiritual needy man, indicates acquired prosperity that has nothing to do with faith or love for God.

Spiritual and material prosperity that is genetically inherited or acquired as a gift, such as the Holy Spirit, can be lost.

Footnote #79

There is no way across Satan's sea [the astral plane], and transfer from the Primordial Serpent's tormenting timeline, into the safety of Abraham's righteous timeline.

What is unsaid here, is that Jehovah always makes a way of escape, which is typified by Lazarus' ascension. Abraham is silent concerning Jehovah's escape plan, because the rich man had rejected the two witnesses already sent to him: (1) Moses and the Prophets, and (2) Lazarus' testimony.

The rich man lost his safe place in Abraham's righteous timeline because he refused to confess the pride of his own heart and repent, and was still denying that he had fallen into this painful place because of his stubborn refusal to deal with his own sin nature.

And the same thing is happening to many in the Church today. There is nothing new under the sun.

Footnote #80

The Primordial Serpent murdered Adam and used his spiritual substance to found this present world. Adam is the one who died when time began, and the one who rose from the dead in Jesus of Nazareth before the physical man, Jesus, was crucified.

Alternate Translation Of The New Testament/ Appendix –
Luke

1 Cor 15:4

⁴ AND THAT HE WAS BURIED, AND THAT HE ROSE AGAIN THE THIRD DAY ACCORDING TO THE SCRIPTURES:

Jesus, the man, rose from the dead because his personality was fully mingled with Adam, the Living One.

Jn 8:58

⁵⁸ JESUS SAID UNTO THEM, VERILY, VERILY, I SAY UNTO YOU, BEFORE ABRAHAM WAS, I AM.

John

Footnote #84

What is wrong with what Nicodemus said?

Miracles do not prove that a teacher is of God, because Satan can perform miracles also.

> **2 Cor 11:14**
>
> ¹⁴ AND NO MARVEL; FOR SATAN HIMSELF IS TRANSFORMED INTO AN ANGEL OF LIGHT.

The only way to know for sure that a teacher or a miracle worker is of God, is to recognize Adam/Christ Jesus doing the work within that man, and only Adam/Christ Jesus in one man can discern Adam/Christ Jesus in another man.

> **1 Cor 2:15**
>
> ¹⁵ BUT HE THAT IS SPIRITUAL JUDGETH ALL THINGS, YET HE HIMSELF IS JUDGED OF NO MAN.

> **2 Cor 5:16**
>
> ¹⁶ WHEREFORE HENCEFORTH KNOW WE NO MAN AFTER THE FLESH: YEA, THOUGH WE HAVE KNOWN CHRIST AFTER THE FLESH, YET NOW HENCEFORTH KNOW WE HIM NO MORE.

Footnote #87

The ***spiritual waters*** of mortal man are the secret of ***mayim nokbim***, the female waters that ascend to arouse the male waters of Ze'ir Anpin to mate with the Shekinah, who then gives birth to Adam. Jesus' response alludes to the restoration of the Shekinah to Israel.

Alternate Translation Of The New Testament/ Appendix – John

The Shekinah is appearing today as the Holy Spirit of Jesus Christ, and Ze'ir Anpin is appearing as Christ Jesus. The Christ child is birthed when the Holy Spirit within the believer mates with Christ Jesus.

Acts 4:27-30

²⁷ FOR OF A TRUTH AGAINST THY HOLY CHILD JESUS, WHOM THOU HAST ANOINTED, BOTH HEROD, AND PONTIUS PILATE, WITH THE GENTILES, AND THE PEOPLE OF ISRAEL, WERE GATHERED TOGETHER,

²⁸ FOR TO DO WHATSOEVER THY HAND AND THY COUNSEL DETERMINED BEFORE TO BE DONE.

²⁹ AND NOW, LORD, BEHOLD THEIR THREATENINGS: AND GRANT UNTO THY SERVANTS, THAT WITH ALL BOLDNESS THEY MAY SPEAK THY WORD,

³⁰ BY STRETCHING FORTH THINE HAND TO HEAL; AND THAT SIGNS AND WONDERS MAY BE DONE BY THE NAME OF THY HOLY CHILD JESUS.

1 Tim 2:15

[15] NOTWITHSTANDING SHE SHALL BE SAVED IN CHILDBEARING, IF THEY CONTINUE IN FAITH AND CHARITY AND HOLINESS WITH SOBRIETY.

Footnote #90

The foundation of fallen man is Cain and Abel, Adam's mortal remains, engraved with the Serpent's nature.

Abel is so overcome by Cain in most people that Cain automatically speaks for the dual being.

But Christ Jesus will speak to Cain only until (through their conversation), Christ is grafted to Abel. This is why, in Verse 16, Jesus says to Cain, the spiritual woman, *let Leviathan withdraw and let [Abel], your [true] husband appear, so that I can address him.*

Footnote #92

Cain interrupted Jesus' conversation with Abel to ask where she could find the spiritual food that would satisfy her thirst to incarnate, because she could not recognize that Jesus' dialogue was setting forth the answer to the very question that she was asking. But Abel (Christ), the male side of John's carnal mind, understood what Jesus (Adam/Christ Jesus) said.

Wherefore, the Scripture says, let the spiritual women (physical men and women who are manifesting the female side of the carnal mind) be silent in the Church, and ask their spiritual husband (physical men and women who are manifesting the male side of their carnal mind) at home,

> **1 Cor 14:34**
>
> [34] LET YOUR WOMEN KEEP SILENCE IN THE CHURCHES: FOR IT IS NOT PERMITTED UNTO THEM TO SPEAK; BUT THEY ARE COMMANDED TO BE UNDER OBEDIENCE AS ALSO SAITH THE LAW.

. . .because only (Christ), the male side of the carnal mind, can understand Adam/Christ Jesus, who is sent to complete them.

Footnote #93

The Devil is the personality that is in full agreement with Satan's nature, and the Scripture likens the Devil to a lion.

> **1 Pet 5:8**
>
> [8] BE SOBER, BE VIGILANT; BECAUSE YOUR ADVERSARY THE DEVIL, AS A ROARING LION, WALKETH ABOUT, SEEKING WHOM HE MAY DEVOUR:

In the Kingdom of Darkness, the female lion is responsible for providing food, but Jesus is the Lion of Judah, and in his Kingdom, the man provides the food.

Alternate Translation Of The New Testament/ Appendix –
John

Footnote #94

Jesus tells Cain, Adam/Christ Jesus' wife, to not interfere with his preaching, but to put her questions to Abel/Christ, Adam/Christ Jesus' root system within John.

The carnal mind (Cain) will never understand the Doctrine of Christ. Wherefore, if Christ is not yet being formed in you, do not expect to learn the Doctrine of Christ directly from the Lord Jesus. Ask the Lord to direct you to a physical person who carries a mature manifestation of Adam/Christ Jesus. Then, submit to that person, and ask them to teach you.

Footnote #99

Christ Jesus is a spiritual man . . .

1 Tim 2:5

> [5] FOR THERE IS ONE GOD, AND ONE MEDIATOR BETWEEN GOD AND MEN, THE MAN CHRIST JESUS;

. . . with spiritual aspects that, for the purpose of understanding spiritual mysteries, can be likened to human body parts.

1 Cor 12:14-17

> [14] FOR THE BODY IS NOT ONE MEMBER, BUT MANY.
>
> [15] IF THE FOOT SHALL SAY, BECAUSE I AM NOT THE HAND, I AM NOT OF THE BODY; IS IT THEREFORE NOT OF THE BODY?
>
> [16] AND IF THE EAR SHALL SAY, BECAUSE I AM NOT THE EYE, I AM NOT OF THE BODY; IS IT THEREFORE NOT OF THE BODY?
>
> [17] IF THE WHOLE BODY WERE AN EYE, WHERE WERE THE HEARING? IF THE WHOLE WERE HEARING, WHERE WERE THE SMELLING?

Alternate Translation Of The New Testament/ Appendix – John

Jehovah is the brain of Christ Jesus, the spiritual man who is rejoining us to the I Am, the highest aspect of the Almighty that is revealed to mortal man.

Footnote #101

Peter did not understand that Jesus, by saying, ***you have a spirit tie with me***, was prophesying that Peter would have a spirit tie with him. Neither did Peter understand that Jesus, by speaking the words, ***minister to those who follow me***, was prophetically investing Peter with the priestly authority necessary to do the job.

But Peter, blinded by Satan, the God of this world,

2 Cor 4:4

[4] IN WHOM THE GOD OF THIS WORLD HATH BLINDED THE MINDS OF THEM WHICH BELIEVE NOT, LEST THE LIGHT OF THE GLORIOUS GOSPEL OF CHRIST, WHO IS THE IMAGE OF GOD, SHOULD SHINE UNTO THEM.

nevertheless, rises to the challenge,

Jn 21:7

[7] THEREFORE THAT DISCIPLE WHOM JESUS LOVED SAITH UNTO PETER, IT IS THE LORD. NOW WHEN SIMON PETER HEARD THAT IT WAS THE LORD, HE GIRT HIS FISHER'S COAT UNTO HIM, (FOR HE WAS NAKED,) AND DID CAST HIMSELF INTO THE SEA.

through understanding,

Matt 15:16

[16] AND JESUS SAID, ARE YE ALSO YET WITHOUT UNDERSTANDING?

. . . after Jesus instructs him.

Jn 21:18-19

[18] VERILY, VERILY, I SAY UNTO THEE, WHEN THOU WAST YOUNG, THOU GIRDEST THYSELF, AND WALKEDST

Alternate Translation Of The New Testament/ Appendix – John

WHITHER THOU WOULDEST: BUT WHEN THOU SHALT BE OLD, THOU SHALT STRETCH FORTH THY HANDS, AND ANOTHER SHALL GIRD THEE, AND CARRY THEE WHITHER THOU WOULDEST NOT.

[19] THIS SPAKE HE, SIGNIFYING BY WHAT DEATH HE SHOULD GLORIFY GOD. AND WHEN HE HAD SPOKEN THIS, HE SAITH UNTO HIM, FOLLOW ME.

Footnote #104

See, ***Anchor of Our Soul*** (Online Meeting 06/14/00), or Alternate Translation of Heb. 6:18-19.

Heb 6.18-6.19 – AT: *[OLM - 06 14 00]*

6.18 *[Knowing that since] it is impossible for God to lie, we, the personalities [who] have fled [from Satan, Leviathan and Cain] in order to seize Christ Jesus [who] stands [in the high place, and] is the fulfillment of the calling to which we are appointed, have a mighty comfort,*

6.19 *That [Jesus Christ, the scout] who entered into [the spiritual city] within [the place between the eyebrows], the veil [of the high place], securely anchors our personality [in the spiritual dimension of the throat], which stabilizes [our volatile emotions].* ***(ATB)***

Footnote #106

Peter is still in unbelief, even after Jesus instructs him in detail, concerning the spiritual ascension he is about to experience.

Jn 21:18-19

[18] VERILY, VERILY, I SAY UNTO THEE, WHEN THOU WAST YOUNG, THOU GIRDEST THYSELF, AND WALKEDST WHITHER THOU WOULDEST: BUT WHEN THOU SHALT BE OLD, THOU SHALT STRETCH FORTH THY HANDS, AND ANOTHER SHALL GIRD THEE, AND CARRY THEE WHITHER THOU WOULDEST NOT.

Alternate Translation Of The New Testament/ Appendix – John

¹⁹ THIS SPAKE HE, SIGNIFYING BY WHAT DEATH HE SHOULD GLORIFY GOD. AND WHEN HE HAD SPOKEN THIS, HE SAITH UNTO HIM, FOLLOW ME.

Footnote #107

The word, *single*, signifies the one mind formed when Christ Jesus subjects, and binds, the carnal mind underneath himself.

Ps 118:27

²⁷ GOD IS THE LORD, WHICH HATH SHEWED US LIGHT: BIND THE SACRIFICE WITH CORDS, EVEN UNTO THE HORNS OF THE ALTAR.

Strong's #572 means *single,*

Eph 6:5

⁵ SERVANTS, BE OBEDIENT TO THEM THAT ARE YOUR MASTERS ACCORDING TO THE FLESH, WITH FEAR AND TREMBLING, IN SINGLENESS OF YOUR HEART, AS UNTO CHRIST;

Col 3:22

²² SERVANTS, OBEY IN ALL THINGS YOUR MASTERS ACCORDING TO THE FLESH; NOT WITH EYESERVICE, AS MENPLEASERS; BUT IN SINGLENESS OF HEART, FEARING GOD;

but is also translated, *simplicity,*

Rom 12:8

⁸ OR HE THAT EXHORTETH, ON EXHORTATION: HE THAT GIVETH, LET HIM DO IT WITH SIMPLICITY; HE THAT RULETH, WITH DILIGENCE; HE THAT SHEWETH MERCY, WITH CHEERFULNESS.

2 Cor 1:12

¹² FOR OUR REJOICING IS THIS, THE TESTIMONY OF OUR CONSCIENCE, THAT IN SIMPLICITY AND GODLY SINCERITY, NOT WITH FLESHLY WISDOM, BUT BY THE GRACE

*Alternate Translation Of The New Testament/ * Appendix – John

OF GOD, WE HAVE HAD OUR CONVERSATION IN THE WORLD, AND MORE ABUNDANTLY TO YOU-WARD.

2 Cor 11:3

³ BUT I FEAR, LEST BY ANY MEANS, AS THE SERPENT BEGUILED EVE THROUGH HIS SUBTILTY, SO YOUR MINDS SHOULD BE CORRUPTED FROM THE SIMPLICITY THAT IS IN CHRIST

liberal,

2 Cor 8:2

² HOW THAT IN A GREAT TRIAL OF AFFLICTION THE ABUNDANCE OF THEIR JOY AND THEIR DEEP POVERTY ABOUNDED UNTO THE RICHES OF THEIR LIBERALITY.

2 Cor 9:13

¹³ WHILES BY THE EXPERIMENT OF THIS MINISTRATION THEY GLORIFY GOD FOR YOUR PROFESSED SUBJECTION UNTO THE GOSPEL OF CHRIST, AND FOR YOUR LIBERAL DISTRIBUTION UNTO THEM, AND UNTO ALL MEN;

and bountifulness

2 Cor 9:11

¹¹ BEING ENRICHED IN EVERY THING TO ALL BOUNTIFULNESS, WHICH CAUSETH THROUGH US THANKSGIVING TO GOD.

Strong's #1520, translated, ***one***, in Jn. 21:25, is another word that means, ***single***.

Jn 21:25

²⁵ AND THERE ARE ALSO MANY OTHER THINGS WHICH JESUS DID, THE WHICH, IF THEY SHOULD BE WRITTEN EVERY ONE, I SUPPOSE THAT EVEN THE WORLD ITSELF COULD NOT CONTAIN THE BOOKS THAT SHOULD BE WRITTEN. AMEN.

Strong's #2596, translated, ***every***, in the phrase, ***every one***, means ***down from***, and is translated, ***every***, only 7 times out of approximately 200 uses of the word. The significance of the phrase, *every one*, in Jn. 21:25, above, is, **the mind that is single because the carnal mind is cast down.**

Footnote #108

The word, ***imagination***, signifies Leviathan's concept of what the creation should be, which idea has illegally formed our mortal, spiritually dead world.

Jer 18:12

[12] AND THEY SAID, THERE IS NO HOPE: BUT WE WILL WALK AFTER OUR OWN DEVICES, AND WE WILL EVERY ONE DO THE IMAGINATION OF HIS EVIL HEART.

Lk 1:51

[51] HE HATH SHEWED STRENGTH WITH HIS ARM; HE HATH SCATTERED THE PROUD IN THE IMAGINATION OF THEIR HEARTS.

Footnote #110

Jesus knew that it was not possible for the disciples to seize Leviathan. . .

Matt 12:29

[29] OR ELSE HOW CAN ONE ENTER INTO A STRONG MAN'S HOUSE, AND SPOIL HIS GOODS, EXCEPT HE FIRST BIND THE STRONG MAN? AND THEN HE WILL SPOIL HIS HOUSE.

Mk 3:27

[27] NO MAN CAN ENTER INTO A STRONG MAN'S HOUSE, AND SPOIL HIS GOODS, EXCEPT HE WILL FIRST BIND THE STRONG MAN; AND THEN HE WILL SPOIL HIS HOUSE.

. . . without the help of his glorified Spirit, but tested them, to see if they would confess their inability to change their own mortal nature.

Alternate Translation Of The New Testament/ Appendix – John

Footnote #111

To cook Leviathan, is a legitimate translation of **Strong's** #4371, translated, **meat**, by the King James translators, but meaning, specifically, **boiled** fish. Satan is the energy sea that this world exists in, and Leviathan, the collective subconscious mind of mortal man, is the fish that plays war games in Satan's sea.

Ps 104:26

[26] THERE GO THE SHIPS: THERE IS THAT LEVIATHAN, WHOM THOU HAST MADE TO PLAY THEREIN.

Acts

Footnote #113

As explained in our message entitled "***The Secret of Cain and Abel***," the Zohar, a Jewish Commentary on the Scripture, teaches that Cain's attack upon Abel began with Cain biting Abel's neck. So we see that Cain within the Jews that Stephen was preaching to, gnashed his teeth into the neck of Abel within Stephen.

Stephen told these men the truth with the hope of convicting them of their sins, but instead of repenting, they thought Cain's thoughts, felt Cain's feelings. And acted out Cain's transgression against Abel within Stephen.

Romans

Footnote #115

Wounded is a translation of the Greek word which is translated ***form of***, in Rom. 6:17.

Rom 6:17

> ¹⁷ BUT GOD BE THANKED, THAT YE WERE THE SERVANTS OF SIN, BUT YE HAVE OBEYED FROM THE HEART THAT **FORM OF** DOCTRINE WHICH WAS DELIVERED YOU.

The wound which resulted in mankind dying to his immortal mind, is appearing as Leviathan, mortal man's fallen, dead mind.

Alternate Translation Of The New Testament/ Appendix – 1 Corinthians

1 Corinthians

Footnote #119

The untranslated article *the* appears before the word **Christ**, indicating a personal Christ.

Israel has had many judges, or messiahs, but only Moses and Elijah had the opportunity to ascend into immortality. Moses did not ascend, but Elijah did.

> **Jude 1.09 – AT:** *Indeed, when Michael, the Archangel, verbally distinguished [between] the Devil, [Moses' emotions, and Christ], Moses' living, [spiritual] body, he dared not bring an official judgment of blasphemy against [the fallen Kings within Moses], but said [to them], the Lord charges you [with blasphemy]; and* **(ATB)**

The Spirit of Elijah incarnated as the man, Jesus. (See, Message #396, ***Jesus & John - Elijah & Elisha???***) And, today, Christ Jesus is incarnating in his Sons.

Footnote #120

Satan dominates the emotional plane, and all who hope to ascend beyond her power, must pass through her sea of spiritual energy. This is the principle that Jesus was talking about when He said, ***I have overcome the world.***

> **Jn 16:33**
>
> [33] THESE THINGS I HAVE SPOKEN UNTO YOU, THAT IN ME YE MIGHT HAVE PEACE. IN THE WORLD YE SHALL HAVE TRIBULATION: BUT BE OF GOOD CHEER; I HAVE OVERCOME THE WORLD.

2 Corinthians

Footnote #Error! Bookmark not defined.

Logos, the Greek word which means *living word*, is speaking about Jesus, the *Word of God*, who is presently appearing as the *Mind of Christ.*

Phil 2:5

⁵ LET THIS MIND BE IN YOU, WHICH WAS ALSO IN CHRIST JESUS:

Footnote #Error! Bookmark not defined.

The term *Heaven* in the *King James* translation of this verse, is speaking about Leviathan, the fallen mind of mortal man, and his image, which is this visible, physical world. (See, study on the *third part of man* being the Satanic [dark, earthen] part of the soul [*Message #48, 6ᵗʰ Trumpets, Part 2*].)

Further, *Strong* says that the Greek word translated *to* in the phrase, *caught up to the third heaven*, *Strong's* #1518, can also be translated *exceeding*; and <u>WEBSTER</u> says that the word *exceed* means *to be greater or superior to; to go beyond a limit set by the existing authority*.

Now, remember that Satan is the God-appointed spiritual authority which rules over this dead, mortal mind, but Paul, Glory to God, was caught up beyond the limit set by Satan, and he entered into the spiritual world of Christ Jesus [Kingdom age], who is the supreme authority over Satan herself.

Rev 14.20 – AT: *And the Lake of Fire crushed the mortal mind of the second generation of Sons, which is the firstborn fruit of the whole creature, and the human spirits of the first fruits of the Lord Jesus Christ increased into, and became one with, Christ Jesus, who has authority over Satan, and they flowed down into the visible, physical world, which is hell, where mortal man strives to attain IMMORTALITY, the prize which is in Christ Jesus, and became the undisputed spiritual authority and ruling law, over [the whole visible world].* **(ATB)**

So, we see that there are not three spiritual worlds, but only two: The spiritual world [heaven] that God rules over [Eden], and the physical world that Satan rules over [Hell]. There is no ***third*** heaven.

The expression the ***seventh heaven*** does not appear in the Scriptures. Some Christians have sought information about such a possibility, including one well-known preacher who accepted it at one time, have rejected it, because there are simply no Scriptures to support it.

The expression ***the seventh heaven*** is speaking about the fullness of the combined two heavens. **The Kingdom of the Two Heavens** is a condition of mind in which the Kingdom of God [Mind of Christ Jesus] is so fully dominating Leviathan [dead mind of mortal man], that the whole man [who is still in a physical body] is incapable of sin [Jesus, who was Christ]. ***The Seventh Heaven*** is the Kingdom of the Two Heavens glorified, that is, the man whose mind is the Kingdom of Heaven, but no longer has a physical body.

The ***seventh heaven*** of the spiritual world of God exists in this hour as the glorified Jesus Christ, but will be expanded to the 42nd Generation, and will eventually exist in its totality as the glorified man of Ezekiel 1.

When this occurs, Hell will have been totally absorbed by the visible, spiritual world of God, and the two shall have become one [a ***renewed heavens*** and a ***renewed earth***].

1 Timothy

Footnote #122

The Greek word translated *not* is a negative particle which is used to describe man's worthlessness in relationship to God. ***Negative particles*** signify the *Serpent* or the ***Devil*** in parable form. (See, word study on ***Message #78, The Harvest, Part 9.***)

The first Adam [the living soul] knew better than to believe the Serpent, but the good judgment of his righteous, but immature mind, was overshadowed by Cain, his lower nature.

The Woman [Cain], on the other hand, did not stand a chance against the Serpent's lies, because she did not have any judgment of her own, but was dependent upon the first Adam [the living soul], the head whose protection she cast off.

Footnote #123

12 Levels Of Consciousness

1. Reconciliation; 2. Justification; 3. Sanctification; 4. Resurrected Christ in the individual marries the Lord Jesus who is above the firmament, and becomes a New Man [Christ Jesus]; 5. Perfection [full stature]; 6. Christ Jesus pierces Carnal mind [Leviathan]; 7. Christ [in the individual] harvested from carnal mind [false vine]; 8. Satan killed; 9. Individual personality marries New Man within himself, and becomes a Glorified Man; 10. Glorified Man marries the Lord Jesus Christ [double portion] and becomes a Magnificent Man; 11. Magnificent Man separates from physical body; 12. Magnificent Man ascends above the firmament.

1 John

Footnote #125

Fathers are mortal men who have the spiritual authority to reproduce the nature of the Lord Jesus Christ in other mortal men.

1 Cor 9:2

> ² IF I BE NOT AN APOSTLE UNTO OTHERS, YET DOUBTLESS I AM TO YOU: FOR THE SEAL OF MINE APOSTLESHIP ARE YE IN THE LORD.

Fatherhood is something we grow into. There are, therefore, young fathers and mature fathers. The English words ***fathers*** in 1 Jn 2, verses 13 and 14, are both translations of the same Greek word. That Greek word, however, is in the present tense in verse 13, meaning **men who are fathers now,** that is **young fathers**, and in a past tense in verse 14, meaning **men who became fathers in the past**, that is, **mature fathers**. Both **young fathers** and **mature fathers** are members of the **two-witness company**, which consists of mortal men whose human spirit [Abel] is **in the process of** increasing into Christ Jesus.

Young fathers are fighting Leviathan within themselves, and **mature fathers** are fighting Leviathan in other men, as well as in themselves.

> **Deut 32.26 – AT:** *[But] I will break the fiery serpent in pieces and deliver the human spirit, [Adam's] mortal remains, of those who are being judged [and are confessing their sins and repenting], that is, the young spiritual men who are fighting the fiery serpent within themselves, and the mature spiritual men who are fighting the fiery serpent within themselves [individual subconscious mind], and Leviathan, the sea serpent [collective subconscious mind of fallen, mortal man], and from the spiritual men who are virgins because they follow Elijah everywhere. **(ATB)***

Alternate Translation Of The New Testament/ Appendix – 1
John

Footnote #127

The Greek word translated ***little children***, in 1 Jn 2, verse 12, ***Strong's*** #5040, means, ***disciple***. The most obvious sign that someone following Christ Jesus has entered into discipleship, that is, training to be like the master, is ***correction.***

Pro 13:24

[24] HE THAT SPARETH HIS ROD HATETH HIS SON: BUT HE THAT LOVETH HIM CHASTENETH HIM BETIMES.

Pro 23:13-14

[13] WITHHOLD NOT CORRECTION FROM THE CHILD: FOR IF THOU BEATEST HIM WITH THE ROD, HE SHALL NOT DIE.

[14] THOU SHALT BEAT HIM WITH THE ROD, AND SHALT DELIVER HIS SOUL FROM HELL.

Heb 12:6-7

[6] FOR WHOM THE LORD LOVETH HE CHASTENETH, AND SCOURGETH EVERY SON WHOM HE RECEIVETH.

[7] IF YE ENDURE CHASTENING, GOD DEALETH WITH YOU AS WITH SONS; FOR WHAT SON IS HE WHOM THE FATHER CHASTENETH NOT?

Footnote #128

Waging war against Leviathan in one's own mind, as well and in other men's minds results in the first Adam [the living soul] rising from the dead as one's own renewed Christ mind, which is in Jehovah's image.

1 Cor 15:3-4

[3] FOR I DELIVERED UNTO YOU FIRST OF ALL THAT WHICH I ALSO RECEIVED, HOW THAT CHRIST DIED FOR OUR SINS ACCORDING TO THE SCRIPTURES;

[4] AND THAT HE WAS BURIED, AND THAT HE ROSE AGAIN THE THIRD DAY ACCORDING TO THE SCRIPTURES:

Alternate Translation Of The New Testament/ Appendix – 1
John

This happened first in Jesus of Nazareth.

Rev 1:5

⁵ AND FROM JESUS CHRIST, WHO IS THE FAITHFUL WITNESS, AND THE FIRST BEGOTTEN OF THE DEAD, AND THE PRINCE OF THE KINGS OF THE EARTH. UNTO HIM THAT LOVED US, AND WASHED US FROM OUR SINS IN HIS OWN BLOOD,

(See, *Message #186*, *The Christ, Parts 8 & 9*.)

FACTS ABOUT THE ALTERNATE TRANSLATION BIBLE

A Brief History Of The Alternate Translation Bible

The Lord gave Pastor Vitale the ability to understand and clarify the Scripture in a unique way which ultimately materialized as *The Alternate Translation Bible*.

Pastor Vitale began rendering *Alternate Translations* of the Scripture as early as Living Epistles Ministries (LEM) Message #18, but she did not realize at the time how unique they were. It was not until a Nigerian man asked her where he could purchase a copy of the *Alternate Translations* that she realized their significance.

Pastor Vitale returned to the USA after that, and it was there in New York that the Lord asked her to gather together all of the *Alternate Translations* that she had rendered since 1988 and put them into a book. She had no idea, at the time, that *The Alternate Translation Bible* (ATB) would, eventually, be published and sought after by many serious students of the Scripture, and the thought of pouring through two years of message notes, extracting the Alternate Translations and entering the hand-written and typewritten *Alternate Translations* into a computer program, was overwhelming.

After that beginning, Pastor Vitale diligently incorporated every *Alternate Translation* that she rendered into one of the two files that comprised *The Alternate Translation Bible* on her computer, either *The Alternate Translation of the Old Testament*, or *The Alternate Translation of the New Testament*. Today, *The Alternate Translation Bible* is printed in three volumes, *The Alternate Translation of The Old Testament*, *The Alternate Translation of the New Testament*, and *The*

Alternate Translation Of The New Testament/ Facts About The Alternate Translation Bible

Alternate Translation of Book of Revelation. All three volumes may be purchased, individually, at Amazon.com.

In addition, *The Alternate Translation of The Book of Revelation* has been translated into Spanish, which may also be purchased at Amazon.com.

What is The Alternate Translation Bible?

Lexicon, the Greek word for dictionary, is used to describe most Hebrew/English and Greek/English dictionaries which have been compiled for the specific purpose of studying the Scriptures. Hebrew/English and Greek/English dictionaries offer many definitions for each word listed, just like English language dictionaries do.

The Alternate Translation Bible is an *original translation of the Hebrew and Greek Scripture* in which the translator has exercised *Translator's License* in selecting different definitions than other translators typically chose for many Hebrew and Greek words.

Translator's License means that the translator chooses the English translation for a Hebrew or Greek word each time it appears. *A usage search* for many Hebrew and Greek words reveals that the translators of the *King James Bible* frequently selected a variety of English translations *for the same Hebrew or Greek word.*

The Alternate Translation Bible is an *Amplified Translation of the Hebrew and Greek Scripture.* The Scripture, especially prophecy, frequently omits one or more steps which lead up to the event spoken about. *Amplification* is the term that indicates the inclusion of implied spiritual principles.

Amplification means that more than one English word is used to translate a single Hebrew or Greek word.

Alternate Translation Of The New Testament/ Facts About The Alternate Translation Bible

Amplification means that the English translation may include words that suggest or imply ideas or accounts of events which are undescribed or unstated in the original language,

Amplification means that ideas and spiritual principles that are suggested but not stated in the Hebrew or Greek text, are added to the English translation.

For example, if you were to read that *Jesus was arrested, crucified and became the Saviour of the world*, Jesus' resurrection and ascension would be implied.

Amplified words are not translations of any specific Hebrew or Greek word. They are English words added by the translator for clarity. The *King James Bible* identifies *amplified words* with italicized print. The *Amplified Bible* (Zondervan Publishers, Grand Rapids, Michigan) identifies *amplified words* with brackets. The *Alternate Translation Bible* identifies unstated ideas, principles or events with brackets, but most **a**mplified words have been incorporated into the text of the translation.

The *Alternate Translation Bible* is a *paraphrased translation* of the Hebrew and Greek Scripture.

Paraphrase means to *restate text or a passage of text in another form*, to clarify meaning, or [to use] *as a studying or teaching device* (Webster's Encyclopedic Unabridged Dictionary of the English Language) (emphasis added).

The *Alternate Translation Bible* is an *original translation of the Hebrew and Greek Scripture* which sounds very different than all the other translations available today.

The *Alternate Translation Bible* reflects the translator's choice of definitions, amplification and paraphraseology which is the fruit of years of deep spiritual communion with Christ Jesus, and long periods of prayer, study and contemplation of the Scripture.

The ***Alternate Translation Bible*** is a spiritual translation of the Bible. It is not intended to replace traditional translations.

Alternate Translation Of The New Testament/ Facts About The Alternate Translation Bible

Statement of Faith

The translator believes that:

There is only One God (Deut 6:4, Mk 12:29, Rom 3:30, 1 Cor 8:4, Gal 3:20, Eph 4:6, 1 Tim 2:5, Js 2:19)

Jesus is the only begotten Son of God (Jn 3:16),

The man, Christ Jesus, is the only Mediator between God and man (1 Tim 2:5),

Elijah came (Matt 11:14) in Jesus of Nazareth (Matt 11:14),

Righteous Adam was regenerated in Jesus of Nazareth (Matt 19:28)

Adam is the Son of God (Lk 3:38)

Questions & Answers

1. Does the Alternate Translation Bible replace the King James and other traditional Bible translations?

No. The Alternate Translation Bible does not replace the King James or other traditional Bible translations. The Bible can be understood on three levels:

1. *Literal*: What you see is what you get. Reading and studying the literal translation of the Bible is powerful. It can build faith, result in salvation and bring deliverance from any affliction, spiritual, physical, mental or emotional.

2. *Moral*: Reading and studying the Bible can strengthen a weak moral center, or build character where none exists. The Bible tells us what is right and what is wrong in clear and certain terms.

3. *Hints*: Reading one passage in the Bible can enlighten us, or clarify a question about another passage.

4. *Mysteries*: Deep spiritual principles underlie everything that is written in the Bible.

The Alternate Translation Bible reveals the mysteries, according to the Doctrine of Christ.

2. I used to read the *Alternate New Testament* for free. Can I still read it for free on your new website?

Yes.

http://www.livingepistles.org/index.php/new-testament

3. Is the *Alternate New Testament* for sale? Sheila Vitale was born into a Jewish family and began her spiritual journey as a child when her mother enrolled her as a student in an Orthodox Hebrew school. She also attended synagogue on Shabbat during that time, where she experienced the Spirit of God for the first time. Such a deep longing for God was stirred up in her that she wept. She was touched so profoundly that she became desperate to attend yeshiva (Jewish high school) but her parents could not afford the fees.

She became very ill around the age of 11 and has battled with chronic illness ever since. Her most recent struggle against premature death came in 1990, when she spent three months in the hospital before recovering and going on to resume teaching and managing *LEM*. Her illnesses led her to cry out to God, seeking a deeper understanding of what was happening to her.

Much later, as an adult, after years of searching, she, once again, experienced the Spirit that had brought her to tears, but this time it was in *Gospel Revivals Ministries*, a Pentecostal church where *deliverance ministry* was emphasized. She had desired a deeper understanding of Scripture since her early years, so she began to attend church regularly. Scripture was difficult for her. She struggled with the task, but read at least one Chapter every day even though she did not understand it. After about six months, however, while reading the Bible, she saw a vision of the angel with the little book described in Chapter 10 of the Book of Revelation, verse 8. She began to understand the Bible after that, but several more years had to pass before she began to receive Revelation knowledge of the Scripture.

Sheila Vitale studied the Bible and *deliverance ministry* for about seven years under the teaching of *Charles Holzhauser*, the Pastor of *Gospel Revivals Ministries*, at Mount Sinai, NY. Sometimes she attended as many as five teaching services each week, as well as studying for endless hours to gain key insight into her faith. She also edited *Pastor Holzhauser's* books during that time. After that, she studied independently under the influence and direction of the Holy Spirit, before founding *Living Epistles Ministries*.

Yes. The Alternate New Testament may be purchased through Amazon.com.

https://www.amazon.com/gp/product/069230973X

4. I used to read the *Alternate Old Testament* for free. Can I still read it for free on your new website?

Yes.

http://www.livingepistles.org/index.php/old-testament

5. Is the *Alternate Old Testament* for sale?

Yes. The Alternate Old Testament is available for purchase from Amazon.com.

https://www.amazon.com/gp/product/0692437347

6. I used to read the *Alternate Translation of the Book of Revelation* for free. Can I still read it for free on your new website?

Yes.

http://www.livingepistles.org/index.php/new-testament

7. Is the A*lternate Translation of The Book of Revelation*

Alternate Translation Of The New Testament/ Facts About The
Alternate Translation Bible

for sale?

Yes.

https://www.amazon.com/Alternate-Translation-Revelation-Jesus-Christ/dp/0692251863

ABOUT THE AUTHOR

Sheila R. Vitale is the Spiritual Leader, Founding Teacher, and Pastor of *Living Epistles Ministries (LEM)*. She moves in the offices of Teacher of Apostolic Doctrine, Prophet, Evangelist and Pastor, has an international following, and has been expounding on the Scripture through a unique spiritual lens for nearly three decades.

She has written more than 50 books based on the Old and New Testaments including *Ephraim, Man of the Earth and The Eagle Ascended (OT), and Salvation* and *Not Without Blood (NT)*. She has also rendered original spiritual interpretations of Biblical texts such as *The Woman in The Well (John, Chapter 4)* and *First Corinthians, Chapter 11*. Her unique, Multi-Part Message style is seen in *LEM* Serial Messages such as *A Place Teeming With Life* (9 Parts) and *Quantum Mechanics in Creation* (18 Parts). Each Part of a Multi-Part Message Series can also be enjoyed as a complete and independent study. In addition, she has defined, explained, illustrated and demonstrated hundreds of spiritual principles throughout more than 1,000 *LEM* Lectures.

Her signature work, however, is the three volumes of *The Alternate Translation Bible (ATB)*: *The Alternate Translation of The Old Testament, The Alternate Translation of The New Testament and The Alternate Translation of the Book of Revelation*. *The Alternate Translation Bible* is a work in progress (*The ATB Project*). Accordingly, additional spiritual interpretations of both whole and partial Chapters are added from time to time, as they are rendered. The most up-to-date versions of *The ATB Project* may be found online at *The LEM* W*ebsite* (*LivingEpistles.org*). *The ATB* is a *spiritual interpretation* of the Scripture and is not intended to replace traditional translations.

She also analyzed the Greek text of *The Book of Revelation* and preached extensively on it in the early years of *The ATB Project*. During that time she produced 197 distinct

Message Parts, under 29 specific *Message Titles*, all of which deal with *The Book of Revelation*. *Also, many* of her books such as, *Adam and The Two Judgment*s and *A Study in Unconscious Mind Control*, have been translated into Spanish, as well as *The Book of Revelation*.

Pastor Vitale is an illustrator of spiritual principles, a researcher, a translator and a reviewer of the Modern Social Trends of Family and Culture, as they are revealed through TV programs *(The Sopranos)*, movies *(The Matrix* and *The Edge of Tomorrow)* and plays *(Wicked)*. She also writes for the LEM *Blog*.

She travels domestically, as well as internationally, preaching and teaching Judeo-Christian Spiritual Philosophy, and has donated Audio Libraries of her Lectures to other ministries in Africa, Asia, Europe and North America,

Pastor Vitale serves *LEM* in a range of spiritual, educational, and administrative functions from *The Selden Centre*, *LEM* headquarters in Selden, New York. She is also a philanthropic individual who supports the *Lighthouse Mission (Patchogue, NY) and HGM – Mission of Hope – Haiti, and other* charitable organizations. She also supports community services such as the *Terryville Fire Department*.

In her spare time, Pastor Vitale enjoys watching movies, attending plays and partaking of cuisines from different cultures. An avid traveler, she has visited several countries in Europe and Africa as well as many cities in the United States.

BEGINNINGS, INSPIRATION AND CALLING

Pastor Vitale began her spiritual journey as a child when her Jewish mother enrolled her in the Hebrew school of an Orthodox synagogue. She experienced the Spirit of God for the first time there in such a profound way that she wept. But after that, when she was only eleven years old, she became very ill and was taken to Mount Sinai Hospital in New York City. She almost died there and has battled with life-threatening health issues ever since. Nevertheless, a deep longing for God continued to pursue her until several years later when she desperately wanted to attend Yeshiva (Jewish high school), but could not. Her secular parents approved of her choice, but could not afford the tuition.

Much later, after years of searching, she once again experienced the Spirit that had brought her to tears in the synagogue of her youth, but this time it was at *Gospel Revivals Ministries*, a Pentecostal church where Deliverance Ministry was emphasized. She had a desire to understand the Bible since she was a child, but Scripture was difficult for her and she struggled with the text. Nevertheless, she read one Chapter of the Bible every day until, one day, *her spiritual eyes opened* and she saw an angel holding a little book.

After that, she attended as many as five teaching services each week for about seven years, the latter part of which she edited *Pastor Holzhauser's* books. But several more years had to pass before *the eyes of her understanding opened even further* and she began to receive *Revelation Knowledge of the Scripture*. She understood at that time that the angel she had seen was the angel of Revelation 10:8.

After about seven years of learning *Deliverance Ministry* and *The Doctrine of Sonship (Bill Britton)* from *Pastor Holzhauser,* she studied the Bible independently under the influence and direction of the Holy Spirit.

In **1988** she began teaching Apostolic Doctrine.

In **1990** she spent three months in Stony Brook Hospital where she recovered from an incurable disease, defeating premature death, once again, and went on to resume teaching and managing *LEM*.

In **1992** she journeyed to Africa for the first time, where she was called to the office of Evangelist.

Alternate Translation Of The New Testament/ About The Author

In the **mid-1990s,** she began to Pastor in addition to being a Teacher of Apostolic Doctrine, a Prophet and an Evangelist, thus, satisfying all five offices of *The Ministry of the Lord Jesus Christ to His Church.*

LIVING EPISTLES MINISTRIES

Pastor Vitale was happy fellowshipping at *Gospel Revivals Ministries* but, eventually, she desired a deeper and more spiritual understanding of the Word of God. One day, after crying out to Jesus about her need, she was amazed to hear Him ask her if she would teach. Her initial response was that she did not see how it would be possible since she was already working a full-time job, despite her poor health. But after the Lord asked her for a second and then a third time, she reluctantly agreed, believing that He would empower her to do the job.

Shortly thereafter, in the latter part of 1987, she began to teach her own brand of Judeo-Christian Spiritual Philosophy, which includes applying Old Testament spiritual principles to unlock the mysteries of the New Testament. She believes that the Scripture is a spiritual document that must be spiritually discerned if it is to be understood correctly, and calls that spiritual understanding **The Doctrine of Christ**. The Lord Jesus Christ named the work *Living Epistles Ministries* in 1988.

The first *LEM* meetings were casual and spontaneous gatherings of friends and fellow deliverance workers in Pastor Vitale's home. After that, they were held in the business office of one of the brethren. Pastor Vitale delivered her first formal message entitled *The Truth About Witchcraft in January of 1988*, followed by *The Seduction of Eve* in April of the same year. After that, she prepared and taught weekly messages including *Signs of Apostleship* and *Lazarus & The Rich Man*. The meetings *eventually* increased to two and then three each week.

Alternate Translation Of The New Testament/ About The Author

LEM publishes a wide range of material, including books, e-books, spiritual interpretations of the Scripture and transcripts of many of Pastor Vitale's Lectures and on-line meetings, all of which, as well as the entire *Alternate Translation Bible,* may be viewed free of charge on the *LEM* website (*LivingEpistles.org*). She also has an *Author's Website* where all of her books, as well as several photographs of herself and a short biography are displayed (Amazon.com/author/SheilaVitale). Paperback and digital versions of *LEM* books may be purchased through *Amazon, Google Books* and *Barnes & Noble.*

LEM provides free video livestreams through YouTube and other Internet Platforms . . .

@LivingEpistlesMinistries (2016 – Sept. 2022)
@LivingEpistlesMinistriesLEM (Oct. 2022 – Ongoing)
@LivingEpistlesMinistries (LEM disciples)

. . . as well as two channels of **Shortclips** where short, focused messages of about 15 minutes each are posted:

@shortclipsbysheilar.vitale3334 (2016 – Sept. 2022)
@ShortClips-SheilaVitale (Oct. 2022 – Ongoing)

LEM donates a significant percentage of its income to other Christian ministries and organizations that advocate for Christian values and defend the United States Constitution.

PASTOR VITALE TODAY

Today Pastor Vitale continues to dedicate her life to teaching the spiritual principles of the Bible and focuses daily on studying, writing and preaching powerful messages from *The Selden Centre,* LEM/CCK's headquarters at Selden, New York.

THE ALTERNATE TRANSLATION OLD TESTAMENT

The Alternate Translation of the Old Testament is an original translation based upon a spiritual understanding of the Scripture that will excite anyone who is looking for a deeper understanding of the Old Testament. *The Alternate Translation of the Old Testament* is not intended to replace traditional translations.

THE ALTERNATE TRANSLATION REVELATION

The Alternate Translation Of The Book Of The Revelation Of Jesus Christ To St. John is an original translation based upon a spiritual understanding of the scripture that will excite anyone who is looking for a deeper understanding of the Book of Revelation. The *Alternate Translation of the Book of Revelation* is not intended to replace traditional translations.

Living Epistles Ministries
Sheila R. Vitale
Pastor, Teacher & Founder
Christian Spiritual Philosophy
PO Box 562, Port Jefferson Station, New York 11776, USA
LivingEpistles.org
or
Books@LivingEpistles.org

www.ingramcontent.com/pod-product-compliance
Lightning Source LLC
Chambersburg PA
CBHW071958150426
43194CB00008B/923